Theatre History Studies

2015 VOLUME 34

Edited by

ELIZABETH REITZ MULLENIX

PUBLISHED BY THE MID-AMERICA THEATRE CONFERENCE
AND THE UNIVERSITY OF ALABAMA PRESS

Template Designed by Todd Lape / Lape Designs
Production by Publications Unit, Department of English, Illinois State University
Production Director: Steve Halle
Production Intern: Caitlin Backus
Typeface: Minion
Essays appearing in this journal are abstracted and indexed in
Historical Abstracts and *America: History and Life*

∞

The paper on which this book is printed meets the minimum requirements
of American National Standard for Information Sciences-Permanence of
Paper for Printed Library Materials, ANSI Z39.48-1984.

MEMBER
CELJ
Council of Editors of Learned Journals

Cover: All Saints Cathedral flag ceremony, 1918; courtesy of Chicago History Museum
Cover Design: Todd Lape/Lape Designs

Theater History Studies is an official journal of the Mid-America Theatre Conference, Inc. (MATC). The conference encompasses the states of Illinois, Indiana, Iowa, Kansas, Michigan, Minnesota, Missouri, Nebraska, North Dakota, South Dakota, and Wisconsin. Its purposes are to unite people and organizations within this region and elsewhere who have an interest in theatre and to promote the growth and development of all forms of theatre.

Theatre History Studies is devoted to research in all areas of theatre history. Manuscripts should be prepared in conformity with the guidelines established in the *Chicago Manual of Style,* and e-mailed to sfreeman@pugetsound.edu, or submitted in duplicate and sent to Sara E. Freeman, Ph.D., Associate Professor of Theatre at the University of Puget Sound, 1500 North Warner St., Tacoma, WA 98416. Consulting editors review the manuscripts, a process that takes approximately four months. The journal does not normally accept studies of dramatic literature unless there is a focus on actual production and performance. Authors whose manuscripts are accepted must provide the editor with an electronic file, using Microsoft Word. Illustrations are welcomed and should conform with the instructions listed on the style guide on the website: http://matc.us/theatre-history-studies-4/theatre-history-studies-the-matc-journal.

This publication is issued annually by the Mid-America Theatre Conference and The University of Alabama Press.

Subscription rates for 2015 are $15 for individuals, $30 for institutions, and an additional $8 for foreign delivery. Back issues are $29.95 each. Subscription orders and changes of address should be directed to Allie Harper, The University of Alabama Press, Box 870380, Tuscaloosa, AL 35487; (205) 348-1564 phone; 205-348-9201 fax).

Theatre History Studies is indexed in *Humanities Index, Humanities Abstracts, Book Review Index, MLA International Bibliography, International Bibliography of Theatre, Arts & Humanities Citation Index, IBZ International Bibliography of Periodical Literature,* and *IBR International Bibliography of Book Reviews,* the database of *International Index to the Performing Arts.* Full texts of essays appear in the databases of both *Humanities Abstracts Full Text* and *SIRS.* The journal has published its own index, *The Twenty Year Index, 1981–2000.* It is available for $10 for individuals and $15 for libraries from Elizabeth Reitz Mullenix, Ph.D., Dean of the College of Creative Arts, Miami University of Ohio, Oxford, OH 45056; (513) 529-3053.

CONTENTS

BOOK REVIEWS

CONTENTS

ILLUSTRATIONS

Introduction

—ELIZABETH REITZ MULLENIX

In the essay that opens this volume, Professor Alan Sikes describes teaching the Abydos Passion Play during the first week of class (as many of us do) because he wants to help students to think about what theatre *is* and what it *does* and how to *recognize it when they see it*. This volume has made me think about theatre history in that way, for it is a different practice now in 2015 than when this disciplinary journal was founded by Ron Engle in 1981. Indeed these essays on the history of performance and theatre are also evocative treatises on historiography, for they all ruminate in their own way about the practice of writing history.

The essays are arranged chronologically, beginning at the beginning with the exploration of the Abydos Passion Play. In a provocative rethinking of this text, Sikes takes a new look at history by questioning our position of inquiry as theatre historians in claiming such an event in our chronology—a query that examines how mythmaking lies at the center of historiography. Sikes's rich contextualization—the work of an expert historian indeed—sheds light on the Abydos ritual and proves that terms like "passion play" and "mimesis" are not relevant signifiers for the funerary expressions of ancient Egyptians. The conceptual tool Sikes uses to unlock this new interpretation is semiotic theory; using sign and referent to revise previous ideas about mimesis, he sheds new light on a familiar subject, the origins of theatre itself. Andrew Gibb also considers sign and referent as he discusses the complex meanings of minstrelsy in antebellum California. For Gibb, previous scholarship that interprets minstrelsy based on its performances in the eastern United States fails to explain the way a white performer in blackface signified to a San Francisco audience, whose ancestries might be Native American, Mexican, African American, or Anglo—or, more likely, representative of a rich intermingling of multiple ethnicities. Through the story of Jewish African Caribbean immigrant William Alexander Leidesdorff, a *californio* elite in Mexican California, Gibb reminds theatre scholars that despite the "national scope of the argument," any performance text is always, "to a greater or lesser degree, played out at a local level." Nicole Berkin's essay, like those of Gibb and Sikes, examines a subject familiar to theatre historians: the antebellum star system. Her study expands our understanding of this well-known practice, however, and contributes to a recent body of work on cultural circulation in nineteenth-century America. Berkin, employing theories adapted from cultural geography, argues that actors and managers attempted to "use circulation to reinforce or re-map the social and cultural categories that circumscribed them, including legitimate vs. popular, respectable vs. scandalous, and star vs. unknown."

The last two essays in the volume reflect current theatre scholars' interest in performance studies, a term not widely in use when this journal began. In 1980, when *TDR* added "a journal of performance studies" as a subtitle, the majority of theatre historians were not engaged in what they would term "performance studies" scholarship despite certain shared methodologies. As the studies by Megan Geigner and Heide Nees demonstrate, theatre scholars now look at a broad range of texts, both dramatic and performative, for unlike that of more traditional historians, our work has *always* been interdisciplinary, relying on diverse approaches and theoretical frameworks.

As you examine this volume of *Theatre History Studies*, you will notice that the typical balance of essays and book reviews is a bit askew. In volume 34, the scale has tipped toward the review; book review editor Rob Shimko and I have decided to include all of the reviews written for the original 2013 issue of the journal, an issue that never materialized due to changes in editorial staff and unexpected circumstances relative to key personnel. I would like to extend my thanks to Rob Shimko, who did the lion's share of editorial work for this issue, and together we would like to recognize the former book review editor Cheryl Black for her expert editorial work on many of the reviews that appear in this volume.

Theatre History, Theatrical Mimesis, and the Myth of the Abydos Passion Play

—ALAN SIKES

The impetus for this essay came from my recent charge to write comprehensive exam questions for one of our Ph.D. candidates here at Louisiana State University. I wanted to write a question on the origins of theatrical practice, but I thought about veering—both culturally and historically—from ancient Athens, the usual locus for speculation on theatre origin theories. After a quick review of suitable source materials, I devised the following question: "What was the Abydos Passion Play? Discuss its content and principal characteristics in context of its production history." It is, admittedly, a challenging question for a Ph.D. candidate, and probably for many credentialed theatre scholars. Still, after composing the question, I decided to try composing a response, one suitable for our "short-answer" exam format: "The Abydos Passion Play is the name given to an event staged during the annual Khoiak festival in the ancient Egyptian city of Abydos. Evidence for this event is found on a stela, or inscribed stone memorial slab, erected by the courtier Ikhernofret during the Middle Kingdom, circa the nineteenth century BCE; but the event was likely staged for many centuries both before and after the dedication of the stela itself. The event commemorated the mythical death and resurrection of Osiris, god of the afterlife, and scholars of the source material claim that it exhibited many elements that we recognize today as theatrical."

I realize that my sample response is quite short, even for a "short-answer" exam, but its brevity is due to the fact that I have supplied nearly all there is to say with certainty about the event called the Abydos Passion Play. I set aside my sample question for the upcoming exam, but I continued to query myself about my drive to develop such a question in the first place, and to query the field of theatre studies about the position of the Passion Play within the discipline. And indeed, after some reflection on the so-named Ikhernofret Stela, the event recorded there, and the specific cultural contexts for them both, I have come to question the designation of the event as a "play" and the stela as a document of "theatrical" practice. Still, I have also come to believe that the Passion Play has an important role in theatre studies: It prompts us to revisit the use of terms most basic to our discipline, as well as the borders that delimit the practices falling within its purview. In other words, rather than undermining our disciplinary claim to archive and investigate the Passion Play, I seek instead to rethink the sort of claim that we might make of it.

Certainly the event described by the Ikhernofret Stela already holds a prominent, if ambiguous, place in narratives on the origin and history of the theatre. Consider these accounts of the event from three popular theatre history textbooks. The tenth edition of Brockett and Hildy's *History of the Theatre* remarks that calling the event a Passion Play "deliberately links it to a European religious drama of the Middle Ages" but notes that scholars are divided as to whether it more closely resembled a public spectacle or a royal funeral. In conclusion, the textbook reports that "information sufficient to resolve the dispute is not presently available, although all apparently agree that some sort of performative event took place." The sixth edition of Wilson and Goldfarb's *Living Theatre* calls this event the Abydos Ritual, in deference to the religious aspects of the Ikhernofret Stela, but states that "it is clear from this account that the ceremony had unmistakable theatrical elements: people played the roles of characters in the story and acted out episodes from the life of Osiris." Finally, the first edition of Zarrilli, McConachie, Williams, and Sorgenfrei's *Theatre Histories* concedes scarce knowledge of this event, noting that "the little that is known to us of this quasi-dramatic commemorative ritual is the information inscribed on a single stele," but offers Ikhernofret performance credit by calling him "both overseer of the ceremonies and a participant/actor playing the role of the Beloved Son of Osiris."[1]

In sum, Brockett and Hildy claim that "Passion Play" may or may not be the right term for the event but argue that it was performative in spirit; Wilson and Goldfarb label the event a ritual but argue that it exhibited theatrical elements; and Zarrilli, McConachie, Williams, and Sorgenfrei claim the event was a commemorative ritual of a quasi-dramatic nature. All the texts, in other words, hesitate to give the Abydos event a definitive description at all, and given the dearth of concrete surviving evidence the authors probably err admirably on the side of caution. Yet more or less implicit in the narratives offered by all three texts is the assumption that the Abydos event prefigures "theatre" in the Western tradition as we understand the term today.[2] Certainly all three textbooks place their discussions of the Abydos event before their introductions to ancient Athenian theatre—a term derived, as we know, from the Greek *theatron*—and given the fact that the Ikhernofret Stela predates Athenian theatre by at least twelve centuries, the placement of their discussions seems justified. Still, the textbooks tell us that the event displayed theatrical elements, or at least performative elements, or at any rate was quasi-dramatic in nature. Perhaps the Abydos event possessed theatrical qualities that somehow predated the advent of Athenian theatre itself; this seems to be the conclusion to derive from the textbooks. Here, however, I offer an alternate possibility. Perhaps our act of placing the Abydos event alongside the term "theatre" embeds in our inquiries a set of guiding assumptions, assumptions with a certain mythmaking power of their own.

To be sure, the Abydos event and Athenian theatre share much in common: both were conducted at specific dates on festival calendars; at specific sites designated for the purpose; and by specific individuals gathered to take part in the unfolding action. Yet one expectation of Athenian theatre is particularly problematic when applied to the Abydos event, namely, the expectation that the acts in question are imitative. Our earliest extant commentaries on the theatre are explicit on the mimetic nature of the drama, its marked difference from an original, discrete reality. In the *Republic*, Plato takes great care to distinguish imitation from reality, famously claiming that the former is so apt to be confused with the latter that he would banish imitation from his ideal state. "As in a city when the evil are permitted to have authority and the good are put out of the way, so in the soul of man, as we maintain, the imitative poet implants an evil constitution, for he indulged the irrational nature. . . . He is a manufacturer of images and is very far removed from the truth." Conversely, in the *Poetics* Aristotle places great stock in imitation and defines tragedy as first and foremost the imitation of an action. Still, he is careful to maintain the distinction between imitation and reality; indeed, tragedy, as the highest form of imitation, is carefully structured and embellished in ways that insist upon its difference from everyday, original reality. "Tragedy is an imitation of an action that is admirable, complete, and possesses magnitude; in language made pleasurable; each of its species separated in different parts; performed by actors, not through narration; effecting through pity and fear purification of such emotions."[3]

I realize that my reliance on the likes of Plato and Aristotle is decidedly "old school" for contemporary theatre studies, but many theatre historians continue to rely upon Platonic and Aristotelian notions of mimesis as central to the nature of theatre itself. Such reliance may be either implicit or explicit on the part of theatre scholars, but it remains pervasive in current critical thought on theatrical practice. Consider the conceptual parallels between ancient theories of mimesis and the insights derived from modern semiotics: specifically, the homology between "imitation and reality," on the one hand, and "sign and referent," on the other. In his famous 1913 *Course in General Linguistics*, Ferdinand de Saussure demands careful scrutiny of the relation between sign and referent; he remarks that "some people regard language, when reduced to its elements, as a naming process only—a list of words, each corresponding to the thing that it names," and then maintains that this view of language "lets us assume that the linking of a name and a thing is a very simple operation—an assumption that is anything but true."[4] Saussure proposes that the sign operates as a conjunction between a communicable "signifier" and a conceptual "signified" that the signifier itself can call to mind. If all goes well with this conjunction, then the sign can successfully designate a referent. Yet Saussure gives almost no consideration to the referent; his concern is with the dynamics of the sign, and this singular attention to the sign dramatically attenuates its relation to the referent it ostensibly designates. In fact, it seems that the very gulf between sign and referent secures their respective identities: sign and referent *are* what they *are* by virtue of their difference, their mutual singularity and specificity.

Here the modern semiotic relation of sign to referent bears a striking affinity with ancient Athenian relation of imitation to reality; indeed, their correlation marks a conceptual inheritance passed from early Western thought to the critical thinking of the present day. Just as the sign maintains its integrity only through its difference from its referent, so the signs employed in the theatre, called "imitations" by Plato and Aristotle, maintain their integrity only in distinction to the reality they endeavor to represent. The one cannot be confused with the other, lest the entire theatrical enterprise be thrown into disarray. Of course, confusions of this nature were ever present in ancient Athens and self-evident to the Athenian philosophers: the false words of the poet elicited real tears from the audience, and the characters of legend were conflated with the personae of performers. Still, the properly ideological insistence on a distinction between imitation and reality remains a hallmark of Western theatrical traditions. And recognition of this insistence in turn prompts me to revisit my approach to my original exam question; perhaps instead of inquiring about the place of the Passion Play in theatre history, we might instead examine its relation to Western concepts of sign and referent, imitation and reality.

Even this new approach to my question poses difficulties, however, as we have no text of the Passion Play itself to peruse for evidence of mimetic practices. We do have the testimony of Ikhernofret, the self-described "sole companion" of Pharaoh Senusret II, who commanded him to visit Abydos and oversee its annual Khoiak festival. We also have the story of the death and resurrection of Osiris, a foundational myth of ancient Egyptian culture. Variations on the story abound; the most complete account is a Hellenized version by Plutarch from the first century CE, though the myth itself is many millennia older. In brief, Osiris was an early divine king of Egypt, a direct descendent of the sun god Re. One day his brother Set, in a fit of jealous pique, locked Osiris in a chest and cast it into the Nile. Isis, the wife of Osiris, found the chest on the shores of Byblos and returned it to Egypt, but Set discovered the chest, hacked the body inside into pieces, and scattered the parts across the land. Isis searched for the missing pieces and reconstituted the body by wrapping it in linen, thereby creating the first mummy; she then buried the body of Osiris at Abydos, which thereafter became the principal site for the Osiris cult. Thanks to the efforts of Isis, Osiris was resurrected as the ruler of the afterlife; with him, she conceived their son Horus, who avenged the murder of his father by defeating Set. Thereafter Horus succeeded his father as king of the living realm, while Osiris reigned in eternity in the land of the dead.[5]

The pivotal Osiris myth laid the ground for the Egyptian preoccupation with death and resurrection. Every pharaoh, and eventually everyone able to afford the basic burial rites, might be resurrected as "an Osiris" and reborn as "a Horus" of the succeeding generation. The issue at hand, however, is whether or not this myth spurred the development of theatre as understood in Western traditions. Certainly some historians have argued that it fulfilled just that function; the most significant among them may be H. W. Fairman, who in 1974 published his edited transcription of the so-called *Triumph of Horus*. It consists of a series of wall carvings, each with accompanying hieroglyphic texts that decorate the Temple of Horus at Edfu in Upper Egypt. The bulk of the images depicts the adult Horus avenging his father, Osiris, by repeatedly harpooning his enemy, Set, who is depicted as a hippopotamus of miniscule proportions; subsequent images celebrate the defeat of Set and recognize Horus as the legitimate pharaoh of the Egyptian lands. As for the Edfu temple itself, construction began in the third century BCE under the reign of the Ptolemies, a Greek dynasty that ruled Egypt between the fourth and first centuries BCE. Fairman calls the *Triumph* a theatrical play, and given its Hellenistic provenance he may have reason to find in it theatrical elements familiar from Aristotle: Fairman claims that as a play it falls on its own accord into distinct acts and scenes; that it develops a central theme, the legitimation of royal authority; and that it displays at least rudimentary attempts at individual characterization and the creation of dramatic tension.[6]

That said, the *Triumph* also displays several features that trouble its designation as a theatrical play. Fairman seeks to minimize the significance of such features, but at times his own efforts throw them into sharper relief. First, Fairman notes that some lines of text appear alongside carved images of deities, and he can with fairness read them as utterances ascribed to the accompanying deities. In itself, however, this hardly offers sufficient reason to call the *Triumph* a play; to risk a contemporary reference, this link between text and image seems more suggestive of a modern graphic novel than of an ancient play. Second, Fairman readily admits assigning many other lines of text to a "Reader" and a "Chorus" who are neither mentioned in the text nor overtly designated in the carvings. The transcription of the *Triumph* produced by Fairman resembles a modern playscript, with each line assigned to specific characters, but often these assignments are interpolations by Fairman himself into the original text. Finally, Fairman notes that the text is written in a hybrid form that inserts characters from the Ptolemaic period into an archaic hieroglyphic system predating the actual carvings by at least a millennium. While it seems clear that the text is partly a transcription of a much more ancient writing, it is equally clear that its antique language would render any performance largely incoherent to a Ptolemaic audience. This also undermines the designation of the *Triumph* as theatre, at least according to the model of Aristotle, wherein theatre offers pleasure and instruction based upon its intelligibility for its audience.[7]

So while Fairman supplies valuable information on *The Triumph of Horus* and useful insights into its possible ritual functions, I cannot help but think that his designation of the text as a theatrical play suggests a desire on his part to find theatre of a Western stamp in a tradition far flung from its Athenian birthplace. More recently, Egyptologist Ronald J. Leprohon has cast further doubt on the existence of an Egyptian theatre—or at any rate one conceived along Western lines—by examining other ritual texts from the Ptolemaic period. The temple of Hathor at Dendera, another Ptolemaic edifice, displays wall carvings reminiscent of theatrical practices, most notably processions of marchers wearing masks of the jackal god Anubis. And several papyri from the Ptolemaic era include lamentations by Isis and her sister Nepthys for the slain Osiris, some of which suggest a dialogue among priestesses during temple ceremonies. Still, Leprohon concludes that none of these sources indicate the practice of theatre in its current Western sense; the rituals were likely performed in closed sanctuaries by a coterie priestly class, for the propitiation of the temple gods, and with no clear reference to mimesis—the conscious imitation of a discrete reality outside the confines of the temple walls.[8]

In light of Leprohon, then, it seems the Ikhernofret Stela invites further inquiry into its status as the record of a passion play. Unfortunately, it offers scant evidence to examine. It does tell us that Ikhernofret completed his mission of adorning the Osiris shrines with gold and gives us an account of his involvement in the Khoiak festival, during which the image of the god was paraded from his temple, transported via ceremonial barques, to his legendary tomb site a short distance away. As this record forms the basis of claims that the Khoiak festival featured a Passion Play, I will cite a few pertinent passages, punctuating my citations with notes on the many terms and epithets mentioned therein. The stela records the labors of Ikhernofret as overseer of the annual Khoiak festival; first among his tasks after the ornamentation of Osiris and his companion gods was the construction of a shrine that would transport the image of Osiris from the inner recess of his temple to the start of the official processional route: "I acted as 'Son, Whom He Loves,' for Osiris, First of the Westerners. . . . I made for him a portable shrine, the 'Bearer of Beauty,' of the 'First of the Westerners,' of gold, silver, lazuli, fragrant woods, carob wood, and meru wood. I fashioned the gods belonging to his divine ennead, I made their shrines anew."[9] Here Ikhernofret claims to act on behalf of the pharaoh in his role as Horus, the beloved Son of Osiris; indeed Ikhernofret seems to assume the role of Horus, at least temporarily, for himself. Osiris is called "First of the Westerners" because all tombs were located on the West Bank of the Nile, and Osiris is of course credited with setting that precedent. The "divine ennead" refers to a set of nine ancient gods present during the early epochs of creation; the lists of "enneads" regularly include Osiris, so we may assume that Ikhernofret also refurbished the images and shrines of his companion gods. "I celebrated the (feast of) 'Going forth' of Upwawet, when he proceeded to champion his father. I repelled the foe from the 'Neshmet' barque, I overthrew the enemies of Osiris. I celebrated the 'Great-Going-Forth,' following the god at his going."[10] *Upwawet* is a very old jackal god, the "Opener of the Way" who stands at the prow of the solar boat as it sails across the sky by day and through the underworld by night. Here he is called the son of Osiris and identified with Horus, who opens the way for the "Going-Forth" of his father into the afterlife. Certainly Ikhernofret suggests the staging of a battle, perhaps led by Upwawet-Horus, as the enemies of Osiris were repulsed from their attack upon his sacred "Neshmet" barque. The term "Neshmet" seems untranslatable at present, but the Neshmet barque was clearly only one of several used during the festival. Ikhernofret continues: "I equipped the barque (called): 'Shining-in-Truth' of the lord of Abydos, with a chapel. (I) put on his regalia when he went forth to . . . Peker; I led the way of the god to his tomb before Peker; I championed Wennofer at 'That Day of the Great Conflict'; I slew all the enemies upon the [flats] of Nedyt."[11] Here Peker is the name given to the traditional burial site of Osiris; scholars believe that it references a collection of nearby tombs from the First and Second Dynasties that by the Middle Kingdom were considered burial places of the primeval gods themselves. At any rate, the god was apparently carried there on his "Shining-in-Truth" barque to receive new funeral rites. Wennofer is an epithet for Osiris, a name that connotes the eternal and incorruptible nature of his body, and Nedyt names the location either where Osiris was slain by Set or where his body was discovered by Isis. At any rate, Ikhernofret again suggests the staging of a battle and the vindication of Osiris. Still unclear, however, is if these stagings were understood by the Egyptians as theatrical imitations designed to depict an earlier historical reality.

Thus the Ikhernofret Stela supplies tantalizing glimpses of the Khoiak festival from the Middle Kingdom era, but it offers neither a comprehensive description of the event nor a claim that the event itself was considered mimetic by its participants. This prompts yet another possible approach to my original exam question: Rather than seeking evidence of mimesis in the Passion Play, perhaps we should read it alongside other ancient funerary texts for evidence of parallel practices. We have a vast wealth of these texts, more than I could ever detail in their entirety, but one abiding aspect of these documents seems particularly pertinent to my present inquiry: a link between sign and referent alien to our current conception of the terms. Recall that modern semiotics since Saussure regards signs and referents as mutually coherent due to their mutual distinction from one another. Egyptian texts, however, conceive the relation of sign and referent in quite another way. I want to consider as one instance of this relation the link held to inhere between the name, on the one hand, and the individual so named, on the other.

To invoke the name in ancient Egypt is not simply to invoke the sign of a referent; the name is in no way so easily divided from the one named. According to the Egyptians, the name is endowed with *heka*, a term translated as "magic" in most studies. I argue, however, that current connotations of the word "magic" give short shrift to the sophistication of the term as employed by the Egyptians. As Erik Hornung notes, the heka of the name is understood as having actual physical properties; it not only constitutes "part of the nature and substance of every living being" but also offers "effective nourishment for the deceased."[12]

Indeed, the heka of the name fulfills multiple functions: It can ensure the preservation, the transformation, even the subjugation of an individual entity. To illustrate the heka of the name, I offer examples from three funerary texts, each from different eras of Egyptian history; even as conceptions of the afterlife change over time, the power of the uttered name retains its potency.

From the Old Kingdom, circa 2700–2200 BCE, we have the *Pyramid Texts*, wall carvings from the burial chambers of the Fifth and Sixth Dynasty pharaohs. The *Texts* are voluminous and vary from one tomb to another, but all are exhortations for the deification of the deceased pharaoh and his ascension into the heavens. A central concern is the preservation of the identity of the pharaoh through the invocation of his name and the divine attributes ascribed to him. As an example, consider this "Spell for Resurrection" from the *Pyramid Texts* of Pharaoh Teti from the Sixth Dynasty; here the pharaoh is identified as an "Osiris" who is welcomed into the heavens by Horus, who also embodies the reborn Teti himself: "Hail, Osiris Teti! Stand up now! / Horus has come to install you among the gods. / Horus has set his love on you and has provided for you. / Horus has fastened his eye to you; / Horus has opened your eye for you that you might see with it. / The gods have raised your face for you, for they have set their love on you."[13]

The Middle Kingdom, circa 2050–1650 BCE, supplies us with the *Coffin Texts*, adaptations of older pharaonic writings that, in a sort of "democratization" of the afterlife, were inscribed on the coffins of private individuals. The famous Spell 148, "To Transform into a Falcon," demonstrates how the assumption of a divine name can effect the transformation of the deceased into a Horus figure. The text begins with a declaration by Isis, who confirms to the other gods that she is pregnant with the son of Osiris. She then entreats Horus to be born, and immediately upon his birth he assumes the guise of a falcon and claims ascendancy over the other gods, particularly Seth. In reciting the spell and in claiming the name of Horus, the deceased can also claim the power and position of Horus: "(Horus says) 'I am Horus, the great Falcon who is upon the battlements of the Mansion of Him-whose-name-is-hidden. My flight has reached the horizon, for I have overpassed the gods of the sky, making my position more prominent than that of the primordial gods—even the Contender bird cannot equal my initial flight. My place is far away from Seth, the adversary of my father Osiris, for I have used the roads of eternal recurrence of dawnlight and by my flight I have become elevated.'"[14]

Finally, from the New Kingdom, circa 1550–1050 BCE, we have the *Book of the Dead*, a collection of spells printed on papyrus and buried with anyone who could purchase a copy of the text. The most crucial section of the *Book of the*

Dead is the "Negative Confession" that promises safe passage for the deceased into the blessed realms of the underworld or Duat. The text takes its name from the denial of wrongdoing that the deceased must pronounce before Osiris. After this declaration, however, the deceased faces a further challenge. Various deities guard the entrance to the blessed realms, and only those who can pronounce their divine names are allowed to cross the threshold. Here knowledge of the name allows the deceased to subjugate these guardians and attain access to a happy afterlife. "'I shall not let you enter by me,' so say the door-posts of this portal, 'unless you have said my name.' / '"Plummet of Truthfulness" is your name.' / 'I shall not let you enter by me,' so says the right door-leaf of this portal, 'unless you have said my name.' / '"Scale-pan which bears Truth" is your name.' / 'I shall not let you enter by me,' so says the left door-leaf of this portal, 'unless you have said my name.' / '"Scale-pan of wine" is your name.'"[15]

These texts, through the heka of the name, are more than merely writings on a wall, a coffin, or a papyrus; they are also understood as utterances, recorded in perpetuity, for the protection and well-being of the deceased. Yet the heka of the name derives its own potency from a more fundamental source: the generative heka that affected the very emergence of the earth from the primeval waters of Nun. As Tom Hare has recently noted—with a nod to Jacques Derrida—the world of the Egyptians is saturated with heka that unites all aspects of existence with one another; the world appears not as a finite collection of static entities but as an ebb and flow of infinite variation: "The break from nonbeing to existence is not at heart a question of *how* many, but rather a question of how *into* many. The One swims inert, and Being is attained only in the overcoming of the One by bridging the *différance* that constitutes stasis-and-movement, body-and-thought, self-and-other, cognition-and-utterance."[16]

Heka, in other words, links individual resurrection through the name to the ebb and flow of the entire world, its eternal cycles of transition and regeneration. In the Old Kingdom, when funerary practice focused mostly on the afterlife of the pharaoh, the dead monarch took the name of Osiris and joined the sun god Re in his celestial barque; there the rising and setting of the sun doubled the death and resurrection of the pharaoh himself. Later, as funerary practices were democratized during the Middle and New Kingdoms, all who could afford a decent burial became "an Osiris" and attained a happy afterlife in the Duat. The central role of Re in earlier Old Kingdom practice was not forgotten, however; Re descended into the underworld each night at sunset; there he became "Osiris-Re" and sailed the length of the Duat, only to rise again at sunrise every morning.

Through the transformations enabled by heka, then, Re is identified with

Osiris; Osiris with the deceased; and the deceased in turn with Re, who likewise undergoes death and resurrection. The Ikhernofret Stela outlines a similar tale of transformation, as the rising Osiris returns to the land of the living in the form of his warrior son Horus. Moreover, it also suggests a link between this individual patrimony passed from father to son, and the daily rising and setting of the sun itself. When Re appears in the eastern morning sky, he becomes Harakhte, one form of Horus triumphant over his enemy Set. When Re reaches the western sky in the evening, he becomes Atum, the creator god who caused the first mound of land to emerge from the primeval waters. And when Atum daily descends into the underworld to become Osiris, the mound of creation also serves as his burial site. The formula for heka is therefore not "either. . . or" but "both. . . and." It does not produce separable and static identities but multiplies them in a promiscuous proliferation of identifications.

The concept of heka thus prompts us to rethink the assumptions of modern semiotics, for through heka the relation of sign to referent becomes anything but stable; the invocation of a sign can effect a transformation of the referent, and the referent itself may become a sign to effect the transformation of other referents, ad infinitum. Moreover, if heka cannot sustain our usual conception of sign and referent, then the heka of rituals like those recorded on the Ikhernofret Stela may not sustain comparison to the theatrical mimesis we have inherited from the Greeks. Rather than mere "imitations" of "real" events lost to a distant past, they may be enactments of events that extend from the creation of the world, and through the present moment, into eternity. And if this is the case, then the labeling of the Ikhernofret Stela event as a theatrical "Passion Play" is an imposition of our own terminology onto practices ill-suited to receive it. The existence of an "Abydos Passion Play" is a myth, and one of our own making.

Newly guided by an understanding of heka, we might seek some final insights from the Ikhernofret Stela by trying to link the event it describes to locations at the ancient sites at Abydos. Once again, however, we confront a frustrating scarcity of extant evidence. The great Osiris temple from the Middle Kingdom era of Ikhernofret was apparently razed to make way for a later New Kingdom structure, itself also largely lost to the ravages of time. There is, however, a well-preserved Abydos temple from the reign of the New Kingdom pharaoh Seti I; dedicated to Osiris, as well as a host of other gods, its wall decorations offer a great deal of information on the rituals of the Osiris cult. Egyptologist Rosalie David has published a detailed analysis of the temple carvings; there she notes that each god worshipped in the temple had its own sanctuary, their walls detailing the daily rituals of waking, bathing, dressing, and feeding the idols housed therein. More significant for my purposes, however, are the decorations of the Osiris Complex, a suite of hidden rooms accessed by a door at the rear of the Osiris sanctuary. The walls of the Osiris Complex suggest a complete cycle of ritual observances, one that David maintains was likely performed as part of the annual Khoiak festival.

The Osiris Complex is composed of two halls, the first larger than the second; each hall contains three niche shrines on their far ends dedicated to images of Horus, Isis, and Pharaoh Seti I deified as Osiris. The smaller Second Hall and its niche shrines are badly damaged. But the larger First Hall is better preserved and boasts wall decorations of the ritual practices conducted therein. The eastern wall shows Seti I presenting offerings to Horus and Osiris in their various guises, along with ancestor gods understood as the forebears of Osiris himself. In this way, the wall decorations confirm the link of Osiris and Horus to their own divine ancestors, just as Seti I was linked to his own dynastic familial forebears. The western wall, while partially destroyed, prominently depicts Seti I assisting Isis in erecting the Djed pillar, a totem for Osiris that likely symbolized the spinal column of the dead god. Erection of the Djed pillar allows Osiris to rise and stand on his own two feet, whereupon he can engender his son Horus and ascend to kingship in the afterlife. Finally, the three niche shrines of the First Hall cement the relation between the living Seti I and his eventual deification as an Osiris. The Horus shrine shows Seti I making offerings to Horus, who in turn presents the pharaoh with royal insignia; similar scenes appear in the Isis shrine. The shrine to Seti I is centrally poised between the other two: one panel of the shrine shows Horus performing funerary rites for the deceased pharaoh; another shows Horus and Isis presenting the risen pharaoh to Osiris, who thereby becomes an Osiris himself.[17]

David maintains that performance of these rituals at the Khoiak festival would cement the link between the risen Seti I and the risen Osiris; and indeed, since the former becomes a version of the latter, celebrants at the Seti I temple likely conducted rituals much like those of the great Osiris temple nearby. Unfortunately, the walls of the Seti I temple have no records of battle enactments or tombsite visits like those recounted on the Ikhernofret Stela; the wall carvings probably depict celebrations held prior to the departure of the god from the temple proper. There is, however, evidence for similar processional rites connected with the Seti I temple. While the Stela recounts a procession of Osiris to his original Peker tombsite, the likely destination from the Seti I temple is the so-called Osirieon, one of the most enigmatic structures extant from the entire Egyptian era. The Osirieon very nearly abuts the Seti I temple, but it sits several meters below ground, buried beneath the surface much like a tomb. And while its outer chambers display decorations credited to the later pharaoh Merenep-tah, its central walls are unlike any other tomb or temple from the period. The walls have no decorations whatsoever; not a single image or inscription appears on the massive, close-set blocks that comprise its interior.

Some Egyptologists speculate that the Osirieon served as a cenotaph or "false tomb" for Seti I himself, but it bears no resemblance to his actual burial site, one of the most lavishly decorated tombs yet found in the Valley of the Kings. David, for one, calls the Osirieon a cenotaph but acknowledges that "the building is unique in Egyptian architecture" and that "both its date and purpose have produced controversial theories."[18] Here David references the findings of Edouard Naville, who first excavated the site in 1914. Naville noted the resemblance of the Osirieon to Old Kingdom temples of the Fourth Dynasty, especially those linked to the Great Pyramids and Great Sphinx at Giza. The blocky, unadorned walls that characterize both the Osirieon and the much older Giza temples led Naville to maintain that "it is not impossible that this is the oldest Egyptian building, of large proportions, which has been preserved."[19] Yet even if the Osirieon does date from the much later era of Seti I, it may purposely recall antique monuments—much like those at the nearby Peker tombsites—as a means to link the life and death of the individual pharaoh to the cycle of death and rebirth ongoing since time immemorial.

The actual layout of the Osirieon merely deepens its mystery, for it too resembles nothing else extant from the period. It consists, in essence, of a raised platform surrounded by a moat fed with water from the nearby Nile. The central island was likely a site for funerary rituals, but the bare walls offer no clue to the nature of the rituals themselves. Still, the singular features of the Osirieon suggest a singular ritual function, and most Egyptologists agree that the island represents the first earthen mound to emerge from the primeval waters. Perhaps, then, the Osirieon invokes heka in its most fundamental manifestation. Inasmuch as this first mound is the locus of every birth and rebirth, it is the source of heka for the entirety of creation; perhaps no wall carvings are needed here, because the structure instantiates the heka that infuses every inscription, in every tomb and temple, throughout the length and breadth of the Egyptian realm. I speculate, to be sure, but if the Osirieon is meant to embody the first earthen mound, then it is a site of simultaneous death and resurrection that unites the past and present, the human and divine, the individual and universal. And if so, then it likewise confounds our modern distinctions of sign and referent, as well as our inherited theatrical distinctions of reality and imitation.

I realize that I have strayed far afield from my original exam question on the

Abydos Passion Play. I have also extended my inquiry far beyond the original source material found on the Ikhernofret Stela. I have done so, however, to discover what may happen when we seek to flesh out such scarce evidence by fitting it into a more familiar theatrical mold. It seems that a meditation on the function of heka suggested by the Osirieon may offer more insight into the event recorded on the Ikhernofret Stela than will their designation as a "Passion Play." Certainly my own investigation of the Abydos Passion Play has spurred me to think carefully about the history we write and the conceptual tools we deploy in the writing; without this careful thought, we may find ourselves engaged in acts of mythmaking without knowing it. And yet, on the other hand, we may also find that acts of mythmaking—a knowing mythmaking—in some sense sustain our scholarly practice. Here I refer to "myth" not as an untruth to be discovered and discredited but as an explanatory mechanism, an axiom, which undergirds our disciplinary presuppositions. In this sense, our concepts of semiotics and mimesis are every bit as "mythic" as the notion of heka was for the Egyptians. Without them, we theatre historians would be unable to identify our field, to mark its boundaries, or to specify its items of inquiry.

Today I include the Abydos Passion Play in my theatre history syllabus; I discuss it during the first week of Theatre History I, as might be expected. I teach it, however, not to inform students of an originary theatrical practice but to provoke them to interrogate their own assumptions about theatre: what it "is," what it "does," and how they can "know it when they see it." I see this sort of interrogation as vital to the future of our field. During my own career as a theatre academic, I have seen the disciplinary borders of theatre studies grow increasingly porous. At times this trend seems the exciting result of greater collaboration across academic fields; at other times it seems a reaction to shrinking budgets and enforced consolidation of formerly independent academic departments. And so at this critical juncture for our discipline, I believe it is all the more important to claim the Abydos Passion Play not only as a legitimate topic for study but also as a crucial opportunity for self-study. In closing, I will also offer a final reconfiguration of my opening exam question: "What was the Abydos Passion Play? Discuss its centrality to theatre history studies in order to demonstrate the utility, and ubiquity, of myth in the production of theatre history itself."

Notes

1. Oscar Brockett and Franklin Hildy, *History of the Theatre*, 10th ed. (Boston: Pearson, 2007), 8; Edwin Wilson and Alvin Goldfarb, *Living Theatre*, 6th ed. (New York: McGraw,

2011), 5; Phillip B. Zarrilli, Bruce McConachie, Gary Jay Williams, and Carol Fisher Sorgenfrei, *Theatre Histories*, 1st ed. (New York: Routledge, 2006), 58.

2. I realize that the invocation of a "Western" theatrical tradition presents many pitfalls even as it operates as a useful shorthand. For the purposes of this essay, I understand Western theatre as marked by production elements that were 1) derived from practices in fifth century BCE Athens and later disseminated throughout classical Mediterranean cultures; 2) revived and reconfigured by European states during the Early Modern Era; and 3) adopted and adapted around the world through the introduction/imposition of imperialist European cultural standards.
3. Plato, *Republic*, selections in *Dramatic Theory and Criticism*, ed. Bernard Dukore (New York: Holt, 1997), 29; Aristotle, *Poetics*, ed. and trans. Malcolm Heath (New York: Penguin, 1997), 10.
4. Ferdinand Saussure, *Course in General Linguistics*, trans. Wade Baskin, ed. Charles Bally and Albert Sechehaye (New York: Philosophical Library, 1959), 65.
5. Plutarch, *On Isis and Osiris*, trans. Charles William King, accessed June 2014, http://www.sacred-texts.com/cla/plu/pte/pte04.htm. See especially chapters XII–XX.
6. H. W. Fairman, ed. and trans., *The Triumph of Horus: An Ancient Egyptian Sacred Drama* (London: B. T. Batsford, 1974), 19.
7. Ibid., 36–41, 56–58. There are, of course, other examples of archaic texts retained in contemporary performance; I think of the Kutiyattam of India and the Noh of Japan. These traditions likewise show marked differences from the Aristotelian model of theatre that Fairman seeks to ascribe to the *Triumph of Horus*, but further inquiry into these traditions is the subject of another essay.
8. Ronald J. Leprohon, "Ritual Drama in Ancient Egypt," *The Origins of Theater in Ancient Greece and Beyond*, ed. Eric Csapo and Margaret C. Miller (London: Cambridge University Press: 2008), 259–91.
9. *Ikhernofret Stela*, trans. J. H. Breasted, accessed June 2014, http://www.reshafim.org.il/ad/egypt/index.html.
10. Ibid.
11. Ibid.
12. Erik Hornung, *Conceptions of God in Ancient Egypt*, trans. John Baines (Ithaca: Cornell University Press: 1982), 89.
13. William Kelly Simpson, ed., *The Literature of Ancient Egypt* (New Haven: Yale University Press, 2003), 251.
14. Ibid., 265.
15. Ibid., 275.
16. Tom Hare, *Remembering Osiris: Number, Gender, and the Word in Ancient Egyptian Representational Systems* (Stanford, CA: Stanford University Press, 1999), 169. "Différance" is a neologism created by Derrida to illuminate his conception of language operations. The word is derived from the French *différer*, which means not only "to differ" but also "to defer." For Derrida, signs generate meaning not only because they differ from one another but also because they defer their ultimate meaning from one sign to the next: A "cat" is a "cat" because it is not a "bat," which is not a "rat," which is not a "hat," etc. The différance that inheres in language ensures the production of meaning, but it also ensures that the meaning of a sign can never be fixed to a single and stable referent.

17. Rosalie David, *A Guide to Religious Ritual at Abydos* (Warminster, England: Aris & Phillips, 1981), 125–51.
18. Ibid., 10.
19. Edouard Naville, "Excavations at Abydos: The Great Pool and the Tomb of Osiris," *Journal of Egyptian Archaeology* 1, no. 3 (July 1914), 166.

William Alexander Leidesdorff and the American 1847

Minstrelsy and Race in California before the Gold Rush

—ANDREW GIBB

In the many excellent theorizations of minstrelsy published over the last few decades, the people and places of the U.S. West appear infrequently.[1] The notable exception is Eric Lott's chapter in *Love and Theft*, titled "California Gold and European Revolution: Stephen Foster and the American 1848."[2] In that piece, Lott conducts a close analysis of the minstrel songs popular in California during the Gold Rush and concludes that minstrelsy acted locally as "the badge of northern sectional formation and its developing struggles over slavery" (203). That explanation figures minstrelsy in California as an extension of the contentious racial politics of the eastern United States. While the point is forcefully argued, it emerges from an assumption that Lott never explicitly acknowledges: that the experience of contemporary white immigrants is of paramount importance to understanding the meanings of minstrelsy in nineteenth-century California.

But minstrelsy did not come to the West Coast with the miners. The first recorded minstrel performance in California was acted by occupying U.S. soldiers in the spring of 1847, at the height of the U.S.–Mexico War, nearly a year before the fateful discovery of gold. J. E. Lawrence of the San Francisco *Golden Era*, writing a journalistic history of California theatre in 1855, recorded the details of that inaugural minstrel show: "During the summer of 1847, some of the soldiers of Company F, New York Volunteers, gave a series of negro minstrel performances at Santa Barbara, where they arrived in April of that year. A portion of this band had previously given four or five entertainments at Liedesdorff's [*sic*] old City Hotel, San Francisco, in March, 1847, immediately after their arrival in the country."[3] Both the public venue (San Francisco's only hotel at the time) and the Volunteers' extended run argue against a show intended solely for the entertainment of fellow soldiers; local audiences no doubt contributed to the show's success. But in the spring of 1847, the local population of San Francisco (then known as Yerba Buena) included few Anglo Americans, and certainly no gold miners. What might non-Anglo local spectators have made of the soldiers' unfamiliar racial mimicry? How might the performance have read within the racial order peculiar to Mexican California? What might the conquering soldier-actors have conveyed to their audiences about a possible new racial hierarchy in California's future? And how are we to interpret the seemingly counterintuitive fact that the host of California's first minstrel show, hotel owner William Alexander Leidesdorff, is today celebrated as one of California's most important African American pioneers? The performance of a minstrel show within this space, so different from the genre's usual venues, throws the assumptions that historians make about minstrelsy into sharp relief.

I suggest that these performances be read as actions performed within a specific, local framework of assumptions about race, society, and power. Those assumptions, it should be understood, were radically different from those commonly held in the eastern United States, from whence minstrelsy emerged. Interpreting the performances within this unique geographical and social context not only offers us further insight into the minstrel phenomenon but also allows us to see how the racial preoccupations of the antebellum United States played out among local, non-Anglo populations at the frontiers of the nation's expanding power.[4] A detailed examination of the 1847 San Francisco minstrel shows reveals multiple, culturally specific notions of race being contested at the local level *before* the Gold Rush brought the region into the center of the slavery debate. What's more, through the unique figure of hotel owner and host William Leidesdorff, we can see how Californians of nonwhite ancestry took an active part in that negotiation. Concentrating on the circumstances of production and reception, I argue that minstrelsy's introduction to California reveals a contemporary struggle about how race was going to signify on the new U.S. frontier.

The minstrel show as understood by producers and audiences in the eastern United States relied upon a number of cultural assumptions commonly held by antebellum whites. Those beliefs are often accepted as given by historians in their discussions of minstrelsy, but they need to be foregrounded if we are to make sense of a minstrel performance outside of the form's original site. The first such assumption was that the notion of "race" was a valid category for differentiating and hierarchizing human beings. Another, which might be considered a corollary to the first, was the idea that different races displayed distinctive characteristics—physical, psychological, moral—and that such characteristics were evident for all to see. For a minstrel show to function as intended, audiences had to bring those assumptions with them into the theatre. Put more plainly, white audiences in the United States of the 1830s and 1840s shared with actors and managers a belief that whites were fundamentally different from (and superior to) the African American characters portrayed onstage. For such audiences, much of the humor of the minstrel show arose from a shared recognition of supposed racial characteristics that demonstrated African American inferiority. While there is little purpose in enumerating those stereotypical characteristics here, it is important to acknowledge their acceptance by eastern minstrel audiences, in light of the historical shift in venue represented by the San Francisco shows. For on the frontiers of the Mexican nation in the nineteenth century, the aforementioned assumptions were far from universal. Whereas some Mexicans may have accepted contemporary beliefs about race's biological basis, there was little agreement as to the signifiers that defined race.

Race on the Frontiers of Mexico

By the time the Volunteers arrived in the Mexican province of Alta California, the territory had been under military occupation since the previous July, when Commodore Sloat of the U.S. Navy, hearing of the outbreak of the U.S.–Mexico War, sent his men ashore at the Mexican Californian capital of Monterey to raise the Stars and Stripes. Occupation would lead inexorably to U.S. annexation following the war, and, driven by the massive migrations of the Gold Rush, to an unprecedentedly swift statehood in 1850.[5] But in the spring of 1847, the war still raged in the heartlands of Mexico, and on the California frontier, life largely continued according to social arrangements that had been in place since before Mexican Independence in 1821.

Beginning with Spanish colonization in the sixteenth century, and continuing into the nineteenth century and beyond, Native Americans and African Americans constituted the largest portion of the population in most Latin American states, from Chile to the northern frontier of Mexico. This demographic preponderance made it impossible for the European-descended minority to enact the kind of rigid controls on interracial procreation that developed in the slaveholding areas of the United States. As a result, the majority of the population of Latin America, including that of Mexican California, could claim indigenous and/or African heritage. Nevertheless, throughout the

Spanish colonial and early republican eras of Latin American nations, European-descended minorities attempted to assert social control by linking power to race, both practically and ideologically. Those of European birth, or whose ancestors were European, assumed that they deserved the highest positions of power, and such offices were reserved for them by law and custom. Offspring of unions between members of this European ruling class and subject Native Americans or African Americans, although not granted access to the halls of highest power, were nevertheless trusted by Euro-Americans with positions of lesser authority, such as that of plantation overseer, or of ranch majordomo. For the most part, those with a fully Native or African American heritage were delegated to positions of manual labor or service. For this pyramidal social structure to function, those at the top had to keep close track of all the possible permutations of human reproduction and delineate the limits of access for each mixture of genetic backgrounds. This need for a method of racial tracking led to the formulation of the *castas*. According to this classification system, all individuals could trace their heritage back to at least one of three racial groups, each considered to have its own separate, unchanging, biologically determined physical and mental traits. These essentialized groups included African Americans (the casta of *negros*), Native Americans (*indios*), and whites (*españoles*). Keeping those categories intact required that the offspring of each potential pairing between the three groups be assigned their own castas: an español and an india would together produce a *mestizo* child. A negro and an española would produce a *mulato*. An indio and a negra would give birth to a *zambo*. Those of mixed parentage might eventually partner with others like them, or with members of the three essentialized groups. Offspring of those second-generation unions were also each given a new casta title.[6] For the sake of the present study, it is not necessary to delve more deeply into this phenomenon but merely to contrast it with the system of racial classification common in the nineteenth-century United States. There, as in Latin America, European heritage was a prerequisite for access to the highest levels of power. But the racial fluidity and complexity that characterized the middling levels of power in Latin America was almost unknown in the United States, where a single African American ancestor, no matter how far back in the family tree, could disqualify one for positions of authority. This far more rigid approach to interracial procreation and its relation to power is often shorthanded as the "one drop rule." Although a good number of mixed-heritage people lived in the United States, they were never granted the same kinds of authority commonly afforded their compatriots in Latin America. The singular exceptions to this general rule were the communities of free people of color within the United States, such as that of New Orleans, which will be discussed in greater detail later. Within such communities a wider range of social mobility was granted to African-descended people, but it is worth noting that the social boundaries of such communities were always sharply delineated and rigorously policed by whites. That outside pressure led to the decline of many such communities in the United States as the nineteenth century progressed.

In the great metropolitan centers of Latin America, the casta system provided a way to identify those eligible to take up the necessary tasks of governance and business and those prepared by birth to provide labor and be governed. But Mexico's northern frontiers were sparsely populated and had been settled primarily by mestizos and mulatos. In such an environment, a direct connection between casta and individual social position could not be rigidly enforced. This situation made exceptional cases possible, such as that of Pío Pico, who became governor of California despite the fact that his grandmother was early mulata pioneer Jacinta de la Bastida.[7] Such examples of social mobility, unthinkable in either the Anglo United States or Mexico City, clearly indicate that strict correlations between race and class were not enforced in frontier Mexican California.

The relative fluidity of racial hierarchy in Mexican California should not, however, be taken as an indication of a race-blind society. Instead, it should be considered as a critical historical factor that led to a very particular employment of race as a tool of social organization. In period California, the most important distinction was a local racialized dualism of *gente de razón* and *gente sin razón*. Translated roughly as "people of reason" and "people without reason," the terms were coined by colonizing Spaniards in order to draw racial distinctions between themselves and Native Californians. The "reason" evoked was the reason of God and civilization, which Native Californians were judged to be born without. Such reason was not strictly essentialized, however, as the evangelizing philosophy of California's missionary priests held that indigenous peoples could be led to the light eventually. Given this theological emphasis on the equality of souls, it is perhaps more accurate to say that, for Spanish and later Mexican Californians, de razón was signaled by a series of performed behaviors. The term generated a distinction between those who lived (or were deemed capable of living) according to Euro-American cultural mores and those who did (could) not. Necessary performances included appropriate religious beliefs, normative sexual and marriage practices, and a suitable respect for established social hierarchy.

These distinctions, formulated during the Spanish colonial period, continued to shape California society during the Mexican period. Following secularization in 1834, the vast land holdings of the famed California missions were divided among a small number of californio (Mexican Californian) landowners, who established great ranchos of thousands of acres apiece. Local life quickly became organized around these sites of agricultural production and their owners. Native and poor Mexican Californian laborers were forced into positions of dependent labor, and in exchange received food, clothing, shelter, and occasional largesse from the landowners. Historians have often labeled this arrangement of California society "feudal," but Douglas Monroy, borrowing from Eugene Genovese, has instead advanced the term "seigneurial culture" as more apt to the description of contemporary labor conditions.[8] The term refers to a system that demonstrates elements of both modern capitalism and medieval feudalism, without really resembling either. "Neither a chattel nor a market arrangement," Monroy writes, "but a relationship of mutual and personal dependency . . . attached the laborers to the rancho" (102). As a culture of elite land ownership developed, the necessity for strategic familial alliances grew, with new partnerships often sealed through marriage. In short order, California society arranged itself around a handful of powerful men, each supporting a large following of retainers and connected by families' ties to a region wide network of fellow elites. In this new environment, local use of the term "gente de razón" shifted toward a more strictly economic meaning, distinguishing the landowning classes from the laboring portions of society. Importantly for the present study, nonwhite heritage did not bar entrance into the top tier of this new hierarchy. As has been noted, Pío Pico obtained the highest office in the land. Manuel Domínguez, one of the region's wealthiest ranchers and a popular local politician, was the child of a Native Californian mother. The prominence of these men was not tied to their race but was prescribed by their social obligations to others within the economic system. Their social identity was determined through their performance of those obligations, and it is through such performances that the local social hierarchy was perpetuated.

William Alexander Leidesdorff and the Performance of Hierarchy

This complex system of race and class signification provided the backdrop against which the New York Volunteers offered their eastern-generated parody of African Americans in the spring of 1847. Their demeaning representation had little in common with the lived experience of the African-descended population of California, which included most prominently the host of the San Francisco shows, William Alexander Leidesdorff. Leidesdorff is today claimed by Californians as one of their most distinguished African American pioneers, a surprising appellation for the man who helped introduce minstrelsy to the state. Yet it is precisely the unexpected nature of that association that makes the contemporary California experience so ripe for analysis. And in the case of the Volunteers' minstrel shows it is Leidesdorff, more than any other participant, who embodies the complexity of the place and the event.

Leidesdorff's African heritage did not come by way of eighteenth-century migration from Mexico, as was the case with californios such as the Picos. And unlike many of California's later African American pioneers, who came with the Gold Rush, Leidesdorff was not born in the eastern United States. In some ways, had Leidesdorff hailed from either of these two constitutive communities, his participation in the minstrel shows—his motives and expectations—might be easier to explain. But once again, the uniqueness of the California situation during the period asserts itself. For Leidesdorff was an African Caribbean by birth. And to make matters even more complex, his father was a European-born Jew. The circumstances of his extraordinary life assured that, wherever he went, he would always to some degree find himself at the fringes of society. And yet, like so many liminal figures before and since, Leidesdorff was able to parlay his ambiguous social standing into positions of cultural influence. At no point in his life was this more true than during his time in California.

Leidesdorff was born in 1810 on the Caribbean island of St. Croix, at that time a Danish colony. His father, William Leidesdorff, was a Danish Jewish sugar plantation owner.[9] When the elder Leidesdorff arrived in the Caribbean is unknown, but he may well have immigrated to St. Croix in the pursuit of opportunities unavailable to him in the mother country. Although Denmark had opened its doors officially to Jews in the seventeenth century, full citizenship rights were not recognized until 1814. The Danish overseas colonies could provide an outlet for Danish Jews who sought to escape legal restrictions at home, which included a ban on land ownership.[10]

Despite his business success in the Caribbean, there is no record that the elder Leidesdorff ever fully integrated into Danish society through marriage. Perhaps this is due to Danish laws forbidding intermarriage between Christians and Jews or to anti-Semitic feeling on the island.[11] He did, however, cohabitate with Anna Marie Sparks, a woman of African and European ancestry, who bore him several children, including William Alexander. Although the planters of St. Croix were as guilty of the sexual exploitation of enslaved black women as their compatriots across the Americas, it appears that Ms. Sparks was a free woman of color. Possibly Cuban by birth, she may have lived for some time in New Orleans before coming to St. Croix.[12]

Information about William Alexander's early life and education is scarce; he may or may not have been sent to Europe for schooling. At some point he relocated to New Orleans, where he must have appreciated the social opportunities open to a man of mixed heritage such as himself. From the 1810s to the 1830s, free persons of color constituted roughly one quarter of that city's population, and they enjoyed a level of freedom and prosperity unparalleled in the United States.[13] But by the time Leidesdorff became a naturalized U.S. citizen in 1834, the community was already under assault by whites eager to bring New Orleans in line with the racial order prevalent in the wider United States. Whether these steadily worsening conditions were the cause of Leidesdorff's departure for California is unknown, but the timing and direction of his move both support that interpretation: Leidesdorff signed on as master of a California-bound ship in 1841, just one year before a new law in Louisiana outlawed business contacts in the West Indies for free persons of color.[14]

While we may have to conjecture about the motive behind Leidesdorff's relocation to California in 1841, the outcome is certain. After only two years of trading up and down California and in Hawaii, he accumulated enough wealth to purchase a town lot in the port town of Yerba Buena, destined to become the harbor of San Francisco. On that lot he built the settlement's first hotel.[15] Leidesdorff quickly realized that his local ambitions would be limited as long as he remained a foreigner, and so in 1844 he applied for and was granted Mexican citizenship.[16] With that move, the Jewish African Caribbean immigrant secured a future in his adopted home, for as a naturalized Mexican he was eligible to receive a land grant, a development that was immediately forthcoming: in the very year of his conversion, he was awarded the 35,000-acre *Rancho Rio de Los Americanos*, initiating him into the ranks of the ruling-class californio elite.[17]

One final honor awaited Leidesdorff in his ascension to local prominence. In 1845, he was offered the position of U.S. vice-consul to California, which he accepted despite his official status as a Mexican citizen.[18] In taking on the post, Leidesdorff agreed to encourage californios to secede from Mexico and join the United States. Leidesdorff's subsequent participation in the events leading up to the U.S. conquest is a clear indication that he embraced the idea of a U.S. California.[19] These actions raise the question of why Leidesdorff would be so eager to see the racist nation he had so recently escaped absorb the haven of relative tolerance he had found in Mexican California.

For our purposes here, the more immediate question is why he would support a local performance of the most theatrical expression of Anglo-American racism, the minstrel show. Surely he had become acquainted with the form while in New Orleans. By the spring of 1847, William Alexander Leidesdorff, once illegitimate and disenfranchised, had found a place of acceptance and distinction in local California society. What's more, he achieved this without attempting to obscure his racial heritage, as all sources indicate that Leidesdorff's African heritage was no secret in Yerba Buena.[20] Takeover by the Unites States had the potential to threaten that hard-won position by reinstating a racial order he had chosen to leave behind. By inviting a minstrel show into his hotel, he ran the risk of drawing the attention of the invaders to his own nonwhite heritage, with possible disastrous effects to his place in local society. Yet he chose that risk, understanding how race functioned differently in California and how the production of theatre fit into the social fabric of Mexican California.

The ritualistic performance of hierarchy and mutual obligation that constructed and maintained californio society could take many forms. Community feasts were a common symbolic expression of social organization. Elites regularly hosted such events, to which it was understood the entire community was invited. Everyone would be fed, but only fellow landowners or important guests would be invited to dine indoors at the table of the californio host. At various points throughout the event, the host would display himself and his family before assembled guests, express his sense of obligation to the community, and receive praise for his generosity by the community's workers, both his own servants and those of his fellow elites. These dependents understood that they were required to respond with a performance of their own: a public display of gratitude and loyalty. Such reciprocal performances adhered them to their californio betters, securing them a continued living for themselves and their families.

Social position was similarly performed at the dances that often accompanied such feasts. Social dance was an extremely popular pastime in Mexican California and marked almost all important community occasions. Such dances could be lavish affairs, fully catered and frequently lasting until dawn, and were occasionally repeated on successive nights. As in the case of holiday feasts, the correct performance of social behaviors at these events clarified and justified the positions of individual attendees within the social hierarchy. The dances of Mexican California were more than mere gestures of charity from landowners to their dependant communities; they were multilayered performances that both reflected and shaped social arrangements.

An example that illustrates this process at work, and speaks to Leidesdorff's assimilation into elite californio society, is an event that preceded the run of the minstrels at Leidesdorff's hotel. On October 5, 1846, Yerba Buena fêted the newly installed commander of the U.S. occupation, Commodore Robert

F. Stockton, in a daylong celebration.[21] The day's festivities were capped with a dance, extravagantly hosted by Leidesdorff in the main room of his hotel. The evening is described in the diary of Yeoman Joseph Downey, a U.S. sailor fortunate enough to be given leave to attend: "But the crowning event was yet to come off and that was the Ball. Talk of your Dignity Balls, your Ball en masque, your Fancy Balls, and your 4th of July Balls—Pshaw. There never was a Ball given since Noah first landed from the ark that could compare in all its details with the 'Reception Ball' at Yerba Buena. The Large Dining Room of the largest house in the city was most brilliantly illuminated, and shone forth in all the blaze and brilliancy of 100 Spermacitte [*sic*] Candles, which reflected from some 30 or 40 mirrors the resplendent countenances of all the assembled beauty of the District of San Francisco."[22] This passage reveals the important function of the californio dance. Downey's description of the space—its size as well as its decoration with rare and expensive spermaceti candles and mirrors—underlines the importance of generous display to these gatherings. Through the dance in honor of Stockton we can see Leidesdorff acting out his role as californio elite, and in doing so midwifing the integration of U.S. national and local California power structures.

The production of theatre in Mexican California fit into the same patterns of power's display that feasts and dances exemplified. Before the Gold Rush sparked massive in-migration, population density in California communities was insufficient to support resident professional theatre companies. This did not mean, however, that theatre was unknown in California before traveling eastern actors followed their audiences to the mines. Prewar californios who hailed from, or traveled to, larger Mexican cities to the south were familiar with theatre and routinely collected playscripts from around the Spanish-speaking world for their libraries.[23] When itinerant performers occasionally visited the region, or whenever californio youths got the notion to put up a show, local elites would eagerly seize on the opportunity to both gratify their love of culture and display their seigneurial benevolence. They would offer the players the use of their homes, often the only structures in the community large enough to accommodate an indoor performance. The entire community would be invited, and no entrance fee would be charged. Workers would receive the gift of the arts, landowners could enrich their lives while seeing and being seen, and all would enjoy themselves at the invitation of their californio host. As with dances and feasts, all who participated would join in performing the social hierarchy of the community.

Ultimately, I contend that the explanation for Leidesdorff's participation in the staging of a minstrel show can be found by contextualizing the event within these local power arrangements. His actions make sense if his worldview is understood as primarily californio in outlook. Given his personal background and the steps he needed to take in order to achieve local prominence, it would have been clear to Leidesdorff that local power relations depended far more upon properly performed behavior than upon ambiguous racial classifications. In the wartime period before gold was discovered, Leidesdorff shared the hopes of his fellow californios that local power structures (and the cultural assumptions that underpinned them) would be integrated into a postwar California. If the patterns of local society were preserved in a U.S. California, Leidesdorff would maintain his position and could even open a new realm of possibility for African Americans in the region. To survive the turbulence of war and annexation, those patterns needed to be reiterated at every possible opportunity. When U.S. soldiers expressed a desire to put on a show, Leidesdorff made sure it would be performed under his roof. Although he may very well have found the minstrel shows personally distasteful, it was the production arrangement of the performances, and not their racist content, that would serve his ultimate ends.

Minstrelsy's Local Reception

When contextualized within local production practices, Leidesdorff's support of the soldier-minstrels can be read as an act of resistance to the eastern U.S. racism he fled by coming to California. By serving as the show's producer, Leidesdorff signaled *who* held the power in 1847 San Francisco and emphasized that local power had little to do with race. But while Leidsdorff may have hoped that his performance as munificent African American producer would trump the racist material staged by the actors, the extent to which it did so depended upon how well spectators understood the expression of power in the local arena. The soldier-actors of the New York Volunteers, for instance, were unfamiliar with Californian social arrangements and likely did not understand how local power was reflected in their choice of venue. But the attitudes of U.S. enlisted men would have held little concern for Leidesdorff. For him, the most important spectators would have been the elites of the town: his fellow californios, foreign merchants of the California trade, and the commanding officers of the U.S. invasion force. These were the men who would decide the future direction of California. How Leidesdorff's personal performance played to this heterogeneous assemblage of power brokers could affect how race and power were going to function in the new U.S. California.

One would assume that Leidesdorff's fellow californios were most likely to comprehend his seigneurial gesture as host, and therefore most likely to discount the shows' racist content. And yet it is precisely among that group that the shows might have done their most profoundly divisive work. For despite the relative acceptance of African-descended people in Mexican California, such heritage was by no means universal among californios. It is possible that those without African ancestry could have read the Volunteers' minstrel show as an invitation to adopt the racial order of the eastern United States.

To understand how such an appeal may have been received by californios, it is worthwhile considering a parallel minstrel performance, staged shortly afterward at another site of U.S. Pacific imperialism. In 1854, Commodore Matthew Perry led a U.S. fleet to Japan, with orders to force that nation's fiercely isolationist government to drop their restrictions on foreign trade. The subsequent monthlong negotiation was punctuated by a number of diplomatic events, among which was a minstrel show performed by U.S. sailors for the benefit of Japanese officials. Writing on that performance, theatre historian Esther Kim Lee suggests that we view it as a "symbolic mediator of political diplomacy."[24] She demonstrates that, even though the Japanese had little direct experience with Africans or African Americans, their mythology and folklore often figured black as evil or dangerous (8). Lee argues that this indigenous "trope of blackness" made minstrelsy's negative representations of African Americans legible to Japanese audiences. The invocation of blackness is critical, in Lee's interpretation, to understanding the crosscultural negotiations of the U.S. and Japanese delegates: "From the initial encounters to the signing of the treaty and to the establishment of formal diplomacy, blackness consistently operated as the target to which white Americans and Japanese could transfer their views of each other as barbaric and subhuman. By mediating through blackness, white American and Japanese were able to understand each other as civilized and worthy of respect" (3). Thus the blackface makeup of the minstrel performers invoked a U.S.–Japanese solidarity based upon a shared nonblackness.

Among Mexican San Franciscans, the makeup conventions and eastern-specific racist humor of the Volunteers' minstrel shows would have been unfamiliar enough to draw attention, and a process such as Lee suggests for the Japanese audiences might well have been at work among nonblack californios. Despite California's unique racial constructions, blackness still carried some negative stigma, enough perhaps to support a bridge between some californios and their Anglo-American counterparts.

That said, given the long history of African-descended people in California, audience reception of minstrelsy would by necessity be a far more complex process than what played out in Japan. If, as has been shown, social status in California was obtained and maintained by the proper performance of that status, and if class and race were intentionally conflated by ideological constructs like the castas, then one might speak of proper performances of race. Certainly a connection between social status and race has a long history in Latin America, where it is often expressed by the phrase *el dinero blanquea*, or "money whitens." For audiences acculturated to see the world in such a way, the racial essentialism trumpeted by minstrel shows must have seemed naïve, or at least unrealistic. Yet herein lies a paradox. For californio audience members could very well have dismissed the racial essentialism inherent to the shows, and still embraced the performativity of the Volunteers' expression of racial difference. In other words, *how* the soldiers' performed blackness might have seemed odd, but the fact that the soldiers were *performing* race might well have been accepted as normal. For locals, the very conventions of minstrelsy could well have resonated with their views about the mutability of race and the attendant ability to choose one's racial identity through performance. To californios of mixed heritage uncertain about the future of their society, the minstrel shows may have been interpreted as assurance that there could be a place for them within the new racial order, as long as they properly performed their white heritage and downplayed their other, particularly African, roots. Taken a step further, it is possible that californios viewed the minstrel shows as an opening through which they might graft onto a larger U.S. society their own local notions of race as a performance, rather than a condition. Perhaps the odd performance practices of these invading thespians suggested an openness on the part of Anglos to the idea of race as performance. For his part, Leidesdorff the producer was intimately familiar with Anglo constructions of race, and he would have fully understood the rigorous essentialism of the invaders' minds on the subject. Yet he may well have hoped that local understandings of race would result in his own performance (as producer) being valued over that of the Volunteers (as performers), at least within the local setting.

No eyewitness accounts from Leidesdorff's californio colleagues have survived, so it is impossible to say whose performance, the hotelier/host's or the soldiers/performers', read most strongly among that demographic. Later evidence does suggest, however, that californios without African ancestry were willing to accept Anglo racism against blacks as long as their Native American heritage was overlooked. The case of californio Manuel Domínguez serves well to illustrate the point. Despite being born to a Native American woman, Domínguez inherited a great rancho and entered local politics, eventually serving as a delegate to the convention that drafted U.S. California's first state constitution, in 1849. During that convention, Domínguez objected to a proposed disenfranchisement of Native Americans. And yet, when the conversation turned to the denial of African American civil rights, Domínguez remained silent.[25] His actions suggest how even those californios whose Native American heritage put them on the firing line of a new U.S. racial order may well have been willing to shield themselves by embracing the antiblack racism of the Volunteers.

The San Francisco venue for the Volunteers' minstrel shows almost certainly ensured that some spectators were neither invading Anglo-Americans nor socially threatened californios. Throughout its Mexican era, the port was unique among California towns in its demographic profile. A good portion of its population consisted of transient foreigners, leading one period commentator to describe the place as "this lively, gossipy, Yankee, British, German, Russian and Mexican town."[26] Any number of visiting Europeans may have attended the 1847 San Francisco minstrel shows, and it is worthwhile to consider what meanings the performances might have carried for them.

In her 2010 study *Racial Geometries of the Black Atlantic, Asian Pacific and American Theatre*, Shannon Steen writes about blackface minstrelsy in the United States between the world wars. She notes an increase in African American performers appearing on U.S. stages during the period and a simultaneous decline of white minstrel performers, a development she attributes to the emergent notion of theatrical authenticity.[27] The notable exception for Steen is Al Jolson, famed Jewish American minstrel performer and star of *The Jazz Singer*, who pointed the way, she argues, toward a new understanding of white minstrelsy: "Following a trajectory inaugurated in *The Jazz Singer*, white characters still blacked up, but almost always as part of a showbiz narrative in which the blackface functioned as a play within a play (or equally commonly, as a play within a movie). In other words, audiences were asked to *see through blackface*" (34–35, emphasis mine). Steen writes about the final stages of white minstrelsy, chronologically far removed from the 1847 performance of the New York Volunteer minstrels. But her notion of "seeing through blackface" may well afford some insight into the reception of the San Francisco shows. The Volunteers were certainly not "asking" their audiences to see through their racial impersonation in the way Steen suggests, or indeed in any other way. But audiences unfamiliar with minstrel traditions and conventions may have "seen through" the soldiers' blackface in a similar fashion. It is an established fact that by 1847 minstrelsy was an international phenomenon, and it must be assumed that minstrel conventions were familiar to some San Francisco spectators.[28] But the specific cultural conditions out of which minstrelsy arose determined how it was seen by its various national audiences. Whites in the eastern United States, who lived in uneasy coexistence with African Americans and saw minstrels as an onstage embodiment of their fears, may have unconsciously discounted the signs of performers' whiteness to a degree impossible for British, French, or Russian whites. If so, European audiences would be far more likely to "see through" the blackface mask than would U.S. theatergoers.

The split reception I'm suggesting here cannot be proven conclusively with respect to the San Francisco shows. Yet such differences are apparent in the wider record of period minstrel shows. In his *Blacking Up: The Minstrel Show in Nineteenth-Century America*, Robert Toll cites several accounts of white U.S. audience members mistakenly believing that the actors they watched were true African Americans, not disguised whites.[29] By contrast British audiences, argues Robert Nowatzki in *Representing African Americans in Transatlantic Abolitionism and Blackface Minstrelsy* (2010), were sensitive to visiting minstrel performers as white Americans from the very first London productions.[30] In the case of the San Francisco shows, then, any British audience member, regardless of previous experience with the form, would have been far less likely to accept the performer's impersonation as reality than would a U.S.-born viewer.

If such a hypothetical British (or Russian, or French) viewer saw through the burnt cork to the bodies beneath, the effect would be to emphasize the whiteness of those Anglo-American bodies and to underline the contrast between them and those of nonwhites. The favored position of Europeans in the period Pacific trade was the result of ongoing cultural negotiations with local inhabitants in the various trading centers. In most cases, Europeans who were engaged in those exchanges acted upon the assumption of white superiority and nonwhite inferiority. British traders had a long history with California but had been deeply invested in intercultural exchange with China and India for far longer. The Pacific fur trade brought Russians to California, but only after a significant engagement with Native Alaskans. The French had only a passing interest in the American West Coast, but they were actively striving for dominance over Polynesians. If British or Russians or Frenchmen saw through the minstrel mask—which could all too easily be substituted for a Chinese, Native Alaskan, or Polynesian face—then perhaps they were relieved to see the familiar face of the Anglo-Saxon conqueror underneath. Even if those Europeans feared or resented the United States as a trade rival, the concession of California to fellow whites at least maintained and strengthened the emerging racial order of the Pacific Rim. In choosing to mount a minstrel show, the New York Volunteers foregrounded their own whiteness and thus signaled to any European audience member that California was now securely under the control of a white power. What is more, through the minstrel act of racial mimicry, the soldier-actors may have signaled to those foreign audiences, however falsely, that U.S. whites possessed an innate understanding of nonwhites and that such a knowledge guaranteed control over nonwhite populations. Such a claim would no doubt have been reassuring to the Pacific's European colonizers.

Leidesdorff's Legacy

Leidesdorff's seigneurial benevolence provided a counterperformance to the dualistic racial model inherent in the Volunteers' representation. Just as the soldier-minstrels' humor relied upon eastern assumptions about race, so the resistant potential of the Leidesdorff's self-representation depended upon particular local assumptions. The production and consumption of the San Francisco shows demonstrate the delicate balance between local californio power and Anglo–American military dominance that characterized the political and social landscape of California in 1847. Had that state of affairs prevailed into a postwar territorial period, a racial order distinctly different from that of the eastern United States might have taken hold on the western frontier. California may have become a model for a relatively more equitable integration of Native and African Americans into the social life of the United States. Had the region not entered into the Union until after the Civil War, pioneers like Leidesdorff might have inspired large-scale African American migration to the West Coast.

Unfortunately, the Gold Rush destroyed those possibilities. Negotiations between national and local formations of race, initiated during the wartime occupation, were swamped by the demographic flood of Anglo Americans into the region following the discovery of gold in 1848. Californio attitudes about race were rapidly and forcefully displaced by those dominant in the eastern states. Within just two short years, California entered fully into the Union as a condition of the Compromise of 1850, guaranteeing that slavery and race would become a central issue for the people and government of the new state. Antiblack legal sentiment was apparent from the first manifestation of an Anglo-American government. The original state constitution, promulgated in 1850, denied the franchise to African Americans. A law passed in 1851 barred blacks from testifying against whites in court, and in 1852 the state legislature passed the California Fugitive Slave Act. The chilling effect of those early exclusionary efforts can be seen in the fact that African Americans represented a flat 1 percent of the California population from 1850 through the 1920s.[31]

Despite the forces driving these measures, it seems possible that African- and Native-descended Californians, especially those with a local power base, could have had some alleviating effect on the trend. Who, for instance, would be better suited to representing San Francisco in the Constitutional Convention than Leidesdorff? And would he not be likely to raise an objection to his own disenfranchisement? Unfortunately, he never got the chance to make that objection. In May 1848, just days after the news of the gold strikes reached San Francisco, William Alexander Leidesdorff fell victim to an acute case of meningitis and died at the age of thirty-eight. With much public fanfare, he was laid to rest among his californio compatriots in the crypt of Mission Dolores.[32] Noted African American historian Sue Bailey Thurman, in her 1952 biographical essay on Leidesdorff, offers this elegiac assessment of the man's effect on San Francisco history: "The citizen of today—whatever racial, creedal or national origin, migrant like himself—may walk 'The City's' streets with dignity, knowing that Leidesdorff helped immeasurably to establish this right, a hundred years ago."[33] Modern Californians, inheritors of 150 years of racial strife, must be left to decide for themselves whether or not Thurman's evaluation of Leidesdorff's legacy rings true. Nevertheless, it is difficult not to interpret the nearly simultaneous events of gold discovery and Leidesdorff's passing as a double blow to the hopes of the region's nonwhite communities.

Irrespective of our judgment of Leidesdorff's actions and their consequences, the San Francisco minstrel shows of 1847 provide an important reminder about the period debate over race and slavery: that despite the national scope of the argument, it always to a greater or lesser degree played out at a local level. Our current understanding of minstrelsy, and of the antebellum period generally, must take the specificities of place into account.

Notes

1. Other than Lott's contribution, discussed in the text of this piece, the only theorization of minstrelsy that takes the U.S. West into account is a short passage from a chapter on minstrelsy in Alexander Saxton's book *The Rise and Fall of the White Republic* (New York: Verso, 1990), 165–82; see pages 171–73. The author would like to thank Leo Cabranes-Grant, William Davies King, and Carlos Morton, who responded to an early draft of this work. The generous comments of Rosemarie Bank, Paul Keith Bryant-Jackson, Dorothy Chansky, Elizabeth Reitz Mullenix, Heather S. Nathans, and Jon D. Rossini were vital to the present version.
2. Eric Lott, *Love and Theft: Blackface Minstrelsy and the American Working Class* (New York: Oxford University Press, 1993), chapter 7.
3. J. E. Lawrence, "Drama on the Pacific: First Theatricals in California, Number 1," San Francisco *Golden Era*, April 15, 1855.
4. Throughout this essay, I employ the term "Anglo" in a manner common to writing on the U.S. West, as a catchall term to refer to European-descended persons, regardless of

their degree of English ancestry, whose heritage can be traced to the eastern portions of the North American continent from the time of English colonization to at least the beginnings of trans-Mississippi expansion.

5. Richard B. Rice, William A. Bullough, and Richard J. Orsi, *The Elusive Eden: A New History of California*, 3rd ed. (New York: Alfred A. Knopf, 2002), 162, 169–70.
6. Jack D. Forbes, "Black Pioneers: The Spanish-Speaking Afroamericans of the Southwest," in *Minorities in California History*, ed. George E. Frakes and Curtis B. Solberg (New York: Random House, 1971), 22.
7. Lonnie Bunch, *Black Angelenos: The Afro-American in Los Angeles, 1850–1950* (Los Angeles: California Afro-American Museum, 1988), 12.
8. Douglas Monroy, "The Creation and Re-creation of Californio Society," in *Contested Eden: California Before the Gold Rush*, ed. Ramón Gutiérrez and Richard J. Orsi (Berkeley: University of California Press, 1998), 173–95.
9. John N. Ingham and Lynne B. Feldman, *African-American Business Leaders: A Biographical Dictionary* (Westport: Greenwood Press, 1994), 424.
10. Conrad Kisch, "The Jewish Community in Denmark: History and Present Status," *Judaism: A Quarterly Journal of Jewish Life and Thought* 47 (1998): 214–31.
11. Restrictive laws in Denmark expressly forbade sexual contact between Jewish men and Christian women (Kisch, "The Jewish Community in Denmark," 216). Neville A. T. Hall cites specific instances of anti-Semitic violence, both physical and verbal, on St. Croix in the late eighteenth and early nineteenth centuries (*Slave Society in the Danish West Indies: St. Thomas, St. John, and St. Croix*, ed. B. W. Higman [Baltimore: The Johns Hopkins University Press, 1992], 104, 244n75).
12. Gary Mitchell Palgon, *William Alexander Leidesdorff: First Black Millionaire, American Consul and California Pioneer* (Raleigh: Lulu Enterprises, 2005), 8, quoting Robert Ernest Cowan, "The Leidesdorff-Folsom Estate: A Forgotten Chapter in the Romantic History of Early San Francisco," *Quarterly of the California Historical Society* 7, no. 2 (June 1928), 105–11.
13. Joseph Logsdon and Caryn Cossé Bell, "The Americanization of Black New Orleans, 1850–1900," in *Creole New Orleans: Race and Americanization*, ed. Arnold R. Hirsch and Joseph Logsdon (Baton Rouge: Louisiana State University Press, 1992), 201–61. See also Mary Gehman, *The Free People of Color of New Orleans: An Introduction* (New Orleans: Margaret Media, 1994).
14. Gehman, *The Free People of Color of New Orleans*, 67, 52.
15. Ingham and Feldman, *African-American Business Leaders*, 426; Palgon, *William Alexander Leidesdorff*, 11.
16. Sue Bailey Thurman, "William Alexander Leidesdorff," in *Pioneers of Negro Origin in California* (San Francisco: Acme Publishing Company, 1952), 1–3. See also Hubert Howe Bancroft's *History of California* (San Francisco: The History Company, 1884–1890), 4:711.
17. Palgon, *William Alexander Leidesdorff*, 21.
18. Thurman, "William Alexander Leidesdorff," 3.
19. Ingham and Feldman, *African-American Business Leaders*, 427.
20. Bancroft, recording the details of Leidesdorff's racial heritage in the 1880s, must have gathered his facts from mid-century sources, or from those who had known Leidesdorff. His ancestry must therefore have been common knowledge in California (Bancroft,

History of California, 4:711). Ingham and Feldman quote two of Leidesdorff's San Francisco contemporaries who claimed open knowledge of his African heritage (426).

21. Joseph T. Downey, *The Cruise of the Portsmouth, 1845–1847: A Sailor's View of the Naval Conquest of California*, ed. Howard Lamar (New Haven and London: Yale University Press, 1963), 149–50; Edward Cleveland Kemble, *A Kemble Reader: Stories of California, 1846–1848*, ed. Fred B. Rogers (San Francisco: California Historical Society, 1963), 45–46; Edwin Bryant, *What I Saw in California* (1848; repr., Minneapolis: Ross & Haines, 1967), 330–31.
22. Downey, *The Cruise of the Portsmouth, 1845–1847*, 150.
23. The perfect example of the theatrically well-read californio is Rafael Guerrero, who in 1852–53 produced a season in Los Angeles that included Spanish playwright José Zorrila y Moral's *Don Juan Tenorio*, which premiered only eight years earlier in Madrid, and *Pablo, o la familia del Mendigo*, published a mere three years before by an eighteen-year-old Peruvian prodigy, José Arnaldo Márquez. Advertisements for these shows appear in the November 13 and 27 issues of the bilingual *Los Angeles Star/La Estrella*. Information on Márquez can be found in Maria Elisa Flores's "Lima en la literatura: análisis histórico bibliográfico, 1535–2002" (Lima: Bibliotécnic Consultores, 2002). Available online at http://biblioteca1.pe.tripod.com/documentos/documento6.doc.
24. Esther Kim Lee, "Ethiopian Concert and Sumo Wrestling: A Study of Theatre and Performance During Commodore Perry's Japan Expedition." Presented at the 27th Mid-America Theatre Conference, Chicago, IL, March 2006, 3.
25. Neal Harlow, *California Conquered: War and Peace on the Pacific, 1846–1850* (Berkeley: University of California Press, 1982), 342.
26. Kemble, *A Kemble Reader*, 35–36.
27. Shannon Steen, *Racial Geometries of the Black Atlantic, Asian Pacific and American Theatre* (New York: Palgrave Macmillan, 2010), 33–34.
28. Early U.S. minstrel star Thomas D. "Daddy" Rice first performed in London in 1836, where he was an immediate success. See Michael Pickering, *Blackface Minstrelsy in Britain* (Aldershot: Ashgate, 2008), 7–8.
29. Robert Toll, *Blacking Up: The Minstrel Show in Nineteenth-Century America* (New York: Oxford University Press,1974), 38, 60n26.
30. Robert Nowatzki, *Representing African Americans in Abolitionism and Blackface Minstrelsy* (Baton Rouge: Louisiana State University Press, 2010), 62–63.
31. Robert L. Carlton, "Blacks in San Diego County: A Social Profile, 1850–1880," *The Journal of San Diego History* 21, no. 4 (Fall 1975), 7–20.
32. Thurman, "William Alexander Leidesdorff," 3–4. See also Frank Soulé, John H. Gihon, and James Nisbet, *The Annals of San Francisco* (New York: D. Appleton and Company, 1855), 201.
33. Thurman, "William Alexander Leidesdorff," 5.

Antebellum Touring and the Culture of Deception

The Case of Master Diamond

—NICOLE BERKIN

In 1821, while performing with James Caldwell's company in Norfolk, Virginia, actor Noah Ludlow first met visiting star Junius Brutus Booth. Ludlow could hardly believe that the short, disheveled man before him was "one of the brightest 'stars' in the Western dramatic horizon." In fact, he had "some doubts whether he was the *real* Booth, or some impudent adventurer, who, having heard that Mr. Booth contemplated visiting America, took this peculiar way of introducing himself, and, if possible, 'humbugging' the Yankees before the real Booth should arrive."[1] It was not until the fourth act of Booth's performance in *Richard III* that Ludlow finally witnessed a great talent and was convinced of the star's true identity. A few years later, while traveling with a small circus, then-emerging entrepreneur P. T. Barnum was also entangled in a case of mistaken identity, but one of a very different sort. Upon arriving in Camden, South Carolina, he was suddenly abandoned by the blackface minstrel dancer in his company, prompting an instance of the showman's characteristic resourcefulness: "I had advertised negro songs; no one of my company was competent to fill his place; but being determined not to disappoint the audience, *I blacked myself thoroughly*, and sung the songs advertised . . . to my surprise, my singing was applauded, and in two of the songs I was encored!" According to Barnum, this act was a bit *too* convincing. Following one evening's performance, he intervened in a dispute between a man and some members of the company. Seeing Barnum, the man pulled out a pistol: "You black scoundrel! dare you use such language to a white man?" Barnum quickly responded: "I rolled up my shirt sleeves, and replied, 'I am as white as *you* are, sir.' He absolutely dropped the pistol with fright!"[2]

Ludlow and Barnum suggest the prevalence of impersonation and detection, not simply onstage in theatrical productions but also in the broader milieu of antebellum performance culture under the star system.[3] Historian James Cook describes the preoccupation with cultural fraud during the period as "artful deception," a paradoxical reception pattern that encouraged the slippage between "truth" and illusion in nineteenth-century popular entertainments. A commercial strategy epitomized by Barnum's elaborately staged public hoaxes, artful deception did not invite audiences to detect the sham, but rather, as the New York showman famously explained, to "let the public decide."[4] Indeed, as traveling performers seeking guest engagements became ubiquitous, so did debates over whether a star's status was deserved, and the term "star" became popularized in quotation marks as an implicit acknowledgment of the title's instability and ambiguity. This hesitation reflects a broader cultural interest in assessing whether stars were *really* stars and whether performers were really who they claimed to be.[5] The growing geographic circulation of performers in the antebellum period, before images to verify their identities were widely available, instantiated debates over their authenticity. Ludlow's suspicion toward Booth conveys the impression that "star" billing or even a famous name was not enough to verify an actor's legitimacy, while Barnum describes an instance of spectators believing a false impersonation rather than doubting the display of "true" identity.

Of course, the cultural interest in authenticity and impersonation—and specifically in racial mimicry—was inherent in minstrelsy. As Eric Lott has argued, the white imitation of nominally black movements, dance, and speech was rooted in *both* disdain *and* desire for black cultural practices. "Minstrel performers attempted to repress through ridicule the real interest in black cultural practices they nonetheless betrayed."[6] Instances when the racial counterfeit supposedly broke down especially revealed this mixture of attraction and repulsion, what Lott calls "love and theft." Like Barnum's outraged spectator, audiences who claimed to have witnessed the unsettling performances of genuine black men, rather than their white imitators, "subtly acknowledged the greater power of the genuine article, a fact that also illuminates the purpose of the diminished copy." According to Lott, minstrelsy was much more than white mockery or derision of black culture; rather, it was "a means of exercising white control over explosive cultural forms."[7]

Despite the obvious differences between Barnum's and Ludlow's stories, they are undoubtedly related as two responses to the new mobility that performers experienced in the decades during the star system. These anecdotes—both certainly embellished and in Barnum's case likely invented—also suggest that questions of legitimacy, of identifying the "real" thing, pervaded both the ostensibly "legitimate" theatre of scripted dramas *and* the realm of popular entertainments, particularly minstrelsy, thus undermining easy distinctions between these two categories of performance. The mixed connotations of stardom, and its potential for misidentification or impersonation, thus reached beyond star actors to encompass a variety of touring performers, and it is well known that during the antebellum period a typical evening at the theatre consisted not only of plays but also of popular entertainments. Blackface minstrels and acrobatic troupes, along with singers and musicians, appeared between the acts of scripted dramas and as afterpieces. Since stock companies primarily consisted of actors and actresses skilled in tragedies and comedies, or "legitimate" theatre, managers usually had to look outside their companies—to visiting performers—in order to present audiences with the popular entertainments that they expected to accompany plays. While jugglers, circus performers, magicians, and minstrels were not directly involved in star-stock dynamics related to lines of business or the dramatic repertoire, they were crucial to the larger frenzy for novel attractions—such as visitors who were new to local audiences—that was enabled by the star system.

In this essay, by examining a series of episodes that took place across the country in 1841, I demonstrate how popular entertainers and theatre managers capitalized on the mobility facilitated by the star system in specific ways, as well as how touring helped to promote and complicate familiar connotations of "popular" and "legitimate." By investigating the relationship between touring and perceptions of cultural legitimacy, I aim to advance the rich body of scholarship concerning the politics of the popular within the antebellum American culture industry.[8] Although cultural historians have long recognized the field of the popular as a mutable category and a site of social formation and struggle,[9] few have examined the crucial role of touring in the production of antebellum popular culture.[10] Taking the lead from cultural geographers such as Doreen Massey and Mark Simpson, who conceive of space as a "product of interrelations," and the movement of people and things as "contestatory processes" invested in the "making and breaking of subjectivities,"[11] I bring the paradigm of mobility to bear on nineteenth-century *theatre* culture. I contribute to the recent body of work on antebellum cultural circulation, which includes studies by James Cook and Daphne Brooks, among other scholars,[12] by focusing on neglected regional entertainment markets and on the transactions between performers and managers. I argue that touring was significant not only for stars of the legitimate stage who were famous enough to undertake transatlantic tours but also for popular performers who operated on the fringes of respectability and who negotiated with managers outside the major northeastern cities.

To Cook's theory of artful deception, I add that touring itself was a mode of cultural fraud. As a commercial strategy, deception was not only a "a perceptual contest played out between showman and viewer"[13] but also a way for performers and managers to compete with one another for cultural and economic control over the theatre business, and specifically for authority over expanding entertainment circuits in the South and the West. Both performers and managers attempted to use circulation to reinforce or remap the social and cultural categories that circumscribed them, including legitimate versus popular, respectable versus scandalous, and star versus unknown. This struggle for cultural power frequently occurred in what we might call the "margins" of the entertainment industry—in the journeys to and from theatrical events, in surrounding business transactions, and in cities outside of the northeastern cultural centers; these practices were not incidental to but constitutive of antebellum popular culture.

In the years following the financial panics of 1837 and 1839, early in his career and before establishing the American Museum, P. T. Barnum frequently managed small troupes of traveling performers. The economic collapse diminished Barnum's career prospects in New York, compelling him to go on the road in search of new regional markets. Although Barnum clearly recognized the opportunities afforded to traveling acts by the star system, he claims to have been "disgusted with the life of an itinerant showman" and "always regarded it, not as an end, but as a means to something better," to future employment in "a respectable, permanent business."[14] Of course, Barnum later became famous for glossing over his mercenary business ventures with the appearance of respectability. By disparaging traveling troupes as illegitimate while also exploiting their novelty and profitably, Barnum promoted his entertainments as both genteel and sensational. Barnum's posture of disapproval reflects a long history of attitudes toward theatrical itinerancy and popular entertainments that were still widespread during the antebellum period.

In the spring of 1840, Barnum set out on tour with singer and Yankee delineator C. D. Jenkins, an "orphan vagabond" named Francis Lynch, and seventeen-year-old Irish-American minstrel performer John Diamond, "the best negro-dancer and representative of the Ethiopian 'break-downs' in the land."[15] Because Diamond was not quite an adult, his contracts and payments were coordinated between his father and Barnum. In addition, due to Diamond's small stature and the potential publicity that came with the exhibition of a dance prodigy, Barnum presented the dancer as being only twelve years old, as "Master Diamond," a title then conferred upon male child performers.[16] In his memoir, Barnum recounts these early-career journeys as a series of adventures and mishaps; as opposed to the lucrative professional tours he would undertake a few years later with General Tom Thumb (Charles Stratton) and opera singer Jenny Lind, these travels were marked by their spontaneity and disorganization. Throughout, Barnum and his performers had to scramble to secure means of transportation, performance engagements, and boardinghouses while already on the road. They ventured through Buffalo, Toronto, Chicago, Springfield, and St. Louis before taking a steamship to New Orleans, where they arrived in early January 1841. By that point, Barnum's company of performers, recalling Barnum's earlier tour and brief foray into blackface minstrelsy, had been "reduced, by desertions."[17] Jenkins and Lynch had abandoned Barnum, and the showman had only $100 in his pocket. Eager to recoup his losses by employing the one performer he had left, Barnum sought an engagement for Diamond. Unlike touring star actors, who at least attempted to book their engagements months in advance, Barnum arranged the New Orleans performances for Diamond only upon arriving in that city. As opposed to actors traveling with their repertoire of roles, minstrels could, on short notice, insert their brief acts into the play billed for the evening. This flexibility also provided minstrel performers with promotional opportunities; before Diamond arrived in New Orleans, the local press took notice of his presence in the region and publicly speculated upon his possible performances in their city. Sending a signal to theatre managers in New Orleans, one reporter wrote: "This young extravaganza singer and dancer was at Vicksburg at last dates. . . . Whether he has an engagement at either of our theatres or not we are unable to say; but at New York he provided a great card to the managers and would doubtless draw here." When Diamond did indeed reach New Orleans, followed by gossip that he was spotted at the St. Charles Hotel, another journalist wondered which of the two rival theatres—the St. Charles, managed by James Caldwell, or the American, managed by Noah Ludlow and Sol Smith—would engage the celebrated performer.[18] Barnum ended up securing an engagement for Diamond at the St. Charles. The impromptu opportunities that arose for traveling popular entertainers seemed to work to Barnum's advantage in this instance, and according to the showman, "the tide began to flow" and he received $500 as half the share of Diamond's benefit, the first of three nights.[19] The press quickly responded with enthusiasm. Of the blackface dancer, one reporter wrote: "No other *diamond* ever cut such *shines*. . . . None but himself can be his parallel." At the end of the St. Charles engagement, another professed that even "lovers of the legitimate" "are waiting for another visitation from Master Diamond."[20]

Although Ludlow and Smith quickly became aware that Barnum and Diamond were engaged at their competitor's theatre, one letter suggests that the dancer was on the managers' minds even before his January arrival in the South and establishes the ambivalent mingling of popular and legitimate in theatrical business transactions. A few weeks prior, Ludlow received a note from his friend, actor Charles Keemle, who was in St. Louis assisting the managers with operations of their theatre in that city while the company was in New Orleans. Ludlow and Smith had instructed Keemle not to rent the unoccupied theatre under any circumstances, and Keemle "therefore declined letting it to any of the numerous applicants in the shape of jugglers, magicians—il est omnes genres."[21] Theatrical companies occasionally rented theatres that were owned or leased by other managers for entire seasons, while traveling popular entertainers often sought space for shorter engagements. As shown by Barnum's travels, in the early 1840s, circus troupes and blackface minstrel performers traveled separately from the larger infrastructure of theatres, visiting stars, and resident company managers, sometimes engaging with these "legitimate" houses but also finding alternative performance venues such as dance halls, taverns, or vacant theatres. Popular entertainers, whether individuals or troupes, could arrange with local companies for lengthy contracts, but were rarely committed to a "home" theatre like members of stock companies were. As Tracy Davis argues, the fact that theatres were never held exclusively to dramatic events and were leased to other kinds of entertainment "demonstrates the fluidity of these enterprises under financial constraint"; her statement, although directed at the nineteenth-century British theatre, applies to the theatre industry in the United States as well, especially during the recession-laden 1840s.[22] Since Ludlow and Smith's firm was in perennial debt, the managers must have had strong reasons for forgoing the extra funds they would have received on rent. Perhaps they preferred to avoid the potential business conflicts that might arise with a tenant. Or they may have explicitly not wanted to be associated with these "omnes genres," for fear that it would tarnish their theatrical reputation. Although circus, minstrelsy, and acrobats were integral to Ludlow and Smith's seasons and appeared on essentially every evening's bill, the managers were ambivalent toward these genres and, like many journalists and cultural critics of the period, often cast them as illegitimate lowbrow "amusements of a rougher nature."[23] Whatever the reasons for Ludlow and Smith's concerns, Keemle thought that Ludlow might want to make an exception for one applicant, "who wishes to *show up Master Diamond* (a sharp youth no doubt) a great actor or 'spouter'—and 'all-fired' relator of Yankee Stories—an *indescribable Dancer*."[24]

Although I have been unable to confirm whether Keemle convinced Ludlow to rent the theatre, their exchange illustrates that, curiously, a young performer wished to challenge Diamond in St. Louis just as the dancer was arriving in New Orleans; perhaps it was Yankee performer and Barnum defector C. D. Jenkins or a dancer hoping to benefit from Diamond's reputation as a formidable minstrel dancer. During the antebellum period, performers' whereabouts were often elusive, and, as this instance demonstrates, popular entertainers were particularly peripatetic, since they usually traveled independently and booked engagements on the spur of the moment. At the same time, Keemle's letter suggests that Ludlow and Smith were quickly made aware of Diamond's, as well as his competitor's, presence in the region, and the series of arrivals and departures that came with itinerancy—while possessing connotations of cultural illegitimacy and impermanence—also generated gossip and press. Ludlow and Smith, through their multilateral presence in the West and the South, as well as through correspondence with their professional network, were better positioned than many to learn about spontaneous arrivals and departures in their regional circuit.

In 1841 then, minstrel performers like John Diamond could be found on tour, performing spontaneously wherever they could find a booking that would subsidize lodging and travel expenses, as well as in established "legitimate" theatres in urban centers. During the antebellum period, traveling popular entertainers operated according to rules that were separate from those governing the institutions of the star system and legitimate theatres; at the same time, they often capitalized off that very network of venues, company managers, and scheduling conventions. Legitimate and popular performers adhered to different touring and booking practices but were also interrelated, both onstage and in business arrangements that occurred behind the scenes. Moreover, although the burnt cork mask made minstrelsy an inherently elusive performance practice, during the early 1840s, it was particularly enigmatic. T. D. Rice had, by the early 1830s, established his reputation for having "jumped Jim Crow," but according to Eric Lott and Dale Cockrell, it was not until the formation of the first minstrelsy troupe in 1843 that the minstrel show became a more codified genre; in the early 1840s, the form was an "interstitial art"[25] characterized by a looser combination of singing and dancing practices that centered on racial impersonation. In addition, although minstrelsy has most frequently been identified with male working-class audiences, such as the sporting subculture of New York's Five Points district, like the series of popular entertainers who attempted to rent the St. Louis theatre, Diamond and his engagement at the St. Charles and his participation in theatrical practices like the benefit system locates antebellum minstrelsy within a variety of cultural spaces. In fact, minstrelsy's generic slipperiness in the early 1840s—its status as disparate song and dance routines rather than as a formalized minstrel show—facilitated its closeness to the "legitimate" stage and "respectable" productions.[26]

Although Ludlow and Smith would come to know Barnum very well, in 1841 the western managers were not personally acquainted with him, and Diamond's performances at Caldwell's theatre provided the perfect introduction to the New York showman, who staged a fake dance contest to showcase Diamond's talents. "Humbug," Smith began his diary entry on January 21. "At the St. Charles, a Yankee Humbugger named Barnum got up a pretender *bet* of $250—on the dancing—negro dancing!! of Master Diamond [*sic*] & a 'Mr. Mercer' of Kentucky (as the bills had it) . . . a supernumerary came out with Diamond & shuffled out, squatted, turned & twisted in imitation of the youthful hero—a tall person came forward & announced that Master Diamond had won the wager & thus ended the humbug!"[27] Clearly perturbed by the event, Smith also wrote about it to his friend and former musical director of his company Edwin Woolf, noting that the supernumerary was beaten by Diamond, "a brilliant star" and "jewel of dancers."[28] According to Smith, in New Orleans, "humbug carried the night," since receipts at the St. Charles totaled nearly $2,000, while those at the American amounted to only $400.[29] The movements that Smith describes—shuffling, squatting, twisting—were associated with cruel imitations of nominally black dances, and racial derision was undoubtedly at the forefront of Diamond's act; Eric Lott has characterized these displays of racial caricature as expressions of the white desire for and containment of black practices. However, Smith seems less preoccupied with the content of Diamond's dances than with the deceptive event—the humbug—and its commercial success. While nineteenth-century audiences mistaking the "seeming counterfeit" of the blackface performer for the "genuine article"[30] was part of the lore and appeal of minstrelsy (as shown by Barnum's reminiscence), for Smith, the humbug lay not in the minstrel mask but in the bogus challenge. Outraged that the dance competition was fixed by Barnum's "pretender bet," Smith exposes Diamond's competitor as sham, suspecting that this "Mr. Mercer" was not an authentic

Kentucky minstrel dancer but a lesser actor in the company with little dancing skill. During the 1840s, Diamond built his reputation on precisely these kinds of potentially deceptive challenges.

Described by James Cook as "highly ritualized cultural phenomena, with multiple judges, elaborate scoring systems (for speed and accuracy), and surprisingly lucrative pay-offs,"[31] the challenges often featured one of the two dancers imitating the other or mimicking other well-known minstrels of the period. Clearly audiences delighted in this interplay of impersonation and competition; indeed, it is likely that spectators, like Smith, recognized that Diamond's competitor was no match for the skilled dancer. Although audience members delighted in the pronouncement of a winner, most were probably able to distinguish between genuine contests between two experienced minstrel dancers and a fixed challenge like the one Smith witnessed. Whereas audiences probably took pleasure in both kinds of performances, Smith was still incensed by Diamond's spurious victory nearly a week following the dancer's engagement at the St. Charles. "Nothing but humbug has been running in my head ever since the Dimond [*sic*] affair," he wrote to his business partner, and proposed an idea for "a most splendiferous *humbug* for next summer." Smith refused to trust his "gigantic views to paper," preferring to speak face-to-face, but was willing to share the hint that if Ludlow would consent to "bring about an engagement with the dark individual I have in view, I'll be d—d f I can't beat Barnum (even) in his own country (Yankee land) & perhaps cross the Atlantic & humbug the English too!"[32] Although Smith's plan and the identity of this "dark individual" are deliberately mysterious, his proposal suggests his willingness to engage in humbug not as a simple act of revenge but as a commercial strategy. Perhaps feeling proprietary over the entertainment scene in the West and the South or betraying his own feelings of regional inferiority, Smith was particularly eager to execute his plan in a more culturally "significant" transatlantic context.

Diamond was not the only popular entertainer exasperating Ludlow and Smith during the winter of 1841. Around the same time that Barnum and Diamond arrived in the South, a traveling circus and equestrian troupe under the management of Fogg and Stickney appeared in New Orleans. Like Barnum, Ludlow and Smith were struggling amid the economic depression and sought opportunities to augment their earnings. Anticipating that the "celebrated circus company," which was "well known throughout the South and West,"[33] would attract audiences away from their theatre, Smith decided to preempt any competition and engage them himself. Despite Ludlow and Smith's frequent disapproval of popular entertainers, they clearly saw them as genuine competitors. The managers arranged a contract for $700 a week to perform at the American and elsewhere in the region until the first of April, with the stipulation that they should perform only at their theatre for the remainder of the New Orleans season and "also that for one year they should not perform in the city of St. Louis except under our direction or in connection with us."[34] Smith determined that he would travel through the South with Fogg and Stickney while Ludlow would carry out the regular season in New Orleans. In fact, Smith read about Master Diamond's performances at Caldwell's while touring with the circus and equestrian troupe. However, the sojourn did not go smoothly, and Smith was continually vexed by the challenges of traveling with a team of horses. "Mud! Mud!! Mud!!!," he wrote in his diary from Natchez. "Last night at 11 o'clock, a cavalcade of 12 horsemen might have been seen, if it had not been so dark that you could scarce see the hand before you! Wending their uncertain way up the hill of Natchez—through mud & mire."[35] Such difficulties were not tempered by profitable returns: Smith complained to Ludlow a few days later, "We have stuck our feet in it by engaging Fogg and Stickney."[36]

But the tour with the circus may not have been all for naught. Reports from the *New Orleans Times-Picayune* suggest that Smith arranged a little side business while en route with Fogg and Stickney from Natchez to New Orleans. On February 9, the paper printed a notice of "another humbugging match" in Vicksburg "between Master Diamond and some fellow probably employed for the purpose." The following day, one journalist noted a rumor that Master Diamond "is to appear at the American Theatre" but that the dancer "most respectfully begs to inform the public that notwithstanding the very urgent solicitations for his services by the managers of that establishment, to perform at their theatres in New Orleans and St. Louis, their offers were not accepted. It is certainly true that Mr. Sol Smith made an engagement with Master Diamond for the Vicksburg Theatre, from which place he has just returned with the most triumphant success. He therefore wishes to remind his numerous friends that it is at the *St. Charles* he hopes to see them again on Wednesday, Friday, and Sunday nights, 10th, 12th, and 14th inst."[37] Advertisements indicate that Diamond likely did appear at the St. Charles on those three nights, along with a subsequent performance at Caldwell's Mobile theatre.[38] Whether or not Diamond was truly behind the report, his deferred and shifting movements around the South provided effective fodder for his own promotion. It appears, then, that after Diamond's debut at the St. Charles in late January, he made an excursion to Vicksburg, crossing paths with Smith and the equestrians and making it back to New Orleans in time to complete an additional run there with Caldwell. Although Smith does not recount the incident, it would not have been out of character for him to try to intercept Diamond; during the period, Ludlow and Smith often tried to poach performers from competitors like Caldwell, even while upholding their own regional "non-compete" stipulation. And, in light of the debacle with the equestrians, Smith would have been on the lookout for other opportunities, and especially one that would irk Caldwell and Barnum. Despite the challenges of traveling during the 1840s, touring offered the possibility of running into colleagues or of making a new professional connection; in a period when most theatrical business was conducted through correspondence, which was often unreliable and lent itself to misunderstandings, spontaneous face-to-face encounters were extremely valuable.[39]

According to Barnum, Diamond had a habit of disappearing, which makes the dancer's alleged encounter with Smith in Vicksburg more convincing. Following the performance at Caldwell's Mobile theatre, Barnum wrote to inform Ludlow and Smith, along with Fogg and Stickney, that Diamond had "absconded" after having "overdrawn the money due to him to the amount of $95 and has during the last week expended a hundred dollars in Brothels and other haunts of Dissipation and vice." Barnum explicitly cautioned his colleagues "against employing or in any manner harboring him on penalty of the law," as Diamond was "lawfully under an unfulfilled contract bound to me by his guardian." Barnum even admitted to taking a particular steamship from Mobile to New Orleans in order to "prevent a person in your company from tempering [*sic*] with Master D. and attempting to seduce him from my employ."[40] Further attempting to preclude any competitors from engaging Diamond, Barnum vowed to publish a notice of the dancer's poor conduct in the New Orleans papers.[41]

Where Diamond went when he abandoned Barnum in late February is unknown, and unsurprisingly, I have found no evidence confirming Barnum's allegations. However, Diamond's desertions and defections, rather than expressions of his poor character or recklessness, may have been efforts to capitalize off the flexible conventions of touring as a popular entertainer. Indeed, Diamond seems to have had the commercial shrewdness to get himself to Vicksburg for a one-night engagement organized by Smith, an event that was quickly noticed by the local newspapers. By accusing Diamond of breaking a contract and engaging in a vice-ridden underworld, Barnum fends off the conclusion that Diamond's behavior may have been the result of his own professional acumen. In addition, although independent popular entertainers adhered to more flexible contracts and business policies than did theatrical companies, Barnum attempts to find recourse in the "official," intractable rules of the law, perhaps in defiance of the very flexibility that he had used to his advantage while traveling with Diamond, Jenkins, and Lynch earlier that year. Barnum's letter also implicates the dancer's age and maturity. Although Barnum had aimed to trade on Diamond's youthful appearance and the appeal of a dance prodigy, the showman surely also appreciated the diminutive moniker's suggestion of the dancer's subservient position. However, Master Diamond behaved with a great deal more independence than Barnum desired. The dancer was evidently capable not only of negotiating with other managers but also of buying tickets for travel and making decisions about which steamboat to take. After Diamond's supposed rebellion, Barnum depicts the performer neither as a "lad"[42] nor as a self-directed adult but as an irresponsible adolescent who can be easily seduced by those wishing to take advantage of his talents. Barnum also expresses widespread assumptions about minstrelsy's illegitimacy and cultural milieu. Scholars have most often contextualized minstrelsy within the male sporting fraternity of working-class neighborhoods like New York's Five Points, described by Dale Cockrell as "a culture of fisticuffs, riotous drinking, gambling, general rowdiness . . . not at all like that of the middle or elite classes" and of "social activities that were unacceptable to those who operated the court system."[43] The subculture most frequently associated with minstrelsy served to legitimize Barnum's charges of Diamond's criminality. However, while minstrelsy was undoubtedly popular within districts like the Five Points, it was clearly also popular among the broadly middle-class theatregoers in New Orleans and other urban centers. Although Barnum was eager to usher Diamond into the legitimate theatre of New Orleans, once the dancer turned against him, Barnum was quick to circumscribe minstrelsy within its "proper" depraved cultural milieu.

Despite Barnum's antipathy toward both his colleagues and Diamond, the New York showman quickly set aside his feelings for the sake of potential profit. A few days after his previous letter, Barnum wrote to Smith again, his threatening tone much diminished and pleased that Diamond had "come to his senses" and returned to him and hoping to secure an engagement at the American.[44] Barnum, betraying little loyalty to Caldwell, proposed that Smith use Diamond to compete directly with the St. Charles. Caldwell was currently presenting the popular Viennese danseuse Fanny Elssler, an attraction for which Ludlow and Smith had unsuccessfully competed. Barnum, always ready with a promotional scheme, suggested that Diamond might not only perform during the same week as Elssler but also impersonate her dances on the very nights that she was performing at the rival theatre; Diamond had presented dances "a la Elssler" during previous engagements in New York, and impersonating famous performers was clearly a strong current within antebellum popular culture. Although Ludlow recounts Diamond's performances at the American in his memoir, evidence suggests otherwise.[45] Despite ample newspaper coverage of theatre listings during this period, the purported performance is absent from available newspapers and from Ludlow and Smith's extant correspondence.

By mid-March, it seemed that Master Diamond had disappeared from Barnum for good. Left without any performers to engage, the entrepreneur departed the South for New York. However, Barnum was not entirely rid of the business with Diamond. On March 30 he arrived in Pittsburgh to learn that someone was performing at the museum in that city under the name of "Master Diamond." Claiming to have visited the performance incognito, Barnum discovered that it was Francis Lynch performing under the management of Jenkins; the two performers, who had fled from the travelling showman earlier that year, were now operating on their own, increasing their earnings by eliminating Barnum's share. Ever skilled at crafting a good story, Barnum reports that he arrested Jenkins, Jenkins arrested Barnum for a supposedly false and unrelated claim, and both were released from prison at exactly the same moment.[46] Of course, with such an array of potential Master Diamonds on the scene that spring, it is unknown which performer Barnum actually saw playing in Pittsburgh.

Diamond's most recent defection from Barnum seems to have been the result of an arrangement with Ludlow and Smith—perhaps negotiated with Smith in Vicksburg—*or* with Fogg and Stickney. A few days after Barnum acknowledged Diamond's disappearance—not only to Ludlow and Smith but also to the circus managers—Matt Field, Ludlow's son-in-law and a longtime member of his company, wrote to his wife, Cornelia, that "Fogg & Stickney have got Diamond with them up the river, and no doubt they are flourishing likewise."[47] It is unclear whether Diamond's journey with the circus managers was orchestrated by or *against* Ludlow and Smith, since at some point that spring, Fogg and Stickney broke their contract with the managers, violating the requirement that they would play in New Orleans or St. Louis only under Ludlow and Smith's management. By the beginning of May, the circus managers had set up a tent in New Orleans, "within a stones throw" of the American. Echoing Barnum's reaction to Diamond's disappearances, Ludlow and Smith took legal action against the entertainers who had wronged them, but, as soon as Fogg and Stickney discovered they were likely to be imprisoned for disobeying an injunction against them, they "absconded," which was evidently a popular tactic of the day. Smith offers a play-by-play of the incident in his diary: "I see the tent of Fogg & Stickney is struck—& they are *off for St. Louis* in the boat which carries this package!!! I can't get the contract out of the court to-day, but will send it immediately—but if you think it is worth while to try to stop them, you can swear to the facts & have contract to show afterwards. If I were you, I would put the Govr. in possession of the facts of the case. . . . I am sick—sick of dealing with rogues."[48] Like Barnum, Ludlow and Smith failed in their attempt to use the law to pin down elusive performers. However in this case, not only did Fogg and Stickney desert Ludlow and Smith but they also took Diamond with them. Smith was determined to stop "the d—d slippery set" from interfering with their St. Louis season, but if he couldn't stop them en route, at least he would get some revenge, advising Ludlow to try to "see Diamond the instant he arrives," in order to "get him on some terms."[49]

The following day, Smith had a new addition to this plan. Rather than try to halt Fogg and Stickney's progress or intercept Diamond, he endeavored to compete directly with the circus company's entertainment offerings. Apparently, either Fogg, Stickney, and Diamond had to travel separately from the equestrian troupe, or Smith decided to hire his own team of horsemen, since he instructed Ludlow, "*To send up the Equestrians immediately without stopping on the way* . . . to close for 3 nights for the purpose of making the circle, & preparing for the horses. With force enough, the alteration can easily be made in 3 days—& by that time, *the troupe will arrive*."[50] Ludlow and Smith's outrageous plan apparently worked. Soon after Fogg and Stickney's arrival in St. Louis, the theatre managers temporarily transformed their theatre into a circus venue and launched a series of equestrian performances.[51] Smith was eager to play the game of theatrical mobility and interception, but his plan was more than a personal vendetta against Fogg and Stickney; it was also a business strategy, and Smith knew from past experience that if a circus was in town, it was sure to compete with the St. Louis theatre. The ad hoc circus seems to have had some measure of success, since by July, Ludlow and Smith's assembled group of equestrians was touring the South, along with none other than Master Diamond.

James Cook's research on the careers of John Diamond and African American minstrel performer William Henry Lane complicates Diamond's whereabouts in the fall of 1841 even further, and casts an enormous shadow of doubt over his already questionable movements around the country that year. According to Cook, in 1840, while managing New York's Vauxhall Gardens, Barnum began promoting Lane. The showman's deception of his audience was twofold: not only did he present the black dance sensation in blackface, leading local reporters to assume Lane was white, but he also promoted Lane as John Diamond. By 1844, Lane, now as "Master Juba," and Diamond were drawing crowds and substantial monetary rewards by competing in dance matches against one another at venues such as New York's Bowery Amphitheater. Moreover, as Cook speculates, "Diamond and Lane may have even conceived of the original contest *together*—as a money-making gimmick to benefit both parties."[52] While he does not discuss Diamond's performances in the South and the West, Cook establishes a timeline in which Barnum commenced his relationship with Lane just a few months before arriving with Diamond in New Orleans. By examining Barnum and Diamond's movements and deceptions outside the Northeast, I introduce several new possibilities into Cook's narrative. Could Barnum have been promoting Lane-as-Diamond slightly earlier than Cook posits, in the winter and spring of 1841? Or perhaps either the "dark individual" involved in Smith's "splendiferous humbug" or the dancer hoping to challenge Diamond by renting Ludlow and Smith's St. Louis theatre was in fact William Henry Lane?

During the fall of 1841, newspaper sightings of John Diamond are similarly equivocal. In August and September, he was reportedly playing with Jenkins in New York, at both Vauxhall Gardens and the Chatham, and by November 27, he was advertised as playing for Ludlow and Smith at the American, along with the equestrians. However, advertisements place Diamond back in New York on the twenty-ninth, making an engagement in New Orleans just two nights prior physically impossible.[53] Acknowledging the confusion over the dancer's whereabouts that fall, the *New York Tribune* announced on November 30 that "[t]he *real* Master Diamond has returned, and performed here [at the Bowery Amphitheatre] last night with great applause," and a few days later the *Dramatic Mirror* advised the managers of New York's Vauxhall Gardens "to withdraw such a humbug as *this* Master Diamond."[54] That week, however, more scandalous reports about Diamond began circulating in newspapers from New York to New Orleans: "Master Diamond, well known as an enacter of negro characters, has been committed to jail in New Orleans, for 'stabbing with intent to kill' Mr. James Barron of that city. He inflicted three wounds upon him with a penknife for some fancied insult at a hall."[55] Echoing Barnum's accusations earlier that year, it seems that Diamond's "abscondings" often coincided with reports of licentious and immoral behavior. The *Times-Picayune* published the piece on December 15, along with an article reprinted from the *Boston Post*: "We rather think this will be news to Master Diamond. He concluded an engagement at Harrington's Museum in this city last Saturday." The *Picayune* summed up the contradictory articles this way: "The sum and substance of the business is, friend Post, your Master Diamond has hooked the name of the Master Diamond in our calaboose."[56] The New Orleans reporter acknowledged that one city's Master Diamond often differed from another's, and that a performer's movements in one city reverberated nationally through expanding networks of antebellum print culture. The minstrel performer's (or performers') activities in the South and the West heightened interest from critics and spectators in New York and Boston, the northeastern cultural centers. Audiences and journalists were less concerned with detecting the "real" dancer than they were with getting in on the hoax. As a commercial strategy, artful deception did not invite audiences to detect the difference between counterfeit and illusion, truth and representation, but to delight in the "blurring of these aesthetic and moral categories."[57]

Referring specifically to "a commercial industry that forced William Henry Lane to imitate 'himself,'" Cook argues, "What also needs to be acknowledged . . . is the enormous market savvy expressed through these stylistic reversals."[58] The episodes in 1841 involving Diamond, Barnum, Fogg and Stickney, and Ludlow and Smith are part of this larger story of geographic and professional mobility within antebellum popular culture; absconding, disappearing, following, and intercepting constituted strategic industry maneuvers that reflected the tenuous cultural hierarchy of the period. Barnum, Ludlow, and Smith all recognized their audiences' desire for circus and minstrelsy and moved from one city to another, arranged impromptu tours, or changed itineraries mid course in order to engage popular entertainers; however, rather than treat these peripatetic performers as business partners or independent agents, they characterized them as pawns to be seized or captured. Although Barnum and Ludlow and Smith repeatedly engaged in precisely the same tactics of mobility and interception as Diamond and Fogg and Stickney, the former group repeatedly denounced the latter as slippery, untrustworthy, and even disposed to criminal conduct; the managers' disavowal of the instability of their own cultural authority was their brand of artful deception. Barnum and Ludlow and Smith wanted to have it both ways: to capitalize off audiences' desire for popular entertainers while persistently dismissing those performers as dependent, unprofessional, and duplicitous. Moreover, while Diamond, Fogg, and Stickney's behavior has generated ample documentation from Barnum and Smith about the events in the South in 1841, I have found no evidence describing these occurrences from the perspectives of the popular entertainers, an imbalance in the historical record that serves to heighten their elusiveness. However, by not only reading individual instances but also patterns of circulation—recurrent and well-timed disappearances and abscondings—Diamond and Fogg and Stickney appear to have employed geographic movements strategically, rather than capriciously.

While it is impossible to distinguish with certainty the "real" Master Diamond from the counterfeits, more important is how Diamond represents the possibilities inherent in antebellum geographic movements and how performers, spectators, and critics relished and capitalized off the dancer's ambiguity. Artful deception was not only about pleasure; it was also about capital—both economic and cultural. Diamond's movements and desertions—and those of his impersonators and imitators—may have secured him additional engagements and therefore higher earnings. Importantly, they also got his name in the papers. Performers' physical movements encouraged publicity and interest far removed from the sites of visiting engagements, facilitating what Joseph Roach defines as celebrity: the circulation of an individual's name or image independent of his or her own person.[59] Nineteenth-century star status was also what Tracy Davis identifies as a kind of "brand name";[60] as a popular entertainer, Master Diamond could not acquire the "official" star position of a leading "legitimate" actor like Edwin Forrest or Junius Brutus Booth, but he could use the exigencies of being an itinerant minstrel performer to secure his own brand. Whether or not all the movements attributed to Master Diamond were in fact those of the "real" John Diamond, reports of his circulation and debates over his legitimacy reified the performer's celebrity, the Master Diamond brand name.

Notes

1. Noah Ludlow, *Dramatic Life as I Found It* (St. Louis: G. I. Jones and Co., 1880), 223.
2. P. T. Barnum, *The Life of P. T. Barnum, Written by Himself* (1855; Urbana: University of Illinois Press, 2000), 189–90.
3. On the theatrical star system, see Simon Williams, "European Actors and the Star System in the American Theatre, 1752–1870," in *The Cambridge History of the American Theatre*, ed. Don B. Wilmeth and Christopher Bigsby (Cambridge: Cambridge University Press, 1998); David Grimsted, *Melodrama Unveiled: American Theater and Culture 1800–1850* (Berkeley: University of California Press, 1968); Beth Holmgren, *Starring Madame Modjeska: On Tour in Poland and America* (Bloomington: Indiana University Press, 2012).
4. Qtd. in James Cook, *The Arts of Deception: Playing with Fraud in the Age of Barnum* (Cambridge, MA: Harvard University Press, 2001), 28.
5. See Karen Halttunen, *Confidence Men and Painted Women: A Study of Middle-Class Culture in America, 1830–1870* (New Haven, NJ: Yale University Press, 1982).
6. Eric Lott, *Love and Theft: Blackface Minstrelsy and the American Working Class* (New York: Oxford University Press, 1993), 6.
7. Ibid., 115.
8. For examples that emphasize performance, see Lawrence Levine, *Highbrow/Lowbrow:*

The Emergence of Cultural Hierarchy in America (1988; repr., Cambridge, MA: Harvard University Press, 1990); Robert C. Allen, *Horrible Prettiness: Burlesque and American Culture* (Chapel Hill: University of North Carolina Press, 1991); Bruce McConachie, *Melodramatic Formations: American Theatre and Society, 1820–1870* (Iowa City: University of Iowa Press, 1992); Lott, *Love and Theft*; Gillian M. Rodger, *Champagne Charlie and Pretty Jemima: Variety Theatre in the Nineteenth Century* (Urbana: University of Illinois Press, 2010); Renée M. Sentilles, *Performing Menken: Adah Isaacs Menken and the Birth of American Celebrity* (Cambridge: Cambridge University Press, 2012); Amy E. Hughes, *Spectacles of Reform: Theater and Activism in Nineteenth-Century America* (Ann Arbor: University of Michigan Press, 2012).

9. Stuart Hall, "Notes on Deconstructing the Popular," *People's History and Socialist Theory*, edited by Raphael Samuel (London: Routledge & Kegan Paul, 1981); Pierre Bourdieu, *The Field of Cultural Production*, ed. Randal Johnson (New York: Columbia University Press, 1993).
10. Recent scholars that have examined touring take a transatlantic approach. See Daphne A. Brooks, *Bodies in Dissent: Spectacular Performances of Race and Freedom, 1850–1910* (Durham, NC: Duke University Press, 2006); Sarah Meer, *Uncle Tom Mania: Slavery, Minstrelsy, and Transatlantic Culture in the 1850s* (Athens: University of Georgia Press, 2005); Marlis Schweitzer, "Networking the Waves: Ocean Liners, Impresarios, and Broadway's Atlantic Expansion, *Theatre Survey* 53, no. 2 (September 2012): 241–67.
11. Doreen Massey, *for space* (London: Sage Publications, 2005), 9; Mark Simpson, *Trafficking Subjects: The Politics of Mobility in Nineteenth-Century America* (Minneapolis: University of Minnesota Press, 2004), xiii, xvi.
12. Cook, *The Arts of Deception*; Cook, "Master Juba, The King of All Dancers! A Story of Stardom and Struggle from the Dawn of the Transatlantic Culture Industry," *Discourses in Dance* 3, no. 2 (2006): 6–20; Brooks, *Bodies in Dissent*.
13. Cook, *The Arts of Deception*, 14.
14. Barnum, *The Life of P. T. Barnum*, 207.
15. Ibid., 210.
16. Mark Knowles, *Tap Roots: The Early History of Tap Dancing* (Jefferson, NC: McFarland, 2002), 86. "Master" was the standard term for an underage heir in England at least as far back as the 1500s. By extension, it was the standard way to list male child actors. "master, n.1 and adj.". OED Online. December 2013. Accessed January 28, 2014, http://www.oed.com/view/Entry/114751?rskey=m72be1&result=1.
17. Barnum, *The Life of P. T. Barnum*, 211.
18. *New Orleans Times-Picayune*, January 1, 1841; January 2, 1841.
19. Barnum, *The Life of P. T. Barnum*, 212.
20. *New Orleans Times-Picayune*, January 12, 1841; January 30, 1841.
21. Keemle to Ludlow, 12/13/1840, Box 2, Ludlow Field Maury Family Papers, Missouri History Museum and Library.
22. Tracy Davis, *The Economics of the British Stage, 1800–1914* (Cambridge: Cambridge University Press, 2000), 163.
23. "Winter Life in New Orleans," *New Orleans Times-Picayune*, January 22, 1845.
24. Keemle to Ludlow, 12/13/1840, Box 2, Ludlow Field Maury Family Papers, Missouri History Museum and Library.
25. Lott, *Love and Theft*, 112.

26. Dale Cockrell, *Demons of Disorder: Early Blackface Minstrels and Their World* (Cambridge: Cambridge University Press, 1997), 29.
27. Sol Smith Diary, January 21, 1841, Box 6, Solomon Smith Collection, Missouri History Museum and Library.
28. Smith to Woolf, n.d., Box 5, Solomon Smith Collection, Missouri History Museum and Library.
29. Sol Smith Diary, January 21, 1841, Box 6, Solomon Smith Collection, Missouri History Museum and Library.
30. Lott, *Love and Theft*, 113.
31. Cook, "Master Juba, The King of All Dancers!," 12.
32. Smith to Ludlow, 1/24/1841, Box 2, Solomon Smith Collection, Missouri History Museum and Library.
33. *New Orleans Times-Picayune*, September 27, 1840.
34. Sol Smith Diary, May 3, 1841, Box 6, Solomon Smith Collection, Missouri History Museum and Library.
35. Sol Smith Diary, January 22, 1841, Box 6, Solomon Smith Collection, Missouri History Museum and Library.
36. Smith to Ludlow, January 24, 1841, Box 1, Solomon Smith Collection, Missouri History Museum and Library.
37. *New Orleans Times-Picayune*, February 10, 1841.
38. *New Orleans Times-Picayune*, February 9, 1841; February 10, 1841; February 11, 1841; February 12, 1841; February 14, 1841; February 23, 1841.
39. See David M. Henkin, *The Postal Age: The Emergence of Modern Communications in Nineteenth-Century America* (Chicago: University of Chicago Press, 2007).
40. Barnum to Smith, March 3, 1841, Box 4, Solomon Smith Collection, Missouri History Museum and Library.
41. Barnum to Ludlow & Smith, Fogg & Stickney, February 27, 1841, Box 4, Solomon Smith Collection, Missouri History Museum and Library.
42. Barnum, *The Life of P. T. Barnum*, 210.
43. Cockrell, *Demons of Disorder*, 70.
44. Barnum to Smith, March 4, 1841, Box 4, Solomon Smith Collection, Missouri History Museum and Library.
45. Ludlow, *Dramatic Life as I Found It*, 533.
46. Barnum, *The Life of P. T. Barnum*, 212–13.
47. Matt Field to Cornelia Field, March 16, 1841, Box 2, Ludlow Field Maury Family Papers, Missouri History Museum and Library.
48. Sol Smith Diary, May 3, 1841, Box 6, Solomon Smith Collection, Missouri History Museum and Library.
49. Smith to Ludlow, May 2, 1841, Box 1, Solomon Smith Collection, Missouri History Museum and Library.
50. Smith to Ludlow, May 3, 1841, Box 1, Solomon Smith Collection, Missouri History Museum and Library.
51. Matt Field to Noah Ludlow, May 14, 1841, Box 2, Ludlow Field Maury Family Papers, Missouri History Museum and Library.
52. James Cook, "Dancing Across the Color Line," *Common Place* 4, no. 1 (October 2003), part IV.

53. *New York Evening Post*, August 23, 1841; September 23, 1841; *Boston Daily Atlas*, August 24, 1841; *New Orleans Times-Picayune*, November 27, 1841; *New York Evening Post*, November 29, 1841.
54. *New York Tribune*, November 30, 1841; "New York Theatricals," *The Dramatic Mirror and Literary Companion* 1.17 (December 4, 1841): 134.
55. *Albany Evening Journal*, November 30, 1841; *New York Dramatic Mirror and Literary Companion* 1.17 (December 4, 1841): 134; *Connecticut Courant* (Hartford), December 4, 1841; *Albany Argus*, December 7, 1841; *Centinel of Freedom* (Newark), December 7, 1841.
56. *New Orleans Times-Picayune*, December 15, 1841.
57. Cook, *The Arts of Deception*, 16.
58. Cook, "Dancing Across the Color Line."
59. Joseph Roach, "Emergence of the American Actor," in *The Cambridge History of the American Theatre*, ed. Don B. Wilmeth and Christopher Bigsby (Cambridge: Cambridge University Press, 1998), 352; Also see Roach, *It* (Ann Arbor: University of Michigan Press, 2007).
60. Davis, *The Economics of the British Stage*, 339. On nineteenth-century celebrity, also see Sara Babcox First, "The Mechanics of Renown; or, The Rise of a Celebrity Culture in Early America" (Ph.D. diss., University of Michigan, 2009); David Haven Blake, *Walt Whitman and the Culture of American Celebrity* (New Haven, CT: Yale University Press, 2006); Sharon Marcus, "The Theatrical Scrapbook," *Theatre Survey* 54, no. 2 (May 2013): 283–307.

Performing the Polish-American Patriot

Civic Performance and Hyphenated Identity in World War I Chicago

—MEGAN E. GEIGNER

In the years directly preceding World War I, American immigration numbers soared, with Italians, Jews, and Poles leading all other groups.[1] Concerns about the numbers and the fact that these new arrivals did not conform to "native-born" Americans' ideas of the nation's citizenry—namely, these immigrants were not Anglo-Saxon Protestants—resulted in Americanization campaigns that hoped to instill white middle-class values in immigrant communities.[2] As news of the war filled the papers between 1914 and 1916, concerns surfaced about immigrant loyalty, causing many émigrés to disband their national societies, Anglicize their names, and cease staging national holiday celebrations and ethnic theatre to avoid harassment.[3] History documents well these instances of immigrants erasing the traces of their ethnic heritage to dispel suspicions of disloyalty during the war.[4] Fewer stories persist, at least in the popular imagination, of the inverse: instances of immigrants presenting their ethnic heritage to allay fears rather than provoke them. The Polish immigrant community in Chicago, the third largest national group in the city, embraced what I will call their Polishness,[5] and, instead of fomenting suspicion of Polishness as something anti-American, it read as a truly patriotic American expression.

The Polish community turned to theatre and performance to reframe the discourse of assimilation. By shifting from performance practices that presented exclusively Polish identity (1914–1916) to performance practices that presented a Polish-American identity (1917–1918), Chicago's Poles successfully redefined American patriotism, furthered the homeland cause, and prepared for U.S. entry into World War I. Drawing on their decades-long tradition of Polish-language plays and Polish national holiday celebrations, the Polish community created and made visible a new hyphenated identity, that of the Polish-American patriot. These performances not only demonstrated a resistance to Americanization campaigns but also indexed changing American foreign policy and renegotiated the relationship between "immigrant" and "American."

By analyzing Polish civic performance during World War I, I show the potential for performance as an intervention in debates about immigration and nativist rhetoric. By civic performance, I mean those performances that helped define the city by bringing together a large, heterogeneous audience and putting the city's values on display. Civic performances were usually experiments in sociality. As Jill Dolan states, "performance offers a way to practice imagining new forms of social relationships."[6] I show here how the Polish immigrant community learned to use performance to contest the rhetoric that Polishness was inherently non-American. Polish parades and exhibitions showed Chicago what Poles looked like, where they lived, and what their values were. Instead of allowing nativists and Americanizers to generate the discourse of alien national disloyalty, these Poles used performance to subvert dominant power relationships and become the subjects of the discourse instead of the objects. Furthermore, the community shifted from private, community-based performance practices to broader, city wide performance practices to help audiences reconceptualize immigrant bodies. By parading down Chicago's streets or participating in patriotic choruses, the Polish community used Polish bodies as a surface to rework immigrant identity and refute negative stereotypes of non-Anglos.[7] I argue here that by engaging in a range of embodied practices, the Polish immigrant community performed the possibility of ethnic-Americanness in a time when Americanness increasingly excluded immigrants.

Americanization

The first Americanization campaigns were the result of the U.S. Immigration Commission, or Dillingham Commission, a congressional subcommittee led by Senator William Paul Dillingham. The commission spent three years (1907–10) investigating American immigrants and published a forty-two-volume report in 1911. A large portion of the report was dedicated to a "Dictionary of Races of Peoples," which used William Ripley's hierarchies from his book *The Races of*

Europe. In the "Dictionary," the most "advanced" race was the Anglo-Saxon, which enjoyed a majority in the United States, Britain, Germany (and the German-speaking lowlands), and the Scandinavian Peninsula.[8] Anglo-Saxons, argued the report, proved their civilized acumen in their laws and democratic institutions, whereas non-Anglo groups, such as the Poles (as Slavs), were "still backwards in Western ideas, appliances, and forms of government."[9] The *Dillingham Report* warned that "the original Anglo-Saxon ancestry in America" would be overwhelmed by new non-Anglo immigrants who "were backwards" because they did not "abandon native customs and standards of living."[10] In an attempt to assimilate newcomers into a unified, white, Anglo-Saxon American culture, the commission recommended stronger Americanization efforts.

Americanization marked the confluence of worries about immigration, anxieties about the erupting war in Europe, and Progressive Era concerns about human rights and behavior.[11] Christina Zeigler-McPherson defines Americanization as "a U.S. social and political movement that promoted American citizenship among immigrants in the early 20th century," that debated conceptions of American citizenship, and that "sought to more clearly shape American national identity by aggressively lobbying aliens to naturalize and assimilate into a culture predefined by the country's tradition heritage."[12] Americanization efforts began as early as 1910 but increased during the war, using foreign policy as a means to discredit the idea of hyphenated Americanism. Politicians who had reaped the benefit of immigrant support prior to the war walked the line between celebrating immigrants' ethnic heritage and warning them to be loyal Americans. In May 1915, President Woodrow Wilson said to a group of newly naturalized American citizens: "While you bring all countries with you, you come with a purpose of leaving all other countries behind you—bringing what is best of their spirit, but not looking over your shoulders and seeking to perpetuate what you intended to leave in them. . . . You cannot become fully Americans if you think of yourselves in groups. America does not consist of groups. A man who thinks of himself as belonging to a particular national group in America has not yet become an American, and the man who goes among you to trade upon your nationality is not worthy to live under the stars and stripes."[13] Wilson's speech implied that new citizens who claimed a "conjunctive identity between their countries of descent and their new, adoptive home" through the hyphen demonstrated divided allegiance.[14] By qualifying themselves as a certain type of American, they disrupted unified American culture. In a speech later that year, Theodore Roosevelt famously added:

> There is no room in this country for hyphenated Americanism. When I refer to

> hyphenated Americans, I do not refer to naturalized Americans. Some of the very best Americans I've ever known were naturalized Americans . . . but a hyphenated American is not an American at all. . . . We must unsparingly condemn any man who holds any other allegiance. . . . The one absolutely certain way of bringing this nation to ruin, of preventing all possibility of its continuing to be a nation at all, would be to permit it to become a tangle of squabbling nationalities, an intricate knot of German-Americans, Irish-Americans, English-Americans, French-Americans, Scandinavian-Americans or Italian-Americans, each preserving its separate nationality, each with more sympathy with Europeans of the nationality, than with the other citizens of the American Republic. . . . The man who calls himself an American citizen and yet shows by his actions that he is primarily the citizen of a foreign land, plays a thoroughly mischievous part in the life of our body politic. He has no place here; and the sooner he returns to the land to which he feels his real heart allegiance, the better it will be for every good American. There is no such thing as a hyphenated American who is a good American.[15]

The xenophobic U.S. nationalism conjured by these speeches resonated in Chicago, a city that hundreds of thousands of immigrants and hyphenated Americans called home.[16] When the National Americanization Committee met in Chicago in February 1916, Frances Kellor, the leader, explained that failing to naturalize and Americanize Chicago's immigrants would result in the country being "an aggregation of people instead of a nation."[17] Articles in the *Chicago Tribune* took up Kellor's language and demanded the city "get rid of alien nationalism" and eliminate "German clubs, Swedish clubs, Polish societies, Bohemian societies, etc."[18] Editorials instructed Chicago's immigrants "to forget their extra territorial affiliations as rapidly as decently proper . . . so the United States could be a nation."[19] The call to eliminate alien nationalism in Chicago broke with the city's long tradition of honoring its majority foreign-born population and alarmed its many immigrants.[20]

Chicago's Poles and Americanization

Chicago's Polish immigrant community did not have a sovereign nation in Europe to call home. At the end of the eighteenth century, the Prussian, Russian, and Austrian Empires conquered and partitioned the Polish-Lithuanian Commonwealth. Under Russian and Prussian rule (1775–1919), European Poles could not teach Polish in the schools, practice their religion, or rally for Polish independence. Poles twice attempted to reestablish a free Poland—in the November Insurrection (1830–31) and the January Insurrection (1863–65)—but were put down each time. The failure of the insurrections did stop formal and militarized independence movements but did not stop circulation of Polish nationalism, which happened primarily through underground art and literature to elude the ruling governments.[21] Some Polish revolutionaries, including those who founded the Polish community in Chicago, emigrated in order to have freedom to express resistance against the occupying forces at home and openly call for a free Poland.[22]

In contrast to their homeland counterparts, the Polish community in Chicago had a tradition of eagerly and openly expressing Polish culture. By the second decade of the twentieth century, Chicago's Poles were well established, with churches, schools, cemeteries, businesses, newspapers, and a statue to their Polish countryman and American patriot, Tadeusz Kościuszko, in a public park.[23] Because Polishness was banned in the homeland, Poles in the diaspora felt that maintaining Polish culture was a way to maintain a Polish nation. Polish theatre and music in Chicago were an extension of overtly Polish nationalist displays, such as training in Polish paramilitary groups (such as the Polish Falcons or the Polish National Alliance [PNA]) and joining Polish advocacy groups such as the Polish Alma Mater (PAM), Polish Woman's Association (PWA), and the Polish Roman Catholic Union of America (PRCUA). It was these everyday practices—speaking Polish, supporting parish schools, celebrating national holidays, practicing Polish arts, and meeting in Polish clubs—that maintained the claim for an independent Poland and guarded against the elimination of the Polish national spirit.

Although the community was nearly sixty years old, Americanization posed a threat to Chicago's Poles. They sensed themselves "becoming Americanized in spirit, denying [the Polish] language, [and] becoming ashamed of belonging to the Polish group."[24] They also worried that those asking them to disband their societies misunderstood the community's allegiances; Chicago's Poles felt equally dedicated to the United States and Poland, seeing the two "as the natural and necessary allies of [their] national group."[25] For them, simultaneous love of America and Poland was best expressed through Kościuszko, the American Revolutionary War and Polish Insurrection hero, a symbol of the United States' and Poland's shared values. Polish Chicagoans also felt betrayed by Americanization because it resembled discriminatory experiences in the homeland. One Chicago Polish-language newspaper warned, "Americanism penetrates into Polish homes through doors and windows. It does not appear in so brutal a form as Germanization and Russification in Europe, but because of this it is all the more dangerous."[26]

By the time Americanization discourse reached its first fever pitch in the early teens, Polish Chicagoans found that even places of previous refuge were no longer safe. Settlement houses, or reform institutions that provided social services to new immigrants such as childcare and meeting spaces for immigrant clubs, tried, according to Polish journalists, "to penetrate into the Polish community in order to engulf it. They issue pamphlets printed in Polish, urging the reading of English papers, the sending of children to English schools, and the organizing of American societies."[27] One article claimed the settlement house "clubs [will] snatch our children and systematically take away their national identity."[28] Similarly, Polish Chicagoans grew apprehensive of the Chicago archdiocese (although they were the largest national group within it) since the new archbishop, George Mundelein, installed in 1916, was "an Americanizer par excellence."[29] He insisted that all parish schools conduct lessons in English exclusively and that the city's Catholics should abandon parish national organizations to join English-speaking archdiocese societies such as the Holy Name Society, the St. Vincent de Paul Society, and the Catholic Youth Organization.[30] Suddenly the Catholic Church, which had long been a stalwart of Polish-American nationalism, was a threat to Polish culture in Chicago.

Americanization also threatened the community because it was tied to the push for more immigration restriction, which had the potential to divide families. Using the findings of his report, Dillingham cosponsored the Burnett-Dillingham Bill to limit immigration based on literacy, which was vetoed in 1911 but reintroduced in 1914.[31] In its wake, Chicago's Poles held a mass protest meeting in which Bishop Paul Rhode, the first Polish bishop in the United States; the presidents of the PNA, PAM, PWA, and PRCUA; editors of the local Polish newspapers; Polish alderman, city workers, and other community leaders rallied against the bill.[32] The protest at the end of 1914 depicted the complicated nature of Polish-American identity during World War I Americanization efforts: The community still believed in their efficacy as American citizens and held the protest as a means to affect legislation, but the legislation itself marked them as foreigners who destabilized the American nation. President Wilson ultimately vetoed the bill on January 28, 1915, saying it would "close the gates of asylum which have always been open to those who could find it nowhere else."[33] This act foreshadowed what would become an important relationship between the Polish-American community and President Wilson, one that granted them access to American patriotism when the United States entered the war.

Performing Polishness, 1914–1916

Increasing calls to abandon their national heritage had the opposite effect on Chicago's Poles: instead of disbanding societies or eliminating Polish theatres, the community retreated into Polish culture in an attempt to keep their nation alive. One means to access Polish nationalism was through Polish-language theatre and holiday celebrations, and in 1914 the community staged "the most magnificent nationalistic manifestations of the present time in Chicago."[34] The best example of these kinds of celebrations was the November Insurrection celebrations in 1914. The community held elaborate programs for the holiday in many of the Polish parishes (St. John Cantius, Holy Trinity, St. Helen's, St. Adalbert's) and at the large Polish national societies (the Polish Falcons, PNA, PWA, and PRCU).[35] The events included Polish songs, recitations, speeches, skits, and tableaux, which had been popular at these types of events in Chicago since the 1890s, but they also functioned as fund-raisers for the new Polish Independence Fund and the Polish Central Relief Committee.[36] Stanley Osada, secretary of the Polish Central Relief Committee, told the crowd it was their duty as Poles to give because Poland had only its people, not "a government to raise taxes."[37] In other words, the Polish audience served as surrogate for the outlawed Polish government, displaying their Polish citizenship by paying "a tax" in the form of war relief. In contrast to these events before Americanization, the speakers did not emphasize their duties as Americans nor did they tout Polish contributions to the United States. The homeland took priority.

Although Poles dismissed Americanization rhetoric, the speeches at the celebrations showed the influence of its propaganda in their use of racial nationalism and preparedness tropes. Mr. K. Zychlinski, president of the Polish National Alliance, said to the audience at St. Adalbert's that the war was based on race—it was the result of the aggressive Teuton wishing to destroy all that was not Teutonic—and Chicago's Polish men had a duty to save their race.[38] At the same event, Mr. John Smulski, owner of the large Polish bank in Chicago and a well-known community leader, told the men to prepare by joining the Falcons and other military societies so they could "be ready when the homeland calls."[39] The speeches situated Poles in the audience as Poland's largest resource: they were the makers and upholders of the race, they were "tax-paying" citizens, and they would be Poland's army. No one spoke of America, which was a shift for Polish national celebrations in Chicago, because prior to 1914 they often included some mention of gratitude to the United States or recognition of the American flag.[40]

Despite representing themselves as Poles instead of Polish-Americans for the November Insurrection programs, the events of the war in 1915 demonstrated a gulf between the experiences of Poles in the homeland and Poles in the United States. For example, when the *Chicago Tribune* asked Smulski if Poles preferred the (Russian) czar's or the (Austrian) Hapsburgs' promise for Polish freedom, he responded by saying he "could not speak for Poles in Poland."[41] For some, the distance between themselves and the ground war in Europe was so unbearable that they enlisted in foreign armies, a process available through the Polish National Alliance headquarters in Chicago.[42] Furthermore, because the war pitted the Russian and Germanic partitions against one another, Chicago's Poles had difficulty creating community consensus. Acknowledging this issue, community leaders held a meeting at St. Stanislaus, the center of Polish culture in Chicago, after Warsaw fell to the Central Powers in August 1915. Using categories reminiscent of the *Dillingham Report*'s race distinctions, they decided that Polish "sympathy lies with England and France, as our culture is Romanic rather than Teutonic."[43] By focusing on Western European countries instead of Russia, Chicago's Poles attempted to defray intergroup conflict and align themselves with the "more advanced" races of the West.

Perhaps because of these newly clarified differences between Poles in Europe and Poles in Chicago, Polish theatre in the 1916–17 season—before the United States entered the war—focused on old Polish stories and fears of immigration. Three new drama groups dedicated to Polish-language theatre debuted in that season: a new amateur group at St. Casimir's, who performed at a "magnificent" vaudeville hall; an amateur group called the Followers of Dramatic Art, who performed at Walsh's Hall just south of Holy Trinity; and a new professional company, the Fedro Theatre, who performed at St. Stanislaus.[44] In addition to groups using parish halls and existing theatres, Chicago's Poles also built a new theatre and movie house, The Chopin Theatre, named for one of Poland's most renowned musicians, in the heart of the largest Polish neighborhood.[45]

Plays presented by these groups expressed concerns for Poland's vulnerability instead of stories of Polish triumph in Europe or in America, which had been popular in the years before. For example, St. Casimir's new drama group opened with *The Murder of the Czar of Russia*, "a three-act play based on conditions in the Russian Court."[46] Although the script is lost, the story of the play told in newspaper articles depicts a fantasy for Polish sovereignty; without a czar, Russians could not maintain their hold of Poland. Another group, the Esperanto Dramatic Circle performed the four-act drama *Na Zawsze* (*Forever*), which portrayed a Polish man condemned to Siberia by the Russian government, and The Polish Singer's Alliance produced *November Night*, a play about a servant being conscripted into the Russian army.[47] The plays resonated with members of the immigrant community who had left Poland to avoid military service: Chicago Pole Joseph Arendt remembers his father deciding to bring the family to the United States immediately upon his release from the Russian army so he would not have to fight again, and Anna Blazewich explained that she and her brother emigrated so he could escape Prussian army service.[48] Plays about assassinating the czar or about Poles drafted into foreign militaries showed a community focused on the European homeland and using theatre as a place to meditate on Poland's fate with their conationals.

The one play listed in the Polish press that showed Poles in Chicago also focused on Polish vulnerability. The Followers of Drama's debut play was titled *The Sidewalks of Chicago*, in which "exploiters" of newly arrived Polish immigrants extorted "the hard-earned money of ignorant Polish peasants in a truly shameful and disgraceful manner."[49] A "Jewish tradesman," a peddler, a "quack" doctor, gypsies, and "gangs of cheats" ran roughshod over the new immigrants until the police stopped them.[50] This play reveals contradictory concerns with regard to Americanization and Polishness. On the one hand, it critiqued the United States as a hospitable host land by focusing on the menace of the city. On the other hand, the play expressed embarrassment and frustration with new Polish immigrants, therefore advocating for some degree of Americanization to acclimate the newly arrived. Arendt remembers this as a real problem; he describes other Polish children calling him "greenhorn" and other names because he had yet to Americanize his way of dressing.[51] *The Sidewalks of Chicago* demonstrated a growing concern of the Polish immigrant community: if the war eliminated all hope for a sovereign Poland and if the United States succeeded in fully Americanizing new arrivals, then Polishness would be lost. Polish-language theatre provided a space for the community to collectively consider the issues of war in the homeland, of Americanization in the host land, and of Polish identity during the war.

Theatre also provided access to Polishness by providing a setting in which American-born children of Polish parents might be initiated into Polish culture. Polish theatre was a prime site for youth recreation. Parents encouraged their children to attend Polish plays because they reinforced Polish-language skills and depicted homeland history.[52] Helena Chrzanowski remembers going to see Polish plays as a child that depicted the "ideal of the resurrection of Poland: everybody believed that Poland would be resurrected, so most of those plays were around that theme."[53] Plays were also a means for the youth to celebrate the Polish national holidays. The November Insurrection celebrations in 1916 included two plays—*For Faith and Freedom* and *The Tenth Pavilion*—in which the youth embodied Polish heroes and revolutionaries by stepping into their roles in the depiction of the insurrections.[54] In the years before the United States entered the war, Polish holiday performances and theatres acted as a shield against Americanization. They provided a site of the nation, a resource for the homeland, and a place for immigrant youth to retain their Polish heritage.

Performing Polish-Americanness, 1917–18

As the United States readied to enter the war in 1917, Chicago's Polish performances of national identity shifted from that of the Polish diaspora living in Chicago to Polish-American patriots loyal to the Allied Powers cause. The earliest evidence of this shift was at the Allied Bazaar held at the Chicago Coliseum January 10–25, 1917.

The Allied Bazaar was a way to sympathize with, fundraise for, and give thanks to the many Allied Nations who had sent money to Chicago after the Great Fire in 1871.[55] The event was much like a miniature world's fair; each Allied Nation had a booth that represented their culture, sold goods, and demonstrated their contributions to the war effort. In addition to featuring nation-states like France and Belgium, the Allied Bazaar recognized "the Lithuanians, Slovaks, Bohemians, and Poles, whose countries have been made destitute by the war."[56] The booths were arrayed around a central concessions area that housed a buffet, tea café, cabaret, shooting gallery, "side show, grocery store, fortune teller stand" and art displays.[57] Proceeds from each booth and concession benefitted the Allied armies and various war relief funds. The bazaar encouraged each group to celebrate their national pride, to raise awareness of the effects of war on their country, and to show how they would triumph over the Central Powers. In addition to the booths, groups had special days at the bazaar to host meals, choruses, bands, and speakers in the communal areas.[58] The bazaar hosted nearly fifty thousand people daily and raised $535,000 in its two-week run.[59]

As an example of civic performance, the Polish immigrant community's participation in the Allied Bazaar presented Polishness as part of the coming American war effort and introduced the rest of the city to Polish Chicago's contributions. The planning committee for the Polish booth (members of the Polish Falcons, PNA, PAM, PWA, PRCUA, Polish National Council, Union of Polish Priests, Polish Businessmen's Association, and Polish Relief Committee) stated one goal for the exhibit: to portray Polish Americans as "a cultured and united community, conscious of its national and social duties, in the eyes of the people of other nationalities."[60] The community was aware of the importance of image maintenance and presented themselves as fellow Allies. They stood out, however, by making Polishness something that was located in Chicago. In contrast to the booths from other countries that imported all their goods from the homeland, the items for sale in the Polish booth were made in Chicago.[61] Local Polish stores provided goods, local women contributed "delicious cakes and pastries," and a local Polish restaurant sold "national dishes of Poland."[62] Local Polish theatres also participated, donating their profits to the Allied armies.[63] On Polish Day, sixty thousand patrons attended the bazaar, one third of which, according to the Polish newspaper, were Polish.[64] The day ended with a mass chorus singing "God Save Poland" and "Poland Is not Lost."[65] These anthems spoke to the goals of the bazaar in two ways. For the Americans in attendance, the lyrics situated Poland both as a sympathetic country oppressed and devastated by the Central Powers and as a fellow comrade-in-arms. For the twenty thousand Polish Chicagoans in attendance, hearing the national anthem in a large, centralized city venue (as opposed to in their neighborhood parish) made them feel like part of the social fabric of Chicago. The Allied Bazaar provided the first opportunity for the community to participate in a civic performance during the war and to perform their Polish-American patriotism publicly.

When the United States entered the war on April 6, 1917, Polish Chicagoans found ample opportunity to perform their Polish-American patriotism. One way was to join the U.S. Army in a public and performative way. Rather than simply enlisting, Polish-American soldiers paraded from their neighborhoods to Chicago's downtown to catch their train for boot camp, escorted by Boys Scouts and bands.[66] Polish national holiday celebrations also became sites to perform Polish-American patriotism and to recruit for the armies. This is evident in St. Casimir's celebration for the most important Polish national holiday, Polish Constitution Day, on May 3. For the holiday in 1917 the parish hosted a large parade and program wherein three thousand people listened to a large Polish chorus sing a medley of "The Star-Spangled Banner," "The Battle Hymn of the Republic," and "America."[67] The church's rector, Reverend W. Furman, made a speech in English, rather than in Polish, to appeal to the Americans in the crowd.[68] As the event finished with "God Save Poland," women passed out Polish and American flags. The children's skit performed at the Polish Women's Alliance event provides another example. There, during a recitation, "The curtain was raised on a tableau portraying 'Rising Poland.' . . . Three little girls . . . all dressed in Polish costumes—removed the crown of thorns and the shackles from the figure representing Poland in the tableau, placing a laurel wreath on her head and a scepter in her hand. The flag of the United States was hung above the tableau. Those present were deeply moved on seeing these Polish children performing, under the protection of The Star Spangled Banner, the symbolic act of the 'Resurrection of Poland.'"[69]

Chicago's Poles did not celebrate the November Insurrection in 1917, but they did hold three huge army recruitment rallies in June, September, and October to show onlookers Polish bodies morphing into American and Allied soldiers. On June 3, the community marched to the Kościuszko statue, a symbol of Polish-American military heroism, to pledge their support to "President Wilson and the nation."[70] Local Polish newspaper editor, Anthony Czarnecki, proclaimed to the thousands gathered, "Let the Polish people of Chicago be the first to spring to this call to arms. Let them rise up as Americans to do battle."[71] The Poles marching to the park were no longer immigrants incapable of assimilation; they were Americans fighting for the Allies. Fifteen thousand Polish Chicagoans gathered at the same statue on September 9 and twenty-five thousand gathered at a local hall on October 16. Both events were opportunities to recruit for Haller's army, a French army unit led by General Józef Haller and comprising entirely of Poles, the first of its kind in over one hundred years. At the event in October, the stage was packed with American and foreign dignitaries, blurring the lines between the nationalities.[72] In the parade, Polish societies and Polish soldiers from the U.S. and French armies marched alongside the American National Guard.

The meaning of the flag at these civic performances demonstrates the changing conceptions of the Polish immigrant community in the city. For example, whereas Polish flags had been potentially anti-American a few years before, at these events the streets were a sea of American, Polish, and French flags that indexed subsections of American army recruits.[73] Now Polish flags symbolized people fighting as Allies and for the American cause instead of a stubborn immigrant group "looking over [their] shoulders and seeking to perpetuate what [they] intended to leave behind them," as Wilson had previously stated. As figure 1 demonstrates, children now raised American and Polish flags, side by side, at holidays to show their Polish-American allegiance. A group of local Polish women and girls literally embodied a living American flag to the delight of the crowd at the recruitment event in October 1917.[74] For Poles, the American flag became symbolic of promised Polish sovereignty because American intervention in the war gave hope to the community that the Allies would triumph over the Central Powers and put Poland back on the map. Near the end of the program, a local Polish-American girl, Emily Wisla, presented a new Polish flag to Ignacy Paderewski, a famous Polish pianist and national leader, who instructed the crowd "to give testimony that the American Pole is a worthy heir to the glory of Polish arms."[75] The mixing of flags mirrored the way the line separating Polishness, Americanness, and Polish-Americanness was becoming more difficult to discern, disrupting the clear stratifications in the *Dillingham Report*.

Figure 1. All Saints Cathedral flag ceremony, 1918. Photo courtesy of Chicago History Museum, DN-0070203. *Chicago Daily News*, photographer.

In January 1918, President Wilson formally combined the goals of Poles, Polish-Americans, and American foreign policy by including an independent Polish state as one of his Fourteen Points. With U.S. war aims publicly supporting a sovereign homeland, Chicago's Poles all but eliminated their traditional Polish holidays in order to focus their resources on an Allied victory. January Insurrection celebrations garnered few attendees in 1918, but Chicago's Poles rallied en mass for the Liberty Loan Drive in March.[76] At one planning meeting, Smulski said, "The Americans of Polish blood in Chicago did their share in the last two Liberty Loan campaigns and have done their part gladly for their country since the war began."[77] His language shows a marked shift from speeches in 1914 wherein the Polish audience was addressed as Polish citizens exclusively. Now they were Americans helping the United States as "their country." The community gave generously in Liberty Loan and Red Cross drives, in part by using existing Polish cultural institutions. Polish theaters, particularly vaudeville theaters, showed "moving pictures early in the evening followed by dramas as well as short one-act sketches" and asked for donations between the acts.[78] Polish parishes also served as sites for collection. Immaculate Conception made their parish school, hall, and rectory into headquarters for various "Red Cross activities, drives for Liberty Loans, [and] Freedom Bonds and Stamps," and parish youth got involved.[79] Lillian Cwik remembers making care packages for soldiers and going from house to house with a band in the Polish neighborhoods to "get the people out, you know, to not only help Poland, but also to buy Liberty Bonds here in the United States."[80] The front page of a Polish newspaper showed "certificates received by the Polish National Alliance from the government of the United States for having purchased war-savings stamps" and called for "Every Polish organization . . . every larger association or even wealthier Polish family" to possess such a certificate to show "proof of loyalty to this country which has shown itself a sincere sister nation to Poland."[81]

Polish holidays were also a time to raise money for the Allies. Polish Constitution Day in 1918 inspired a new campaign called "American Poles for Poland on the Third of May."[82] Contributors had their names entered on "The Golden List," which was to be taken to the Polish capital by Paderewski and deposited there among the "ancient and important national treasures."[83] That a list of Polish Americans would be considered a national treasure of Poland demonstrates the way Polish-Americans thought of their hyphenated identity. Their affinity for the United States was created in part by the United States' support of Poland. Polish-Americanness went both ways: it was President Wilson advocating for a free Poland and it was Poles in Chicago giving money to the United States. These acts demonstrated a hyphenated identity in which both sides of the hyphen had importance.

The community reprised their success from the Allied Bazaar at the War Exposition in September 1918. Over thirty-five thousand Polish Americans attended on Polish Day, and they cheered as their flag flew over city hall for the first time.[84] In the Exposition hall, a Polish soldier spoke in English about the conditions in the trenches and a huge choir of seven hundred Polish Americans sang Polish anthems along with the "Star-Spangled Banner" and "My Country 'Tis of Thee." The Polish National Department made a show of sending a telegram to President Wilson expressing the American Pole's unwavering loyalty to America and to American ideals. One of the Polish newspapers called Polish Day at the War Exposition "a national holiday of primary importance," one wherein "the voice of the Polish-American citizens . . . [will] prove to the world at large that the aims of Poland are identical with those of America. Let our people show by their attendance their loyalty to the Star-Spangled Banner and to the Polish white Eagle."[85] In this moment, the broader audience had the opportunity to see Polish immigrants as fellow America countrymen fighting for democracy and freedom.

Conclusion

The examples above show the way that Poles transitioned from performances of Polishness to performances of Polish-American patriotism during the war. When faced with Americanization, they withdrew into their national culture, but once they could see themselves as Allies, they could see themselves as Americans, and non-Polish Americans could see them as Americans, too. By 1918, instead of fearing Americanization rhetoric, Polish Chicagoans denounced it as un-American. In an editorial in *Dziennik Zwiakowy*, the writer said of Americanization,

> This movement has in it not the smallest particle of the true American spirit, the spirit of freedom, the brightest virtue of which is the broadest possible tolerance, no one can deny. And when did this movement begin? It is, as a matter of fact, beginning now, at the moment when America is sealing the brotherhood of nations with its heroic blood, when it is tying unbreakable knots of friendship, when it is fighting for principles of world citizenship. The present war shows that the American "melting pot" is entirely superfluous. No language or "melting pot" can change or make into one the individual and anatomical virtues of temperament and blood. But the love of liberty, the love of ideals, the love of a great country of freedom and honor for its traditions and past have united the spirits of many nationalities, of which America can be proud. And America is proud of its brave citizen-sons who, although of various descents, are fighting on the fields of France as one under the spirit of Americanism, even those who were not originally born here.[86]

Yet even as Americans, Chicago Poles were careful to keep the hyphen. The hyphen—demonstrated in civic performances—brought the idea of the non-Anglo immigrant patriot into being. Hyphenated immigrant identity destabilized Americanization's racial nationalism rhetoric and constructed the Polish-American patriot. As Roosevelt said, some of these foreign-born immigrants became the "very best Americans" ever known to the city, and they did so by utilizing theatre and performance to illustrate the hyphen, not eliminate it.

Notes

1. Immigration Commission, *Abstracts of the Reports of the Immigration Commission with Conclusions and Recommendations and Views of the Minority* (Washington, D.C.: Government Printing Office, 1911), 214.
2. Christina A. Ziegler-McPherson, *Americanization in the States: Immigrant Social Welfare Policy, Citizenship, and National Identity in the United States, 1908–1929* (Gainesville: University of Florida Press, 2009), 10.
3. See John Higham, *Strangers in the Land: Patterns of American Nativism, 1860–1925* (New Brunswick, NJ: Rutgers University Press, 1998), 195–98.
4. For more on Americanization and immigrant assimilation during World War I, see Leslie V. Tischauser, *The Burden of Ethnicity: The German Question in Chicago, 1914–1941* (New York: Garland Publishing, 1990); Philip Gleason, "American Identity and Americanization," in *Harvard Encyclopedia of American Ethnic Groups*, ed. Stephen Thernstrom (Cambridge, MA: Harvard University Press, 1980), 31–58; Ziegler-McPherson, *Americanization in the States*; and Higham, *Strangers in the Land.*
5. "Polishness" in this context is a historically specific term that refers to an imagined, affective community of conationals. Although Poland was not a sovereign nation between 1795 and 1919, the Polish-speaking inhabitants of the historic lands of Poland (and émigrés from the region) still imagined themselves as a nation or a collective bound to one another by a shared language, history, and folklife. Polishness at this time was the consciousness of a shared culture coupled with the desire to be a political nation-state. This consciousness was aided by industrial technologies of nationalism such as widely disseminated print media, education and training systems, and new means of cataloging race and ethnicity.
6. Jill Dolan, *Utopia in Performance: Finding Hope at the Theatre* (Ann Arbor: University of Michigan Press, 2005), 90.
7. For more on the connection between bodies and identity, see Stuart Hall, ed., *Representation: Cultural Representations and Signifying Practices* (London: Open University, 1997), 51; Judith Butler, *Gender Trouble: Feminism and the Subversion of Identity*, 2nd ed. (New York: Routledge, 2006), 96; Linda J. Tomko, *Dancing Class: Gender, Ethnicity, and Social Divides in American Dance, 1890–1920* (Bloomington: Indiana University Press, 1999), 5; and Robert Clyde Allen, *Horrible Prettiness: Burlesque and American Culture* (Chapel Hill: University of North Carolina Press, 1991), 153.
8. William Z. Ripley, "Race Progress and Immigration," *Annals of the American Academy of Political and Social Science* 34, no. 1, Race Improvement in the United States (July 1909): 130–38.
9. Immigration Commission, 234 and 274.
10. Ibid., 2.
11. Ziegler-McPherson, *Americanization in the States*, 9.
12. Ibid., 1–2.
13. *Americanism: Addresses by Woodrow Wilson at the Convention Hall, Philadelphia, May 10, 1915; Franklin K. Lane, New York, January 11, 1919; Theodore Roosevelt, New York, October 12, 1915* (Washington, D.C.: Americanization Department, Veterans of Foreign Wars of the United States, 1926), 2.

14. Berral Lang, "Hyphenated-Jews and the Anxiety of Identity," *Jewish Social Studies: History, Culture, Society* n.s., no. 1 (Fall 2005): 1–15.
15. "Americanism," Theodore Roosevelt address delivered before the Knights of Columbus, Carnegie Hall, New York, October 12, 1915.
16. Ziegler-McPherson, *Americanization in the States*, 88.
17. "Americanization," *Chicago Tribune*, February 23, 1916.
18. "The Hyphen in Politics," *Chicago Tribune*, June 19, 1916.
19. "Nationalism," *Chicago Tribune*, July 6, 1916.
20. John J. Flinn, *Chicago, the Marvelous City of the West: A History, an Encyclopedia, and a Guide, 1892* (Chicago: The Standard Guide Company, 1892), 82; and see Edward R. Kantowicz, *Corporation Sole: Cardinal Mundelein and Chicago Catholicism* (Notre Dame, IN: University of Notre Dame Press, 1983).
21. William R. I. Thomas and Florian Znaniecki, eds., *The Polish Peasant in Europe and America*, vol. 2 (New York: Alfred A. Knopf, 1927), 1440.
22. Miecislaus Haiman, "The Poles in Chicago," in *Poles of Chicago, 1837–1957* (Chicago: Polish Pageant Inc., 1937), 5.
23. "Something about Poles Living in Chicago," *Narod Polski*, October 22, 1913.
24. "We and the Americans," *Dziennik Związkowy*, November 11, 1914.
25. Ibid.
26. "Americanization." *Dziennik Zwiazkowy*, December 5, 1911.
27. Ibid. Several Chicago settlement houses operated in heavily Polish districts: The Northwestern University Settlement House was (and is) just south of two major Polish parishes—St. Stanislaus and Holy Trinity; the University of Chicago Settlement was in the heart of Back of the Yards, a largely Polish area; and Hull House, in West Town, was in a neighborhood with a growing Polish population.
28. Ibid.
29. Kantowicz, *Corporation Sole*, 67.
30. Ibid., 72 and 74, and Stephen J. Shaw, "An Oak among Churches: St. Boniface Parish, Chicago, 1864–1990," in *American Congregations*, ed. James P. Wind and James W. Lewis (Chicago: University of Chicago Press, 1994), 367.
31. Michael LeMay and Elliott Robert Barkan, eds., *U.S. Immigration and Naturalization Laws and Issues: A Documentary History* (Westport, CT: Greenwood Press, 1999), 103–6.
32. "Polish Delegation Calls on Senator Lewis Purpose of Society to Fight Dillingham Bill," *Dziennik Zwiazkowy*, December 15, 1914.
33. "President Wilson's Veto Message of the Immigrant Literacy Bill, January 28, 1915," in *U.S. Immigration and Naturalization Laws and Issues: A Documentary History*, ed. Michael LeMay and Elliott Robert Barkan (Westport, CT: Greenwood Press, 1999), 107.
34. "Circuit Ii of the Alliance of Polish Falcons Commemorates the Anniversary of the November Insurrection," *Dziennik Zwiazkowy*, November 30, 1914.
35. "Honoring Our Hero Celebration of the November Insurrection at St. Adalbert's Parish," *Dziennik Zwiazkowy*, November 30, 1914; "Commemoration of November Insurrection," *Dziennik Zwiazkowy*, November 18, 1914; F. K. Wyra, "Commemoration of November Insurrection at St. Helen's Parish," *Dziennik Zwiazkowy*, November 30, 1914; "Circuit Ii of the Alliance of Polish Falcons Commemorates the Anniversary of the November Insurrection," November 30, 1914.
36. Ibid.

37. F. K. Wyra, "Commemoration of November Insurrection at St. Helen's Parish."
38. "Honoring Our Hero Celebration of the November Insurrection at St. Adalbert's Parish," *Dziennik Zwiazkowy*, November 30, 1914.
39. "Commemoration of the November Insurrection at St. Adalbert's Parish," *Dziennik Zwiazkowy*, December 2, 1914.
40. "November Insurrection Commemorated at St. Stanislaus Kostka Parish," *Dziennik Chicagoski*, November 28, 1892; "November Celebrations," *Dziennik Chicagoski*, December 1, 1893; "St. Casimir Parish Patriotic Program," *Dziennik Chicagoski*, December 1, 1897.
41. "Polish Kingdom Plan of Austria; Coronation Near," *Chicago Tribune*, February 13, 1915.
42. John Madro, interviewed by Anthony Fico, Oral History Archives of Chicago Polonia Project, Chicago History Museum, June 1977.
43. "Poles of Chicago Rejoice over the Fall of Warsaw," *Chicago Tribune*, August 6, 1915.
44. "New Theatrical Company in St. Casimir's Parish," *Dziennik Zwiazkowy*, March 27, 1917; "'The Sidewalks of Chicago' Followers of Dramatic Art Give Poor Performance," *Dziennik Zwiazkowy*, March 28, 1917; "The Polish Press Club," *Dziennik Zwiazkowy*, October 11, 1916.
45. Chicago Building Permit #44808, December 13, 1916; and Leona Hojnacka, interviewed by Oral History Archives of Chicago Polonia Project, Chicago History Museum, 1977.
46. "New Theatrical Company in St. Casimir's Parish."
47. "Esperanto Dramatic Circle Presents 'Forever,'" *Dziennik Zwiazkowy*, February 19, 1917; "November Night," *Dziennik Zwiazkowy*, January 29, 1917.
48. Joseph Arendt, interviewed by Anthony J. Nowak, Oral History Archive of Chicago Polonia Project, Chicago History Museum, April 4 and 20, 1977; Anna Blazewich, interviewed by Mary Cygan, Oral History Archives of Chicago Polonia Project, Chicago History Museum, November 11, 1977.
49. "'The Sidewalks of Chicago' Followers of Dramatic Art Give Poor Performance."
50. Ibid.
51. Joseph Arendt, interviewed by the Oral History Archives of Chicago Polonia Projects, Chicago History Museum, 1977.
52. Veronic Siwek, interviewed by Edward H. Pieraszek, Oral History Archives of Chicago Polonia Project, Chicago History Museum, June 20, 22, and 24, 1977; John and Tillie Rutowski, Lillian Cwik, and Leona Hojnacka interviewed by Oral History Archives of Chicago Polonia Project, Chicago History Museum, 1977.
53. Helen Chrzanowski, interviewed by Oral History Archives of Chicago Polonia Project, Chicago History Museum, 1977.
54. "Commune Iii [Polish National Alliance] Holds November Exercises," *Dziennik Zwiazkowy*, December 6, 1916; Cornelia J. Muchowski, "November Exercises Held in St. Adalbert's," *Dziennik Zwiazkowy*, December 8, 1916.
55. "Meet Us at the Big Allied Bazaar Tonight," *Chicago Tribune*, January 11, 1917; Allied Bazaar, *Report of the Allied Bazaar: The Coliseum, Chicago, Illinois, January 11–20, 1917* (Chicago: The Bazaar, 1917), 7.
56. Ibid.
57. "Meet Us at the Big Allied Bazaar Tonight," *Chicago Tribune*, January 11, 1917.
58. "Bazaar Closes: City's Greatest Charity Effort," *Chicago Tribune*, January 21, 1917.
59. "Fifty Thousand in One Day See Allied Bazaar: Doors Closed Three Times," *Chicago*

Tribune, January 16, 1917; "The Allied Bazar," *Dziennik Zwiazkowy*, January 22, 1917; "Allied Bazaar Profit Fixed at $535,293," *Chicago Tribune*, April 20, 1917.

60. T. M. Helinski, K. Zychlinski, J. F. Smulski, P. Rostenkowski, and H. Setmajer, "A General Appeal to Chicago's Polonia," *Dziennik Zwiazkowy*, December 9, 1916.
61. Cinderella, "Gossip of the Allied Bazaar," *Chicago Tribune*, December 28, 1916.
62. Cinderella, "Bridge Is Bazaar's Latest 'Big Idea,'" *Chicago Tribune*, December 29, 1916.
63. "The Allied Bazaar," *Dziennik Zwiazkowy*, December 14, 1916.
64. "The Allied Bazaar," *Dziennik Zwiazkowy*, January 22, 1917.
65. Ibid.
66. "Chicago Ships 475 Recruits for Regulars in a Day: City Gives 3,200 to U.S. Army," *Chicago Tribune*, May 2, 1917.
67. "Third of May Celebration at St. Casimir's Parish $105.44 Collected for Polish Relief," *Dziennik Zwiazkowy*, May 7, 1917.
68. Ibid.
69. G. Thierse, "Exercises Commemorating the Third of May Sponsored by the Main Educational Department at the Polish Women's Alliance," *Dziennik Zwiazkowy*, May 11, 1917.
70. "Thousands of Poles Pledge Loyalty to the U.S.: Clubs and Societies Gather at the Kosciuszko Monument," *Chicago Tribune*, June 4, 1917.
71. Ibid.
72. "War Secretary Coming to Urge Poles to Enlist: Baker and Paderewski to Speak at Rally Here Next Sunday," *Chicago Tribune*, October 7, 1917; and "25,000 Poles Honor Polish Army Dexter Pavilion Filled to Capacity Collection for Polish Army Nets Thousands of Dollars," *Dziennik Zwiazkowy*, October 15, 1917.
73. Ibid.
74. "French Deputy Here to Enlist Polish Army: Franklin-Bouillon Speaks to 15,000," *Chicago Tribune*, September 10, 1917; "War Secretary Coming to Urge Poles to Enlist: Baker and Paderewski to Speak at Rally Here Next Sunday," *Chicago Tribune*, October 7, 1917; "Solemn Rites Today as Poles Ask Volunteers: Paderewski Battle Hymn Will Be Sung for the First Time," *Chicago Tribune*, October 14, 1917; and "25,000 Poles Honor Polish Army Dexter Pavilion Filled to Capacity Collection for Polish Army Nets Thousands of Dollars," *Chicago Tribune*, October 15, 1917.
75. "25,000 Poles Honor Polish Army Dexter Pavilion Filled to Capacity Collection for Polish Army Nets Thousands of Dollars" and "Solemn Rites Today as Poles Ask Volunteers."
76. Maximilian Hencel, "January Exercises Held at Pulaski Hall," *Dziennik Zwiazkowy*, February 25, 1918; "Council Iii, Polish National Alliance, Holds January Exercises," *Dziennik Zwiazkowy*, January 28, 1918; "Loan Campaign Enlists Aid of 4 Organizations: Political Parties, Poles, and Unions Lay their Plans," *Chicago Tribune*, March 22, 1918.
77. "Poles Organize to Stir 400,000 in Loan Drive: Men Named to Form First Plans for City and County," *Chicago Tribune*, March 23, 1918.
78. Halina J. Majewska, "The Polish Stage in Chicago," *Poles of Chicago 1837–1937* (Chicago: Polish Pageant Inc., 1937), 92. Although secondary sources such as this one suggest there was Polish-language theatre happening in 1918, the Polish press does not report on it. Articles like those reporting on the 1916–17 season do not exist.
79. *Immaculate Conception Diamond Jubilee Book* (Chicago: Immaculate Conception, BVM, 1957), 32.

80. Lillian Cwik, interviewed by Oral History Archives of Chicago Polonia Project, Chicago History Museum, 1977.
81. "The Third of May," *Dziennik Zwiazkowy*, May 3, 1918.
82. "An Appeal to the Poles of America," *Dziennik Zwiazkowy*, March 20, 1918.
83. "The May Campaign of the American Poles for Poland," *Dziennik Zwiazkowy*, May 2, 1918.
84. "Daughter of Stars," *Chicago Tribune*, September 14, 1918; "War Exhibition Ticket Campaign Off with Rush," *Chicago Tribune*, Aug 18, 1918; "The Polish Day at the World War Exhibition," *Dziennik Zwiazkowy*, September 14, 1918.
85. Ibid.
86. S. Z., "Americanization Temptations," *Dziennik Zwiazkowy*, August 7, 1918.

New Paths to Representation; or, How *Under the Cherokee Moon* Broke the Outdoor Historical Drama Mold

—HEIDI L. NEES

But the beauty of theater is that it doesn't need much resource beyond the imagination, the strength of which, well exercised, outdoes anything the makers of those huge mechanized spectacles . . . can do.
MICHAEL FEINGOLD

Thinking about history, especially about the historical discourses of non-Western societies, is too important to be left to historians alone..
PETER NABAKOV

The act of representation in performance is complex, a thorny terrain that theatre scholars and practitioners must navigate with care. Even more difficult is the act of changing existing (and widely accepted) representations that satiate audience expectations. The politics of representing the cultural "Other," as well as "history," are particularly challenging. Nonetheless, many outdoor historical dramas try to tackle both subjects, which often results in problematic representations that tend to cater to audience expectations built on generalizations and stereotypes rather than accurate depictions. As Philip Deloria puts it, "Even in the wake of decades of stereotype busting, a beaded buckskin dress and a pair of braids continue to evoke a broad set of cultural expectations about

Indian people."[1] This is the case I encountered on numerous occasions while conducting research on representations of Native American cultures in outdoor historical dramas.[2] Most of the dramas I witnessed featured stereotyped native characters such as the Noble Savage, the Savage Indian, and the exotic Indian Princess. Furthermore, many of these dramas adopted a Western-based approach to native histories; that is, they favored positivistic, linear notions of history based on progress revealed through Western customs of storytelling. More specifically, these notions of history were most often arranged in a traditionally Western narrative arc based on exposition, rising action, climax, and resolution. In terms of production elements, most of these dramas relied on a similar formula that involved the narrative structure just described, a cathartic experience for the audience, singing and dancing, and an abundance of spectacle. Of the numerous productions I viewed and studied, one deviated from this outdoor drama mold. *Under the Cherokee Moon*, and other programs offered by the Cherokee Heritage Center in Tahlequah, Oklahoma, provided alternatives not only to the traditional outdoor drama format but also to how these productions construct and disseminate representations of Native American figures and histories.[3] In this essay, I explore the ways in which *Under the Cherokee Moon* provided alternative modes of representation and opened new paths for other outdoor dramas to consider. To do so, I draw from close readings of multiple outdoor historical dramas, personal interviews with production participants, and archival research.

Since the emergence of outdoor historical dramas in the late 1950s and 1960s as popular summer tourist fare, Indian characters have played a dominant role in many of these entertainments. This theatrical genre is dependent on the outdoor element, staged annually for summer audiences, and is usually produced in amphitheaters, often built exclusively for one drama. Mountainside Theatre (see figure 1), for example, serves as the site of *Unto These Hills* and can seat over 2,000 people (though in 2013 the show averaged only 425 audience members per night). In 2013, over 280,000 people attended outdoor historical dramas across the country, and over 80,000 attended the productions I witnessed in 2011.[4]

One of the attractions of these dramas is the pageantry and spectacle involved. Unsurprisingly, spectacle is viewed as necessary by most of the producers with whom I spoke, because of the need to fill the vast performance space. Large casts often fill the stage for not only crowd scenes but also song and dance numbers. Most of the dramas I encountered included at least one "settler" dance in which white characters celebrated together through reels, jigs, and/or square dances. Additionally, all the dramas I saw involved a "native" dance in which the

Figure 1. Mountainside Theatre, site of *Unto These Hills*. This type of outdoor amphitheater is the typical theatrical structure I encountered during my research. All the outdoor dramas I researched, with the exception of *Under the Cherokee Moon*, took place in spaces like this.

Indian characters performed a variation on "ritualistic-esque" choreography. This number usually involved fire (sometimes characters danced around a fire, other times fire batons were used) and the light of the fire against the night sky enhanced the spectacle. In most cases, the dances performed by Indian characters were choreographed by nonnatives and were based on research conducted through books and sometimes videos.[5] Because these dances were created through Western lenses and reflected Western styles of movement, the results often fail to accurately resemble native dances. Instead, they fulfill nonnative audiences' preconceived notions of native movement, which are usually built upon images of stomping and whooping Indians culled from movies and television.

In addition to large casts and choreography, battle scenes provide the spectacle many producers seek. These battle scenes depict clashes between native and nonnative forces and involve gunshots, bows and arrows, and hand-to-hand combat. In *Tecumseh!*, the Shawnee leader's tribal confederacy fights U.S. military forces in a scene that involves actors on horseback who utilize the entirety of the outdoor space including wooded trails that encircle the audience and an onstage pond. The negotiation of space and the inclusion of horses, weaponry, and a large ensemble of actors in live battle scenes provide grand exhibitions for the audience.

In addition to spectacles and the large playing spaces in which they are housed, another trademark of most outdoor historical dramas is the narrative structure used. Producers typically retain a traditionally Western narrative structure presented through the theatrical mode of realism. The method of disseminating the histories depicted relies upon a linear, cause-and-effect structure that is dependent upon benchmarks including an inciting incident, climax, and resolution. Love stories are also often inserted into the historical figures' lives. The native histories told are most often constructed and communicated through nonnative sources and often reflect inaccurate depictions of native cultures including costume, societal structures, ritual, dance, and characterizations. Furthermore, the views of history presented in these dramas are based on Western, not indigenous, perceptions of history. The positivistic notions of history depicted focus on progress and are troubling for native cultures because they end with the disappearance of the Indian, either through death or relocation. This problematic "Vanishing Indian" trope is especially embedded in the stereotypes featured in these productions, including the Noble Savage and the Savage Indian. The Noble Savage, a popular character type since the nineteenth century, is simultaneously admired and feared by whites; he is admired for his courage, pride, and conviction and feared for the primitive and unpredictable savage beneath those praiseworthy traits. The uncivilized nature of the Noble Savage prevents him from assimilating into advanced Western society, despite his desirable attributes. The Savage Indian does not demonstrate the laudable qualities of the Noble Savage; instead he violently preys upon innocent whites (especially women and children) and gives in to his unrefined and uncontrollable urges and passions. Both stereotypes persist in entertainment today, including outdoor historical dramas. In both cases, the only suitable result is the destruction of the Indian, thus communicating to the mostly nonnative audiences the erroneous notion that Native Americans are no longer part of contemporary American culture.

In most of the cases I investigated, the plotline revolves around a Noble Savage whose experiences and conflicts result in a cathartic experience for the mainly nonnative audience. Usually, this catharsis is the result of the hero's death or other form of departure and is viewed by many as a way to purge audiences of any white guilt over the mistreatment and expulsion of Native Americans.[6] This type of catharsis reinforces the notion that Native Americans either have no place in modern-day American or are relics of the past living in the ways of the past and thus lack agency in contemporary society. The narratives used in these dramas provide dominant (nonnative) cultures with tools to continue to oppress and/or ignore native communities in the United States today. This format dominates most of the outdoor historical dramas I encountered and has become the approach accepted and expected by audiences and producers. During my research, however, many participants in these dramas expressed a desire to make changes to their productions.

In my conversations with numerous people involved in outdoor historical drama, the comment I heard most was that to survive the current economic climate, productions needed to seek and embrace change.[7] For some this means change at the administrative level, while for others it means change at the production level or in the organization's mission. For all, the change was aimed at combating the decreasing attendance numbers most productions have faced during the last decade. Of greater significance to this study are the cases that involve addressing the issues surrounding inaccurate and oftentimes offensive representations of native cultures and histories. Interestingly, though I heard most people say that change is necessary for various reasons, many also articulated a perceived *resistance* to change in the field. Perhaps such opposition results from a lack of ideas about how to change. Perhaps some producers don't believe they have the financial means or resources necessary to make changes, or they share the view of Jeffrey Jones: "Theater has become uniquely convention-bound and resistant to innovation. It is convention-bound because it relies on familiar and well-understood forms, structures, and dramaturgical principles in order to make it as easy as possible to figure out what's going on, pay attention, and not feel bored."[8] It may be that outdoor historical drama has become so institutionalized that it is bound to its conventions and thus "resistant to innovation." Another possibility surrounds the many complex issues facing producers, they prefer the audience to witness easily consumed, traditional formats and stories charged with enough spectacle to keep spectators from feeling bored.

It may seem easier to some producers to ignore the issues of representation in many outdoor historical dramas, especially since the issues are complicated by the need to sell tickets to nonnative audiences who arrive with their own expectations of what both an outdoor drama and a Native American should look and sound like. Ignoring the issues and continuing with the palatable presentations previously displayed, however, is a choice that is by no means innocuous. The issues facing producers with regard to representation include harmful stereotypes, cultural and historical (in)accuracies, and authenticity. The challenges facing these dramas are complex, and rarely are there simple answers. Therefore, I recognize that the examples I share here are by no means void of their own issues; however, they are, I believe, ways to expand conceptions of outdoor dramas and their representation of Native American cultures.

Once a particular approach is institutionalized, adopting new programming and strategies is challenging. Susan Phillips at the Institute of Outdoor Drama in Greenville, North Carolina, stressed the need for additional programming at outdoor historical drama sites: "Being able to offer something more, offering a children's show, offering little workshops . . . it's just interesting things so that when you come here it's a whole experience for the audience. It's not just going to see that show and you leave. There's so much more to offer."[9] New programming is important not just for bringing in new audiences but also for rectifying some of the harmful images presented by the old programs. After a ten-year struggle to change the drama, the Cherokee Heritage Center in Oklahoma abandoned its previous drama *Trail of Tears* in 2005 and incorporated new programs in the late 2000s. *Trail of Tears*, which had run since 1969 in the Tsa-La-Gi Amphitheatre (see figures 2 and 3), was originally written by Kermit Hunter and left many in the surrounding Cherokee community feeling uneasy over the depictions of Cherokee culture and history. In 1996, Nat Eek, the director of the show, wrote to Scott Parker of the Institute of Outdoor Drama and noted, "The Kermit Hunter script is serviceable but old-fashioned, predictable, lacking in character development (as is most historical drama), and certainly out of sync with the current Native American concepts."[10] Several of the people I interviewed in Tahlequah, Oklahoma, explained that many local residents were frustrated by the inaccurate depictions in Hunter's script. Numerous incarnations of the premise and framework set by Hunter's *Trail of Tears* were staged in the early 2000s, followed by a brief hiatus. More recent programs adopted by the Cherokee Heritage Center, however, offered an alternative to the previous drama and emphasized audience interaction and Cherokee methods of storytelling.

The Cherokee Heritage Center introduced a family-oriented piece in 2011 called *Legends at Dusk* that focused on oral storytelling.[11] Tonia Hogner Weavel, who compiled the traditional Cherokee stories for the piece, explained that it was her realization that "you have to squeeze in little things of history without people even realizing it" that sparked the idea for the show.[12] The performance took place in the Ancient Village site, thus breaking away from the amphitheater, and began with an introduction to the village and eighteenth-century Cherokee life in an attempt to integrate history into the production. After the introduction, the piece shifted to storytelling. Weavel described the appeal of the storytelling aspect: "We do mostly animal tales, but in that it was every story has a lesson and those Cherokee stories have lessons like onions. Like you'll learn a lesson at age twenty-eight and your eight-year-old daughter will learn a lesson from the same story. Your lesson's a little more *fancy* than her lesson. But it *still* is a lesson. And so that's the magic of those stories is that they're multi-faceted and can mean different things to different people."[13] Several storytellers, who were also employees from the Ancient Village, shared various stories and pulled audience members onto the playing space to help enact the tales.

Figure 2. Tsa-La-Gi Amphitheatre. At the time I took this picture in September 2011, the theatre had not been used for several years.

For instance, a child was asked to act like the turtle in the "Why Turtle's Shell Is Cracked" story. Weavel remarked of this interactive component, "People ate it up!"[14] Weavel also pointed out that the show taught audiences about Cherokee culture, explaining that the producers wanted to insert a "cultural hook" into the show. One reason for this, she asserted, was to counteract existing negative images of Native Americans, some of which have been perpetuated by outdoor dramas. She cited an incident in which one of the performers wore face paint that included a white arrow pointing to his eye. She described her reaction thusly: "I was like, 'Why would you do that?' . . . Well, that's just nothing I'd ever heard of before. And I was like—what I wanted to say is, 'You're Cherokee, you don't have to put that on, just being us is *enough*.' We don't have to be *over*—and I think that's what a lot of dramas do. They miss the simplicity and the nature-istic, if that's a word, humble-base of Indian people. It's we're greedy or we want to kill everybody on the prairie. . . . That wasn't it at all. And I think a lot of people miss this real soft, subtle, calmness about Indian people."[15] For Weavel, tapping into the repertoire by pulling traditional Cherokee stories from the oral tradition and using that format to transfer knowledge about Cherokee culture

Figure 3. Tsa-La-Gi Amphitheatre. View from house, looking onto stage.

to audience members helps to combat misunderstandings of Native Americans. The show helped to counteract stereotypes such as the Savage Indian. Also, in Weavel's response to the face paint incident, she touches on the idea of authenticity. The storyteller did not need to subscribe to a white perception of what a "real Indian" looked like by putting on face paint. To Weavel, being himself was all the authenticity the storyteller needed.

The storytelling approach not only allows the producers in Tahlequah to teach audiences about Cherokee culture in embodied ways but also provides an opportunity to expand the audience base. Some outdoor historical dramas prominently feature violence, which may deter people from bringing young children. The storytelling-based shows provide a family-friendly alternative and can assist in an organization's outreach (in this case, reaching out to nonnative audiences in an attempt to educate them about Cherokee culture).

In 2011 the Cherokee Heritage Center commissioned a new, trimmed-down version of their drama *Under the Cherokee Moon*. Written, directed, and featuring Laurette Willis, the drama offered alternatives to the traditional outdoor drama in terms of scale. While Willis set out to create a more manageable and innovative way to relay the area's history, she also created new approaches to representing the local native cultures and history. Whether these innovations were intentional or not, the work provides useful lessons in the politics of representation in performance.

As noted above, although some of the outdoor dramas experienced changes over the years (most notably *Unto These Hills*), they all followed a similar formula that included exposition, rising action, climax, and denouement and featured a protagonist versus antagonist conflict.[16] Furthermore, with the exception of a narrator in some productions, the characters maintain the fourth-wall convention. The productions are representational and feature spectacle, rather than being abstract and featuring avant-garde staging practices.[17] After seeing five different productions and researching others that followed this format, I expected the same from *Under the Cherokee Moon*. This drama, however, discarded the traditional format and style of outdoor historical dramas and instead offered new considerations of how to present Native American histories and cultures in ways that address both the practical and theoretical issues at stake.

I pulled into the large parking lot of the Cherokee Heritage Center and was reminded me of the lots I had seen at the other dramas; the vast number of spaces was a testament to the large crowds that poured in during the drama's heyday, and the disproportionately small number of vehicles actually occupying spaces testified to the present-day struggles of many dramas. I expected to walk into the large Tsa-La-Gi Amphitheatre, since every other show I had seen was staged in a similar space. Instead, the production was staged in the Adams Corner Rural Village, a replica of a late nineteenth-century Cherokee community before Oklahoma became a state. The village consists of several buildings, including a church, a schoolhouse, a general store, and residences. Chairs were set up for approximately seventy-five audience members in the grass in front of the general store (see figure 4). I was surprised not only at the intimate space established but also at the small number of audience members expected. As I sat down, I was handed a program. Unlike the glossy-paged booklets sold at the other dramas, this program was a double-sided single sheet of paper, with one side offering actor bios and pictures and the other side (fashioned after the "Cherokee Rose Buds," a nineteenth-century Cherokee Female Seminary publication), providing context for the show. This context included actual articles from the historical publication, such as poetry, a Secretary's report, a segment in Cherokee language, and information about the publication, and also the song "Amazing Grace," with lyrics in English and Cherokee. Additionally, this side of the program provided a brief introduction to the drama itself: "Welcome to the Cherokee Female Seminary in the late 1800s. You are a resident of Cherokee Nation, Indian Territory, out to enjoy a pleasant evening's entertainment of music and storytelling on the grounds of the Seminary—the first school of higher learning for women west of the Mississippi River."[18] A description of each act and the characters therein followed this introduction. The description concluded with a warning, "If you thought you were just an ordinary citizen, think again (*you look an awful lot like a member of the Doolin gang escaping from U.S. Marshalls!*)."[19] In a move reminiscent of Bertolt Brecht's discouragement of

Figure 4. The General Store at Adam's Corner Rural Village, site of *Under the Cherokee Moon*.

passive audience members, this production broke representational conventions and involved the audience from the start. This direct implication of the audience as active participants in the evening's fare, and not just as detached observers, differentiated this production from the others I had witnessed.

Audience engagement extended beyond the program as actors, costumed in period attire, began to appear on each side of the audience before the show began and conversed with the audience members, asking questions (in character) about where they had traveled, why they had come to the Cherokee

Heritage Center, what they do for a living, and so on. After mingling with the audience for several minutes, the actors disappeared and a man dressed in contemporary clothing appeared on the porch of the general store, which served as the stage. The emcee began by addressing the audience in Cherokee. After a few bewildered looks among audience members, the emcee taught the audience some words of greeting in Cherokee, such as "hello" and "how are you." The emcee then took several minutes to work with the audience in refining their new vocabulary, teasing some on their pronunciations. At this point, he proceeded to welcome the crowd in both Cherokee and English and turned to humor in the form of contemporary Cherokee jokes (most of them at the expense of whites). S. Elizabeth Bird regards this type of humor as an enactment of increased agency on behalf of Native Americans, with which "they can wield that power to fight back." Bird explains, "At the informal, interpersonal level, Indians have been doing that for years, creating a rich humor that plays on and subverts dominant stereotypes, mocking White attitudes, federal agencies, and so on."[20] In this case the emcee, a Keetoowah Cherokee man named Charles Foster, subverted expectations by humorously pointing out white attitudes and perceptions, thus "wielding" the power to call these attitudes into question. Most of the audience, which appeared to be a diverse mix of native and nonnative members, laughed in response to Foster's jokes even though the nonnatives were the targets of much of the humor. Foster also provided background information and history to prepare the audience for the show. This use of a contemporary Cherokee man—dressed in contemporary attire, speaking in contemporary vernacular, and discussing both contemporary and historical culture, events, and figures—addressed issues of temporal dissonance that often arise in productions. Oftentimes, native characters are portrayed as figures trapped in the past rather than as members of contemporary society. In this case, however, audiences were reminded from the beginning that Native American cultures, in this case Cherokee, are not relics of the past, nor are they present-day people living in the ways of the past. The emcee presented viewers with an example of a contemporary native man who is an active member of the local community. Furthermore, the emcee, along with the mingling instigated by the actors before the show, set the tone for the interactive, nontraditional performance that followed. Fourth-wall expectations were dispelled from the start, allowing audiences to open themselves to a new form of outdoor drama.

Following the emcee's introduction, Laurette Willis appeared onstage as Carrie Bushyhead, a graduate of and teacher at the Female Seminary who was of Scottish and Cherokee ancestry. The entire first act revolved around Bushyhead's recollections of the Trail of Tears, the establishment of the Female Seminary, Cherokee leader and Confederate general Stand Watie, and the tribe's divided alliances during and after the American Civil War. Instead of approaching the history of the area and the figures therein through a traditional narrative arc, with events being depicted onstage, *Under the Cherokee Moon* takes a solo performance approach, in which the onstage figure recounts events and people from his or her own point of view. One of the first comments Willis makes as Bushyhead is that she is "escorting" the audience "back in time . . . a responsibility I do not take lightly."[21] In this moment, Willis acknowledges to the audience several ideas. First, she grounds the audience in the present (a notion reinforced by the inclusion of the emcee at the beginning of each act) and acknowledges that through this production they would be revisiting past events and figures through the eyes of the characters portrayed. Instead of becoming enraptured by the replication of past events, the audience remains aware of their place in the present, thus discouraging an Aristotelian style of imitation and catharsis. Second, Willis, as Bushyhead, emphasizes that this time travel carries the "responsibility" of communicating that the stories of the past are important to the present. In my interview with Willis, she explained why she views this relaying of the past as a "responsibility": "We're focused on something greater than ourselves. And that's what this show is about. It's relating that it's not just entertainment. People think maybe they come out for, oh, some fun, something a little different, but its edu-tainment, I guess you could say. It's education, but like I said, the show was just the beginning of the matter, not the end of it."[22] Willis hopes that through the portrayal of historical figures and the relaying of history through their stories, audience members will feel compelled to investigate the histories further, which is why she sees the show as "just the beginning."

Partway through the act, Willis switches character from Bushyhead to Sarah Worcester, an Anglo instructor at the Female Seminary. This process of change is not, however, hidden from the audience through a backstage costume change. Instead, Willis removes Bushyhead's glasses and dons pieces of Worcester's accouterment while singing "Amazing Grace." This musical refrain is used repeatedly throughout the show, as a theatrical transporting device that allows the characters, and at times the audience, to transfer to different times and transform into different identities. While "Amazing Grace" may seem a strange choice (and one potentially tinged by colonialism), the hymn was allegedly sung by Cherokee on the Trail of Tears and is one that is embraced by many Cherokee today.[23] By the end of her musical refrain, Willis's physicality and vocality have changed before the audience's eyes. By exposing the audience to this transformation, Willis allows for a metatheatricality, calling attention to the mechanics of theatre and acting, and reminding audiences that they are viewing constructions that approximate these historical figures but that are not 100-percent replications.

I asked Willis about her process for developing her characters and how she differentiates Bushyhead from Worcester in performance. Willis replied that she establishes a sense of the "weight" of the person through the research she conducts on them. On any of the characters she creates, Willis conducts rigorous research to find photographs of and pieces written by or about the person. She fills in the gaps with her own sense of the figure, which is based partly on her extensive research into accounts of other local events and people. For instance, in the case of Bushyhead and Worcester, there are no remnants of texts they had written. Willis had to rely on other written accounts of the women, but in order to create the character she depended on "journal entries of people who were Trail of Tears survivors and piecing things together of what life was like at the Cherokee Female Seminary."[24] In terms of her performance choices for each character, Willis creates a sense of the weight of the character based on what she knows of their experiences and relationships and begins to construct the physical and vocal presence of the character. She views Bushyhead as having a "weight to her," due in part to her father's role as a judge and her brother's role as a chief. Willis describes Bushyhead as "someone who by her ancestry and by her bearing held a lot of weight both physically . . . and metaphorically . . . so when I walk as her I feel this bearing, I feel this certain way that she carries herself."[25] In contrast, Willis sees a vulnerability and idealism in Worcester and thus decided on a lighter physicality and airier voice for the character. In performing these different characters, Willis creates a palimpsestic effect. Willis layers these two characters on top of each other, as well as on top of herself, in such a way that vestiges of each persona show through in the performance. This effect is exemplified when Willis, as Bushyhead, says, "Let me show you what I mean" as she is telling the audience about Worcester, thus signaling her transformation into the other character. The audience thereby understands the layering of Worcester as an interpretation by Bushyhead, all while recognizing that both are constructs of Willis. The exposed constructedness of this production does not make it questionable as a history lesson but rather suggests that history itself is a construct, thereby opening a space for multiple perspectives and interpretations of the past to emerge.

Although Willis did not cite Brecht as an influence in her creation of the piece, theorists like Elin Diamond apply Brechtian and feminist theory to performance, providing another lens through which to consider Willis's character transformations.[26] Diamond explains that in Brecht's theory of "not, but," the actor alienates the audience and "keeps differences in view instead of conforming to stable representations of identity," thus subverting fixed notions of identity and representation.[27] In *Under the Cherokee Moon*, Willis distances the audience in such a way as to subvert prescribed and stable perceptions of eighteenth-century Cherokee and nonnative women. The constructedness of the performance and the way we interpret identity are rendered apparent by the exposure of difference between and within the characters and actors.

Whether intentional or not, Willis's approach may also be read as postmodern in its view of history. Linda Hutcheon, in her study on postmodernism, claims that many postmodern works "openly assert that there are only *truths* in the plural, and never one Truth; and there is rarely a falseness *per se*, just others' truths. Fiction and history are narratives distinguished by their frames."[28] Unlike other outdoor dramas, which suggest an objective view of past events as they happened and of figures as they were, *Under the Cherokee Moon*, through its metatheatrical awareness and digression from realistic convention, suggests that there are multiple perspectives to history and thus multiple "truths." In many ways, this frees the producers of *Under the Cherokee Moon* from the impossible onus of being 100-percent accurate, whereas other producers are unable to escape debates over accuracy because of their representational style. This freedom does not mean that Willis creates her material without any support. Willis explained that when she pieces together the puzzles of the past to make a show, she conducts a significant amount of research to support the stories her characters share. The scripts she has produced for the Cherokee Heritage Center are reviewed before being approved. Willis noted that when she submits her scripts to Center Board members, "they go over them with a fine-tooth comb and they're submitted to historians."[29] Furthermore, she sometimes has to obtain permission from the principal chief or from tribal elders to depict certain aspects of Cherokee culture. Such was the case during a previous version of the show when she wanted to incorporate a war dance. After gaining permission, Willis was able to consult local Cherokee in staging the dance, thus tapping into what Diana Taylor considers repertoire-based knowledge, in addition to the archive-based written texts she consults. Willis also explained that she tries to use a historical figure's own words as much as possible, and in the scripts she distributes to her actors any words actually attributed to the character are written in blue. Furthermore, she includes a bibliography of the sources she consulted along with the script. While the script recognizes the constructed nature of history, Willis also holds herself accountable for creating productions that are supported by archival accounts of the past, as well as accounts by local Cherokee residents. As she puts it, "I look for the hook. I take what is the history that we know and what is it that we don't know. How can we make what we don't know come to life by what we do know?"[30]

Willis's approach also allows the audience to have an active role in reliving and portraying the past. In addition to breaking the fourth wall through the preshow interaction with the audience and the emcee's dialogue with the audience, actors ask for audience volunteers during the performances. The first time this occurs is after Worcester has transformed back into Bushyhead during "Amazing Grace." Once the transformation is complete, Bushyhead asks for volunteers to try walking with a book on their heads in order to instruct them on good posture. In this case, not only do the actors break the fourth wall but so too do audience members who approach the stage. This type of audience participation is invoked later in the play when the actor playing Will Rogers asks for volunteers to try twirling a rope. Audiences become physically active in creating the performance instead of passively consuming it. By relaying history and culture not just through words and demonstrations but also through audience participation, that knowledge becomes embodied in the audience.

The second act is similar to the first in that it features actors portraying characters who discuss their own histories, as well as the history of the area, in addition to audience interaction and demonstrations. In the case of the second act, however, there are more characters, native and nonnative, including Ned Christie, Will Rogers, Zeke Proctor, Captain John C. West, and Belle Starr. While Willis portrays Starr, four additional actors perform the other roles. The characters do not merely approach the stage, perform their monologue, and exit. Rather, Willis has woven these characters together in such a way that they both monologue and dialogue. She has found and created connections between the characters by looking for links between their lives. For instance, in her research she came across Captain John C. West, who was a member of the Cherokee Light Horse (Cherokee Police). As she continued to dig for information about him, she found Works Progress Administration (WPA) narratives from the 1930s in which West's son was interviewed. It was through that source that she discovered that Captain West's brother, Deputy Marshall Franklin West, died at the hand of Sam Starr, Belle Starr's second husband. Through this connection she was able to piece the characters of Captain West and Belle Starr together and allow them to dialogue onstage. These types of connections allow Willis to bring a plurality of voices together in interesting ways that allow for a multitude of historical "truths." Taking up again Hutcheon's views on postmodern works, Hutcheon avers that they can "also challenge narrative singularity and unity in the name of multiplicity and disparity."[31] In some ways, it may seem that the collection of voices included in this drama are complicit with certain colonial narratives. For instance, the repeated use of "Amazing Grace" and the focus on a Christian Female Seminary can be viewed as advocating for Western influence and intrusion. Voices that oppose American imposition are also included. Ned Christie, a Cherokee senator who was wrongfully accused of murder by the U.S. government and was deemed an "outlaw," is included in the show. Another local historical figure, Cherokee senator and Trail of Tears survivor Zeke Proctor, is also portrayed and rallies support from the audience for Cherokee sovereignty. This variety of perspectives reflects the myriad opinions and experiences that comprise the local community. The tapestry of voices Willis presents challenges "narrative singularity" by introducing native and nonnative voices from various backgrounds. In addition, by making these figures individuals and using a character-driven rather than a plot-driven format, there are no stereotyped characters such as the Noble Savage or Red Savage. Each Cherokee (and non-Cherokee) character has his or her own story to tell.

Disparities between the voices performed onstage is not emphasized, but the script does call attention to disparities between the different accounts these historical figures offer. For instance, Belle Starr tells the audience an anecdote and follows it by saying, "and that's just one of the things they say about me." Other characters make similar statements, including "if you like that story, you should hear what else they say." These lines highlight not only a postmodern view of history but also some particularities of native perceptions of history as articulated by Peter Nabakov. He contends, "When a Navajo storyteller starts his account with 'The way I heard it was . . . ,' as Luci Tapahonso explains, his variant 'doesn't discount other versions, but rather adds to the body of knowledge being exchanged.' It is the innately democratic virtue of much oral tradition that its multiple versions 'enrich the listener's experience,' in Tapahonso's words, and do so by providing cross-referencing native glosses and commentaries that are themselves underlain with complementary fragments or competing claims."[32] The voices that Willis incorporates into *Under the Cherokee Moon* don't discount each other but build upon the histories and cultures depicted in the show. When a character says, "You should hear what else they say," he or she invites viewers to consider the multiple and varied sides to the story, not just the narrative that has dominated historical record. The narratives cross-reference each other in the way the characters dialogue and refer back to each other in their individual monologues. This intertextuality of voices destabilizes what other histories and legends have proclaimed as "Truth." The result is a pluralistic account of the history of the area, the experiences of the individuals therein, and the culture of the Cherokees that "enriches the listener's experience." An authenticity emerges in this case that is based in the lived experience of the characters portrayed and the actors who grew up in the area and within Cherokee culture.

To return to Diamond and Brecht, Diamond says of Brecht's theory of historicization: "In historicized performance, gaps are not to be filled in, seams and contradictions show in all their roughness, and therein lies one aspect of spectatorial pleasure—when our differences *from* the past and *within* the past are palpable, graspable, applicable."[33] *Under the Cherokee Moon* shows audience members that perceptions of the past are riddled with discrepancies while exposing differences and similarities between the past and present. For example, when I attended the drama, the Cherokee Nation was in the midst of unrest regarding voting rights within the tribe. Echoes of the contemporary political controversy were detectable in the lines of characters within the performance who were speaking about nineteenth-century issues. The historicity of the performance, and the differences and contradictions revealed through the script, resonated with many of the locally based audience members, thus making the issues addressed "palpable, graspable, applicable."

The cast of *Under the Cherokee Moon* enriches the audience's experiences further by implicating them in the histories they tell. As in the case of the program, individuals in the audience become members of outlaw gangs, such as Bill Doolin, Rose of Cimmaron, and Cattle Annie, when they are pointed out by Belle Starr. Zeke Proctor treats the audience as fellow members of the Cherokee tribe. Willis revealed to me that she has the actors stand in the back and take note of which audience members are being referenced as which historical figures, such as one of the Dalton gang, so that another actor can reference the same audience member in his monologue. In this way, the audience is not treated as an observer invisible to the characters onstage but rather as a member of the characters' communities. They are thus engaged in the history being presented. Willis explains why this implication of the audience is important to her: "By seeing the history brought to life in this way, the audience is connected to it, they're not divorced from it. Also it *forces* them, and force is almost too hard a word, it *challenges* them, I'd say it challenges them to think. And to feel and to be a part and to ask what would I have done in this situation? We're so used to the techno-sphere and seeing things on television or on the internet where we're divorced from it. But *here*, you're a part of it."[34] Once again, we hear echoes of Brecht in Willis's desire to challenge the audience to think and consider their own actions. As Diamond points out, Brecht's idea of historicization involves a "double movement . . . of preserving the 'distinguishing marks' of the past and acknowledging, even foregrounding, the audience's present perspective."[35] In asking the audience to consider the past through the individual perspectives of various characters while refusing to hide the actor behind that character, Willis hopes audience members will examine and revise their own present-day perspectives. For Willis, involving the audience in this way encourages empathy without resorting to catharsis. And because she believes that "history repeats itself and certain patterns throughout history have been played out," Willis feels that this empathy is a valuable trait for people to develop.[36]

Assigning roles to audience members in this historical drama has another interesting effect on the production. The act of displacing different identities onto the audience members absolves the producers from having to worry about differentiating cast members as "white" and "Indian." Because of the nonrealistic style the show already establishes, audience members understand and "buy" who they are portraying at any given moment based on the designation articulated by the characters. When Zeke Proctor addresses the audience as "fellow Cherokee," we buy it because we understand identity transformation as a convention of this production, in large part because of the transformation we see between Bushyhead and Worcester in the first act. The audience has been prepared for the identity transformations placed on them in the second act. The acceptance and fluidity of this convention of identity transformation eradicates the need for anyone to appear in red makeup and black wigs, actions that have historically occurred in many outdoor dramas and continue to occur in some dramas today.[37] Actors and audience members try on different identities without having to manifest any stereotyped physical attributes. Willis also discourages the assumption of certain physical appearances for Native Americans in her script by subtly revealing details about her characters' backgrounds, specifically Carrie Bushyhead. As Bushyhead, Willis (who identified herself as nonnative) talks about both her Cherokee and Scottish ancestry. Willis admits that she includes this "in case people say, 'she didn't look Cherokee.'"[38] The actors who play Ned Christie, Zeke Proctor, and Captain John C. West are all of various tribal lineages including Cherokee, Osage/Choctaw, and Creek, and all, with their various physical traits, subvert the notion that Native Americans have a uniform look. Willis points out that one of the actors, Joe Weavel, is five-eighths Cherokee and yet has blond hair and blue eyes, citing his looks as a testament to the variety of physical traits in native cultures. By focusing on individuals' stories in this drama, and through the device of identity transformation, the need for a uniform "General Indian" look (which assumes that all Native Americans possess particular features such as black, straight hair, brown eyes, dark skin, and high cheekbones) is eliminated. The script speaks to the idiosyncrasies of individuals and undermines the stereotyped, stock image of the Indian that is presented in many other outdoor dramas. The agency of audience expectations in many ways dictates the General Indian figure in other historical dramas, but here the smaller scale and audience relieves *Under the Cherokee Moon* of some of that pressure.

Hutcheon considers one characteristic of many postmodern works to be the refusal to "hide their interpretative and narrating acts behind the third-person voice of objectivity that is so common to both historical and literary critical writing."[39] In other words, those who pen history traditionally have tried to cover their own biases and perspectives with a mask of objectivity. Oftentimes, history is written in a way that ignores the considerations of the context, intentionality, and the parties that produced and received the statements. According to Hutcheon, "In the postmodern writing of history . . . there is a deliberate contamination of the historical with didactic and situational discursive elements, thereby challenging the implied assumptions of historical statements: objectivity, neutrality, impersonality, and transparency of representation."[40] Outdoor dramas have traditionally adopted a mask of objectivity. The storylines of most of the dramas allow for only one view (most often a white view) of the events depicted, selected, and styled by the playwright. Program notes advertise the historical nature of the piece, and often laud the expertise of the (usually white, male) playwright on both the histories and cultures presented.[41] Furthermore, the representational format of the productions suggests an objective replication of events as they happened, rather than calling attention to the performative and constructed nature of the presentation. In many ways, exposing the multiple perspectives and the lack of objectivity used, as the performances treated in this article successfully do, can be a risk. Producers of outdoor historical dramas risk a loss of authority over the material and of control over the productions and representations therein if they expose the subjectivity, polyvocality, and uncertainties in the historical narratives they have touted for decades. To protect themselves from such risks, many productions have labored to buttress their authority beneath a veneer of accuracy and historical rigor and a seamless, corroborated narrative of agreement. In addition, many producers believe they risk the loss of ticket sales if the production does not meet audience expectations about how an Indian should look, sound, and act. As a result, many continue to deliver stereotyped, inaccurate, and offensive depictions of Native Americans.

Under the Cherokee Moon, on the other hand, does not try to hide behind a mask of objectivity. Instead, it challenges the audience's implied assumptions of history by gleaning the past from a chorus of voices who acknowledge the multiple "truths" that exist concerning their personas and places in history. Furthermore, representation is rendered transparent due to the transformation of identities employed in the play.

The production's approach to history also sets it apart from other outdoor historical dramas in that it does not try to replicate past events. Hutcheon argues that in postmodern considerations of history, "the meaning and shape are not *in the events*." She contends that instead such meanings are "*in the systems* which make those past 'events' into present historical 'facts.'"[42] Hutcheon considers this "an acknowledgement of the meaning-making function of human constructs."[43] Whereas other outdoor dramas such as *Tecumseh!* and *Blue Jacket* are concerned with depicting historical events such as battles, deaths, and treaty negotiations, and with constructing and performing history through those enactments, *Under the Cherokee Moon* is concerned with the accounts that construct histories and make meaning of events. For instance, the audience is not shown a scene from the Trail of Tears in *Under the Cherokee Moon*, as they are in *Unto These Hills . . . A Retelling*. Instead, the characters' narratives reveal information about the event. Because we watch different accounts, and because within each of those accounts the characters acknowledge that others have different stories, the audience sees how the narratives surrounding the event have been constructed and given meaning through the historical record. Through her research, Willis constructed the descriptions of the event she relays as Bushyhead. Therefore, what the audience receives is a network of accounts that demonstrate how individuals perceived the Trail of Tears, rather than a reenactment of the event itself. This maneuvering eschews complete objectivity while acknowledging that 100-percent accuracy is not possible. It is important to reiterate, however, that Willis does not view this as license to completely disregard the notion of accuracy. She stresses, "The history is the foundation of what we do. And we build from there. Because if it is not historically accurate, it reflects poorly on the [Cherokee] Heritage Center."[44] Willis recognizes that *in*accuracies have the potential to be harmful and thus continues to strive for accuracy as much as possible. She also recognizes, as her script demonstrates, that historical "truths" are subjective. Willis's approach to sharing Cherokee history and culture relies upon repertoire-based knowledge transmission and indigenous notions of history to effectively "edu-tain" her audiences.

For many outdoor historical dramas, the outdated, harmful, and negative representations of Native American cultures need to be remedied. In Tahlequah, Oklahoma, after years of struggle over various attempts to change its show, the Cherokee Heritage Center looked to do something else. *Under the Cherokee Moon* is still an outdoor historical drama; it is just not executed in the way it was previously. Nor was it what I expected or had grown accustomed to in my research. *Under the Cherokee Moon* provides alternative modes of representation to those presented in other outdoor historical dramas. By ditching the Aristotelian-based, plot-driven, representational format traditionally used in outdoor dramas, *Under the Cherokee Moon* is able to adopt a metatheatrical style and view of history that allow for a plethora of voices, the transmission of embodied knowledge to audience members, and individual depictions of Native Americans.

And yet, it was not enough. *Under the Cherokee Moon* is no longer in production, closed due to lack of funds and low ticket sales. Perhaps it was too little, too late for the Cherokee Heritage Center. Perhaps there were factors—the long distance between the Center and any major freeway, the lack of tour buses, high gas prices—beyond the producers' control. And as much as I hate to consider it, perhaps audience expectations were not satisfied with these new offerings. This last possibility does not jibe, however, with the reactions I witnessed in my fellow audience members or with the audience's praise-filled evaluations of the show. In these evaluations, audience members lauded the history lessons they learned, the interactive components, the stories shared, and their high level of engagement.[45] Regardless of the reasons, this show no longer plays to audiences. Might vestiges of it still reach producers of other outdoor historical dramas, enabling them to consider the new directions this production set forth? In my initial reaction to this play, I thought *Under the Cherokee Moon* had created viable options in terms of practical considerations (i.e., less spectacle, smaller cast, fewer technical elements, smaller budgets). In this case, the scaled-down version of the outdoor historical drama was not, unfortunately, financially sustainable. What this production can offer to other outdoor historical dramas, however, are lessons about representation. While many of the audience engagement conventions utilized in *Under the Cherokee Moon* may not work in some of the larger amphitheaters, other strategies discussed in this paper can be adopted and adapted in ways that re-present how Native American cultures and histories are portrayed in outdoor historical drama. One can hope that the example given by *Under the Cherokee Moon* will be remembered, as it offers innovative possibilities through which others may navigate some of the representational politics at play in staging Native American histories, figures, and cultures.

Notes

Epigraph 1. Michael Feingold, introduction to *Grove New American Theater*, ed. Michael Feingold (New York: Grove Press, 1993), xxi.

Epigraph 2. Peter Nabakov, *Forest of Time: American Indian Ways of History* (Cambridge: Cambridge University Press, 2002), vi.

1. Philip J. Deloria, *Indians in Unexpected Places* (Lawrence: University Press of Kansas, 2004), 3. Deloria goes on to list other expectations nonnatives often have of Indians, including that they have primitive natures, are ignorant of modern technology, live in the "hinterlands" rather than in metropolitan areas, have "solemn and stoic" attitudes, are unable to handle cash-based economies, and are violent (4–5).
2. The dramas I observed during my research include *Tecumseh!* (Ohio), *Trumpet in the Land* (Ohio), *The White Savage* (Ohio), *Unto These Hills . . . A Retelling* (North Carolina), and *Under the Cherokee Moon* (Oklahoma). I also conducted research on *Trail of Tears* (Oklahoma) and *Blue Jacket* (Ohio), which were no longer in production during my research travels.
3. I should note that the producers of *Unto These Hills . . . A Retelling* have made numerous changes to that production in order to address some of the issues of representation with regard to Cherokee history and culture. After the original *Unto These Hills* drama (written by Kermit Hunter) ran for over fifty years, a new drama, conceived of by Hanay Geiogamah, premiered in 2006. The new production was a drastic departure from the original Hunter script in that, according to many of the people I interviewed, it featured a nonlinear structure, emphasized native dance, and relied on indigenous modes of style and technique. While this new production addressed many of the concerns of the surrounding Cherokee community, it seems to have alienated many (mostly nonnative) audience members. Since 2006, the productions in Cherokee have returned to a format similar to those of the other outdoor dramas I saw, in that they rely on a Western narrative arc. For more information on the changes to *Unto These Hills*, please see Matthew D. Thompson, "Staging the 'Drama': The Continuing Importance of Cultural Tourism in the Gaming Era" (dissertation, University of North Carolina-Chapel Hill, 2009).
4. "Final Report—2013 Outdoor Theatre Attendance, Historical Dramas," *Institute of Outdoor Drama*, December 6, 2013 (publication date), August 8, 2014 (access date), http://9edyy1an29e2gxgy7puvyi8mg.wpengine.netdna-cdn.com/wp-content/uploads/2013-Master-Historical_attendance-Report.pdf.
5. *Unto These Hills* provides an exception, however, as it has been choreographed for several years by native choreographers, performed by native dancers, and features traditional Cherokee dances that have been deemed appropriate for public performance by tribe leaders.
6. This view regarding the release of white guilt through catharsis in these dramas was repeated in some of the sources I consulted regarding outdoor dramas, as well as in several of the interviews I conducted with participants in these dramas.
7. This call for change was echoed in several of the interviews I conducted. Marion Waggoner, who has worked with several outdoor dramas as a producer and director was one of the strongest advocates for change. Marion Waggoner, in discussion with the author, July 2011.

8. Jeffrey M. Jones, "Introduction: How to Read a Curious Play," in *New Downtown Now: An Anthology of New Theater from Downtown New York*, ed. Mac Wellman and Young Jean Lee (Minneapolis: University of Minnesota Press, 2006), xiii.
9. Susan Phillips (Business Manager, Institute of Outdoor Drama), in discussion with the author, June 2011.
10. Nat Eek, "letter to Scott Parker, 11 June 1996" (Institute of Outdoor Drama, Greenville, NC, 1996).
11. The Cherokee Historical Association in North Carolina has also implemented a similar family-centered show that focuses on Cherokee storytelling and includes audience participation.
12. Tonia Hogner Weavel (Education Director, Cherokee Heritage Center), in discussion with the author, September 2011.
13. Ibid.
14. Ibid.
15. Ibid.
16. Some may consider *Unto These Hills* an exception to this claim because it follows a hybrid pageant/narrative plot structure. During the first act, audiences are privy to a series of scenes that present dramatizations of Cherokee history and events since contact with Europeans. Once these scenes reach the nineteenth century, however, the structure shifts and begins to follow one akin to Freytag's pyramid. I would like to stress that the producers of *Unto These Hills* have worked (and continue to work) hard to address issues of representation in the production, and they have been successful in many ways.
17. The naturalistic elements of the dramas can lead to unexpected incidents during the show. For instance, when I saw *Tecumseh!*, one of the horses relieved itself onstage, during a particularly intense scene. The actors did not break, however, and in the subsequent battle scene, one of the actors did not hesitate to fall in the spot where the horse had been standing. The presence of the live horses, the dirt, the pond, and so on onstage infuses traits of naturalism into *Tecumseh!*.
18. "*Under the Cherokee Moon* Show Program" (Cherokee Heritage Center, Tahlequah, OK, 2011).
19. Ibid.
20. S. Elizabeth Bird, introduction to *Dressing in Feathers: The Construction of the Indian in American Popular Culture*, ed. S. Elizabeth Bird (Boulder, CO: Westview Press, 1996), 6.
21. *Under the Cherokee Moon*, by Laurette Willis, directed by Laurette Willis, Cherokee Heritage Center, September 24, 2011.
22. Laurette Willis (playwright, director, and actress), in discussion with the author, September 2011.
23. When I went to see *Unto These Hills*, the Cherokee Nation Children's Choir provided preshow entertainment. "Amazing Grace," sung in both Cherokee and English, was one of the numbers they performed. I encountered this song numerous times in Cherokee, North Carolina, and Tahlequah, Oklahoma.
24. Willis, discussion.
25. Ibid.
26. Elin Diamond, "Brechtian Theory/Feminist Theory: Toward a Gestic Feminist Criticism," in *A Sourcebook of Feminist Theatre and Performance: On and Beyond the Stage*, ed. Carol Martin (Routledge: London, 1996), 122. In some ways I hesitate to call upon

Bertolt Brecht when analyzing a show about native cultures and histories; it feels like I am continuing the tradition of colonization. Just as Diamond refers to her intertextual consideration of feminist theory and Brecht as "strange bedfellows," so too can we consider the juxtaposition of indigenous perspectives and Brecht strange. I feel, however, that Diamond's use of Brecht can be helpful in this examination as well.

27. Ibid., 125.
28. Linda Hutcheon, *A Poetics of Postmodernism: History, Theory, Fiction* (London: Routledge, 1988), 109.
29. Willis, discussion.
30. Ibid. For more information on repertoire-based knowledge see Diana Taylor's *The Archive and the Repertoire: Performing Cultural Memory in the Americas* (Durham, NC: Duke Univeristy Press, 2003).
31. Hutcheon, *A Poetics of Postmodernism*, 90.
32. Nabakov, *A Forest of Time*, 47–48.
33. Diamond, "Brechtian Theory/Feminist Theory," 126.
34. Willis, discussion.
35. Diamond, "Brechtian Theory/Feminist Theory," 126.
36. Willis, discussion.
37. In a longer discussion of this research project, I address the practice of redface to a greater extent. Three of the dramas I watched, *Tecumseh!*, *The White Savage*, and *Trumpet in the Land*, involved white actors donning dark makeup and wigs to differentiate their native characters from the nonnative characters onstage.
38. Willis, discussion.
39. Hutcheon, *A Poetics of Postmodernism*, 91.
40. Ibid., 92.
41. Alan Eckert, author of *Tecumseh!*, and Kermit Hunter, author of both *Unto These Hills* and *Trail of Tears*, were considered by many to be experts on their respective subjects, for Eckert, the Shawnee, and for Hunter, the Cherokee.
42. Hutcheon, *A Poetics of Postmodernism*, 89.
43. Ibid.
44. Willis, discussion.
45. Unfortunately, I was not able to acquire more data on audience reception, aside from my own observations and from reading the evaluations. As I note above, however, the evaluations I read indicated a favorable response from the audience members at the last of eight performances.

BOOK REVIEWS

Russian Culture and Theatrical Performance in America, 1891–1933. By Valleri J. Hohman. New York: Palgrave Macmillan, 2011. pp. 209. $85.00 cloth.

For most of the twentieth century, actors and dancers in the United States have considered Russian training in the performing arts the gold standard. At the Actors Studio in New York City, home of the Method, Lee Strasberg liberally quoted from Stanislavski's teaching and adapted his Russian techniques to American culture. On the top floor of Carnegie Hall, Aleksandra Danilova, formerly of the Ballets Russes, taught ballet while young dancers from other teachers' classes would gather at the doors and greedily watch. Even popular culture treated Russian training and performance as the best available. In the film *Outrageous Fortune* (dir. Arthur Hiller, 1987) two would-be actresses compete for places in an acting workshop, run by a demanding Eastern bloc teacher whose name sounds suspiciously like "Stanislavski." Similarly exacting is Lucille Ball's Russian dance teacher in *Dance Girl Dance* (dir. Dorothy Arzner and Robert Wise, 1940), played by actress Maria Ouspenskaya, who had begun her career in Stanislavski's Moscow Art Theatre. In *Russian Culture and Theatrical Performance in America*, Valleri J. Hohman explores the genesis of this widespread perception by "chart[ing] the development of America's interest in the performing arts from the Russian Empire" (2).

Hohman has uncovered archival information about touring artists from Russia, Russians who emigrated to the United States and brought their art with them, and the producers and writers who promoted their work. She chooses to focus on the years between 1891 and 1933 because Russian modernism was especially vibrant and influential in that period. Her book begins with the large influx of Jews who fled from pogroms in Russia, settled in New York's lower east side, and founded a flourishing Yiddish theatrical culture there. She ends just as Stalin was about to impose Socialist Realism on all Soviet artists, thus effectively killing off artistic experimentation for the next few decades.

Hohman's book includes a broad range of historical figures. She focuses on artists who were highly influential but are less often examined by scholars than the larger-than-life figures like Stanislavski. Among those she treats in depth are the playwright Jacob Gordin, who collaborated with the famed Yiddish actor and theatre manager Jacob Adler; the actress Alla Nazimova, who eventually settled in Hollywood; Nikita Balieff and his cabaret the Chauve-Souris; a number of ballet dancers including Michel Fokine, Mikhail Mordkine, and Adolf Bolm; Nahum Zemach of the Habima Theatre, which performed in Hebrew; and the proletarian artists of Artef, the first workers' theatre to appear on Broadway.

Even more significant are her portraits of those who hailed Russia's performing arts in the United States as hallmarks of great value. Hohman profiles in depth the conservative banker Otto Kahn and the impresario Morris Gest, himself Russian and a sometimes con artist. These two men financed tour after tour, bringing major ballet dancers and the Moscow Art Theatre to the United States for the first time. In these sections of the book, Hohman explores "the commodification of Russian performance" (58), a topic of great importance but one usually overlooked by scholars who treat artistry alone. Journalists and writers like Oliver Sayler, Huntley Carter, and Hallie Flannagan also prominently figure into Hohman's story. Their descriptions of Russian performances they had seen and admired in Europe prepared the American spectators to receive Russian experimentation on home ground more enthusiastically than they might have otherwise.

The book organizes this vast amount of material chronologically in three multisectioned parts. Because some sections focus on playwriting and theatre design, some on business and publicity, and others on specific performances, reading Hohman's book is an interesting and varied experience. At the same time, the parts do not always build neatly upon one another. Part 1 works as a short book on Yiddish theatre, part 2 as a separate exploration of the financial machinations behind the tours of Russian performing artists to the United States, and part 3 as an aesthetic analysis of early Soviet theatrical experimentation on American stages.

What holds the book together, however, is Hohman's second major goal; in addition to charting Russian performance in America, she provides "an analysis of the American reception and adaptation of these performances" (5). In this layer of the book, she raises a number of significant leitmotivs to which she returns often. Among these are the ways that Russian artists succeeded or failed through the management of publicity, the influence of Russian modernism on American art, and what it means to be Russian in the United States.

In my view, this last topic is Hohman's most significant and sustained contribution. As she points out, "The concept of 'Russian' came to connote a variety of ethnicities and ideas in America" (13). Jews, Czechs, Hungarians, Poles, Gypsies, Serbians, Croatians, Romanians, and so on were all deemed Russian. So too were any number of liberal ideologies. In short, "Russian culture and theatrical performance in America turns out to be a story of a multiethnic, adapted, often belated, and sometimes questionably *Russian* culture in America" (143).

Hohman's book belongs to the Palgrave Studies in Theatre and Performance History series, which provides scholarship that is "accessible and free of jargon" (i). The author fulfills both of these promises. She has written an intriguing book full of interesting new information, lively descriptions of performances, and thoughtful insights into a major cultural influence on American theatre during the twentieth century. The book is also a handsomely produced volume with black and white illustrations and a useful appendix that lists many performances that featured the work of artists from the Russian Empire.

In short, Hohman has contributed a fine book to the fields of theatre arts, Russian history, and cultural studies.

—**SHARON MARIE CARNICKE**
University of Southern California, School of Dramatic Arts

Staging the People: Community and Identity in the Federal Theatre Project. By Elizabeth A. Osborne. New York: Palgrave Macmillan, 2011. pp. xi + 240. $85.00 cloth.

In *Staging the People: Community and Identity in the Federal Theatre Project*, Elizabeth A. Osborne expands familiar perceptions and alters common assumptions regarding the Federal Theatre Project (FTP). As to the former, Osborne shifts the focus away from the FTP's efforts in New York City—the region that has, along with the Living Newspapers, received the most scholarly attention by far—and instead considers a wide range of projects in Chicago, Boston, the American South, and Portland, Oregon, as well as two tours. In drawing attention to the FTP's work in these regions and tours, Osborne shows its expansive reach, and, in so doing, demonstrates the ways in which it sought to fulfill national director Hallie Flanagan's hope for a nationwide federation of theatres.

More importantly, Osborne convincingly argues that the FTP was an extraordinarily complex and vexed endeavor, one that sought to balance the agenda and aspirations of its national office—which was itself seeking to balance its efforts with the goals of the immense bureaucracy of the WPA and its subgroup, Federal Project Number One, which had direct oversight of the FTP—with the actions, hopes, and living and working conditions of regional and local artists, administrators, and audiences.

Without question, Osborne's effort to expand the vision of where the FTP did its work, how that work in regions outside of New York was often in tension with various national and regional offices, and what that work constituted leads to a more complete picture of the project as a whole. Additionally, however, in the course of painting this more complete picture, Osborne also asks us to reconsider the way in which the FTP is frequently characterized—that is, as a "successful failure." Instead, Osborne argues that it was "a viable enterprise that in many ways attained its primary objectives: to achieve a theatre that could represent the nation while putting Americans back to work in their fields" (2). Building on this hypothesis, Osborne's case studies reveal that when these regional efforts and tours are evaluated in light of the FTP's professed goals, the "so-called failures might more correctly be designated as successes" (13). In this regard, then, *Staging the People* may rightly be called a "game changer." Indeed, by expanding the vision of what the FTP involved and complicating the frequently one-dimensional suppositions about it, *Staging the People* alters in profound ways the received history of the project.

In terms of structure, following a very useful introduction—wherein she outlines her endeavor to provide a "detailed cultural study of the FTP" (9)—Osborne divides the book into five chapters. Chapter 1, which focuses on two productions in Chicago, stands as a good example of how the whole of the study works. The first half of the chapter centers on *Oh Say Can You Sing*, staged in 1936, while the second spotlights *Spirochete*, staged in 1938. Regarding the former, Osborne carefully explicates the composition history, deftly demonstrating how various political pressures unique to Chicago led to radical revisions of the text. She shows that, in effect, the various changes altered the very ethos of *Oh Say Can You Sing*, making it not a biting piece of political satire but an insipid comedy.

As counterpoint, in the second half of the chapter Osborne turns to *Spirochete*, which took as its subject the syphilis epidemic, a national crisis that had a particularly devastating effect in Chicago. Though not an enormous box-office success, *Spirochete* nonetheless did inspire accolades from the local and national press, as well as local and national health officials, and was held up as an example of the type of socially vital theatre a federally funded producing organization could create. Throughout the chapter, Osborne situates her readings of these texts and productions within the social and political context of Chicago, circa the mid-to-late 1930s. Additionally, she convincingly argues that these productions were subject to competing agendas between artistic and administrative personnel, at both the local and national levels, as well as varying concepts of what constituted success.

This structure of two contextually rich case studies per chapter is repeated in the balance of the book, with each chapter focusing on a particular region or, in the case of chapter 5, touring productions. Chapter 2 highlights two Boston productions: *Created Equal*, produced in 1938, and *Lucy Stone*, in 1939, both of which sought to stage history pertinent to New England but did so in ways that, as Osborne argues, "surrendered the more controversial elements of that history" (84). Chapter 3 charts endeavors in the American South: *Altars of Steel*, produced in 1937 in Atlanta (after having been moved from its location of origin, Birmingham, Alabama), and the so-called Georgia experiment of 1937, wherein the FTP sent five theatre artists into communities in rural Georgia to create local theatre. These productions/programs were, Osborne notes, a "powerful response to the political and cultural issues of the South," and yet, because of local and national events, they stand as "icons of possibility rather than the realization of the FTP" (119).

Chapter 4 looks at two of the offerings produced by the FTP in Portland, Oregon: *Yellow Harvest*, produced in 1936, and *Timberline Tintypes*, in 1938. Osborne persuasively contends that both of these productions were created by a group of artists who, more often than not, successfully navigated the bureaucracies above them; as such, the Portland FTP stands as an example of "a decentralized, yet cooperative unit" that "was able to conduct its business with little interference from the FTP national administration" (146–47). Finally, chapter 5 explicates the fascinating history of two FTP touring groups: the *CCC Murder Mystery*, performed at CCC camps in 1936 and 1937, and the variety show that toured the cities, towns, and camps affected by the Great Flood of 1937. While the whole of the study is strong, I found this final chapter particularly moving and was thoroughly convinced by Osborne's assertion that these long-ignored efforts—tent troupes and traveling theatres—stand as wonderful success stories of the FTP and demonstrate powerfully how the project was, indeed, able to meet the needs of audiences, by way of government support, and thereby achieve the goal Flanagan set.

Deeply researched, cogently argued, expertly documented, and beautifully written, *Staging the People* provokes scholars and students to think anew about the Federal Theatre Project. As such, it seems certain that it will become a foundational text in the study of the one real attempt to create a national theatre in the United States.

—**JOHNATHAN CHAMBERS**
Bowling Green State University

Comedy: A Critical Introduction. By Eli Rozik. Brighton: Sussex Academic Press, 2011. pp. x + 242. $37.95 cloth.

The contemporary resurgence in theorizing about comedy as a genre began with Erich Segal's *The Death of Comedy* (2001), which argued that the classical tradition of comedy died with the advent of the absurdist movement. Two books followed that developed the path Segal established of examining longitudinally the field of comedy: Andrew Stott's *Comedy* (2005), part of Routledge's New Critical Idiom series, and Eric Weitz's *The Cambridge Introduction to Comedy* (2009). While both books have their disadvantages, they are instrumental in explaining early theoretical work, delineating the various forms and subgenres of comedy, and offering potential new areas to study. Eli Rozik's new book, *Comedy: A Critical Introduction*, unfortunately neither helps the reader comprehend comedy nor offers clear insights into the genre.

Concerned that comedy is typically defined in opposition to tragedy, Rozik's main purpose is to find a new way to define comedy. Thus, he first establishes how the two forms are similar: they both involve *hamartia* (he misunderstands the term to mean "flaw" as opposed to "mis-step"), they both share "structures of action," and they both elicit laughter from spectators. Rozik posits that both tragedy and comedy offer "holistic catharsis" in purging the spectator of unsettling emotions. But after admitting that purging "pleasure and laughter" might be unwarranted (71), Rozik explains that comedy rouses and purges "anxiety" during the final *peripeteia* (71). He subsequently characterizes the defining elements of comedy as the "comic mood" and the creation of a fictional world, as well as an "absolute preference for an archetypal structure of action" (81). The "sub-species" of comedy, according to Rozik, are farce, romance, and sketch comedy, while the fields that are not comedy but are "tangential" to it consist of satire, grotesque, and stand-up. That satire and grotesque are distinct from the category of comedy is an interesting perspective—as these kinds of comedy evolved from Aristophanic, or Old Comedy, whereas farce, romantic and festive comedy, and sentimental and social comedy developed from the New Comedy of Menander—but Rozik does not pursue this trajectory further. His discussion of satiric laughter provides an area of potential exploration, for he persuasively argues that laughter cannot work toward social correction if we laugh at the on-stage character without identifying those characters with ourselves.

Like a taxonomist, Rozik dissects the multiple layers of comedy. He argues that the deep structure of any fictional world can be divided into seven layers, but he does not cite any foundational theory for this classification (such as the work of narrative structuralists like Gérard Genette) and quotes only from his own, earlier works. The seven layers—the personified, mythical, praxical, naïve, ironic, aesthetic, and modal—provide the means by which to analyze any fictional comedy; furthermore, the same seven layers can be applied to the analysis of comedic characters. However, the value of such a framework is implicitly limited when the only examples he offers to demonstrate such application are from Molière's plays, *The School for Wives*, in particular. Toward the end of the book, he criticizes other scholars for theorizing about comedy without offering any practical application to dramatic texts, but in chapter after chapter, Rozik summarizes the plots of a few comedies without applying his corresponding analysis.

The book jacket touts this study as useful for undergraduate education, but the obtuse prose would prohibit such use. Oftentimes the circular nature of Rozik's sentences make them redundant, "A fictional world should thus be seen as a mechanism that manipulates the audience into a preconceived perspective on a fictional world" (48–49), or tautological, "a character is a fictional construct and the result of a process of personification that reflects the spontaneous creativity of the psyche; i.e., the basic and essential trait of a character is its humanity. This trait justifies the interpretation of its behavior as human" (99). The book's usefulness is further limited by its lack of diverse examples, as well as by its production photographs, which represent plays from only one theater (the Khan Theater of Jerusalem). Rozik weakens his reading of the comedies by failing to provide sufficient substantiating knowledge; he does not provide scholarship on any of the playwrights he analyzes, such as Plautus, Shakespeare, Goldoni, or Wilde, and his contextualization of Molière derives from one article in a collection of essays on comedy, Robert Corrigan's now out-of-print anthology, *Comedy: Meaning and Form* (1965).

Rozik considers all the prominent theorists within the field of comedy studies, such as Aristotle, Henri Bergson, Mikhail Bahktin, Eric Bentley, Martin Esslin, Northrop Frye, and Susanne Langer, summarizing their arguments in order to dismantle them. Like some Johnny-come-lately battling with the precursor, he provides an aspect of comedy, such as Freud's "safety-valve" theory or Shaw's "life force," only to mitigate the idea to make intellectual room for himself. He corrects Segal for considering Euripides's *Ion* a forerunner of a new type of comedy; he considers Bergson's "mechanical elasticity" too limited an explanation for laughter (33), proposing that the reason for laughter is witnessing "foolish failure" (38–39); and he questions Patrice Pavis's definition of comedy as involving humble or "low characters," preferring instead to identify the genre's "lowly mode" (116). He sets up straw arguments so that he may appear to offer new ideas: by adjusting Bentley's definition of farce, he can argue that farce is "indeed crude and violent, but not aggressive" (117), he can explain why Esslin "errs" by not considering the grotesque as an element of the absurd (141), and he can negate Freud's explanation of how laughter originates (Rozik insists that "the lifting of an inhibition produces additional tension, and that this accumulated tension is released by means of a *peripeteia*" [180]). Even Aristotle comes under question for neglecting "the grotesque" as a form of comedy (139).

One of Rozik's final chapters takes umbrage with the philosophical belief in the genre's comic vision; he criticizes Langer for considering tragedy a genre that focuses on death rather than perceiving that she is talking metaphorically about tragedy's sense of fatality and finality versus comedy's open-ended potential. While the book has some helpful areas, such as a rare discussion of plays that mock religious practices, it seems as if Rozik deliberately works to discard others' contributions to the field, which suggests a negation of the comic ethos of collaboration, creativity, and community.

—**MIRIAM CHIRICO**
Eastern Connecticut State University

The Politics of the Pantomime: Regional Identity in the Theatre, 1860–1900. By Jill A. Sullivan. Hatfield, England: University of Hertfordshire Press, 2011. pp. 288. $29.95 paper.

Jill A. Sullivan's *The Politics of the Pantomime* details the diverse methods by which Victorian provincial pantomimes expressed regional economic, political, and cultural circumstances or interests to the delight (and on occasion, dismay) of local audiences. In focusing on late-nineteenth-century annual pantomimes in Nottingham, Birmingham, and Manchester, Sullivan refreshingly redresses two common critical devaluations of the popular entertainment: that the generic "advances" of pantomime during the Victorian period denigrated the ideal form of the eighteenth and early nineteenth centuries, and that a history of pantomime necessitates as its centerpiece a study of the famed pantomimes of London's patent theatres, a prevalent scholarly strategy that "to an extent, [assumes] homogeneity of those productions that occurred beyond Euston station" (2). As Sullivan notes, provincial pantomimes and their capital counterparts differed in far more than production budgets and technological capabilities. Unlike the specific, localized references in provincial pantomimes, London pantomimes tended toward generalized, nationalistic allusions that represented London as the undisputed epicenter of the Empire. Moreover, with their theatres leagues away from the Lord Chamberlain's office, provincial pantomime authors and managers could engage in more overt and playful political satire without fear of significant censure, an enterprise that was further safeguarded by willingly complicit audiences. Citing pantomime playtexts, as well as numerous promotional materials and contemporary press reviews, Sullivan argues that theatre managers, authors, dramatic critics, performers, and audiences alike participated in the forging of regional identity through pantomime.

Chapter 1, "The Gorgeous Christmas Pantomime," delineates the traditional pantomime format of the Victorian period, focusing on the transformation scene and the harlequinade as the primary suppliers of spectacle. As in London, provincial managers labored to outdo competing theatres' pantomimes, as well as to surpass their own offerings from previous years; this required striking a delicate balance between satisfying audiences' expectations for "traditional" pantomime fare and combating conventionality with innovative stagings, scenery, songs, and the inclusion of local references. Chapter 2 considers the various approaches individual provincial theatres took to cope with growing demands for spectacle, efforts that in turn "[established] specific local identities for their theatre, based on traditions of status and expenditure" (51). "Because spectacular theatre as a whole was predicated on scale," Sullivan writes, the relative ostentation of pantomime spectacle "highlighted the financial and physical resources" of the producing theatre and, by extension (as was the case with Theatre Royal, in Birmingham), the city it called home (58–59). Other provincial theatres promoted their regional identity through the employment of local artists and authors, an initiative that also proved financially advantageous. Theatres that lacked the resources to buy spectacle in the form of extravagant design elements offered supplementary spectacle in the form of lively dances and grand processions performed by adult and juvenile supernumeraries. Ultimately, Sullivan writes, as managers attempted to appeal to audiences by blending tradition with novelty "according to available income and the practicalities of staging, new traditions, features and reputations were formed" (97).

These first two chapters, which together form the book's first section (unified by the idea of "spectacle"), have much to recommend them. Sullivan demonstrates a masterful culling and employment of research in service of her history, and she proceeds through her arguments with clarity and fluidity. Sullivan is careful to acknowledge the dangers of relying too heavily on newspaper reviews before making regular (and effective) use of Victorian theatre critics' flowery, adjective-laden accounts of unimaginable pantomime pageantry: cascading waterfalls, processions of children and live animals, mechanical wonders, and even the infusion of enchanting perfumes into the auditorium. Although the writing in part 1 occasionally lacks animation, as if Sullivan were wary of competing with the Victorian critics' grandiloquent turns of phrase, this is not the case with part 2, in which Sullivan's enlivened and clever prose complements the whimsical character of pantomime entertainments and better communicates her enthusiasm for her subject.

Part 2, titled "The Social Referencing of Pantomime," takes as its focus the "variety of references in local pantomimes and the way in which a local identity could be projected through the use, not just of spoken references, but of visual representations, themed scenes, tableaux, dance and dialect" (15). In the first of two chapters, Sullivan isolates within several decades of provincial pantomimes topical references with unmistakable ties to regional socioeconomic identities. In localizing their pantomimes, managers and authors devised allusions to a wide range of relevant regional concerns, from "minor irritants of everyday [urban] life" to the perceived effects of the 1870 Education Act, from local charitable giving to unemployment (122). In a particularly effective comparison, Sullivan notes that different trade practices and issues in Manchester and Nottingham inspired contrastive pantomime references. The prevalence of cotton and spinning puns in the Theatre Royal Manchester's pantomimes in the 1860s, when America's Civil War "halted the supply of raw cotton to Britain, paralysing the Lancashire mills," was absent from those produced in Nottingham, which often boasted their own unique combination of rural and urban topics to please the town's blended audience (139). The chapter concludes with an appendix of topical songs with helpful commentary. Sullivan's final chapter, "The Politics of the Pantomime," is her most complex and features several compelling case studies. In it, the author examines the role political satire played in forging regional identity; enumerates the varied ways satire was presented to audiences (spoken word, visual references including masked caricature, and performer "gags"); and offers explanations for why provincial theatres evaded official censorship. As Sullivan argues, the repeated, successful inclusion of political satire in provincial pantomimes had much to do with complicit audiences and vocal advocates within the press, and individual theatres' political party allegiances were often acknowledged and accepted by local audiences. Meticulously researched and cogently argued, *The Politics of the Pantomime* will be a welcome addition to the book collections of Victorianists, theatre historians, and pantomime enthusiasts alike.

—MEREDITH CONTI
James Madison University

Performing Gender Violence: Plays by Contemporary American Women Dramatists. By Barbara Ozieblo and Noelia Hernando-Real, eds. New York: Palgrave Macmillan, 2012. pp. 204. $80.00 cloth.

The Research Group on American women writers, coordinated by Barbara Ozieblo at the University of Málaga, continues to foster impressive scholarship on American drama and theatre. The group has been the driving force behind four international conferences in Andalusia, as well as resulting publications of expanded conference essays. Scholars in the group also have published widely on American women dramatists, most notably on Susan Glaspell and Sophie Treadwell. *Performing Gender Violence: Plays by Contemporary American Women Dramatists*—a collection of nine essays and an introduction—proves yet another valuable contribution by this research team to the latest theoretical discourse on women and American theatre.

The book's subject, sadly, remains insistently current. As the editors, Ozieblo and Noelia Hernando-Real, note in their introduction, "Violence against women, in the home or outside the home, in peace as in war, a result of fanaticism or of structural inequality in society—in every part of the world—continues to confound our civilization" (1). By embracing the inclusive concept of "gender violence," the authors of these essays emphasize the interconnectedness of various forms of aggression toward women, uniting in a continuum such diverse acts as "rape, psychological violence, battering, female mutilation and others" (20). The volume focuses on plays written during the last forty years and includes close analyses of plays by both well- and lesser-known dramatists: Julia Cho, Pearl Cleage, Maria Irene Fornes, Rebecca Gilman, Carson Kreitzer, Heather McDonald, Emily Mann, Susan Miller, Marsha Norman, Lynn Nottage,

Linda Park-Fuller, Suzan-Lori Parks, Heather Raffe, Cheryl L. West, Paula Vogel, and Stefanie Zadravec. The editors' goals in this volume are not only to situate recent plays by these women within the evolving theory and practice of feminist theatre, especially since the 1960s, but also to interrogate the potential effect of these plays specifically on audiences and more generally on American society at large.

Most of the essays posit a belief in the efficacy of theatre to initiate reform of a patriarchal society that subdues women into passive roles and whose legal system fails to offer sufficient protection to women as targets of gender violence. As stated in the introduction, "The theater, particularly women's theater, has been a useful tool in awakening awareness of violence" (2). The various essays draw upon multidisciplinary research to demonstrate how groundbreaking women dramatists have helped bring taboo or silenced subcategories of gender violence, such as breast cancer treatment and family abuse, into a wider public arena. This optimistic celebration of the act of performance as a tool to ignite social reform proves one of the book's greatest strengths.

Another strength is the overall unity of the structure and tone of the essays. Most chapters follow a similar pattern, which includes an overview of the subcategory, clear definitions of key concepts, theoretical antecedents, social statistics and behaviors, and detailed interpretations of select plays. After the introduction, which lays out the scope of the book, each chapter builds upon the next, with the authors cross-referencing concepts and conclusions presented elsewhere in the volume. The two opening essays provide an overview of forms and responses to violence against women in critical theory and society, as well as the emergence and evolution of violence as a key theme in women's drama. The essays then progress to discussions of violence in the family (authored by Hernando-Real), the role of female bonding (María Dolores Narbona-Carrión), psychological abuse (Miriam López-Rodríguez), biomedical violence (Marta Fernández-Morales), survival strategies in African American plays (Inmaculada Pineda-Hernández), and war violence (Ilka Saal). Although the book does not contain a concluding chapter per se, Ozieblo's essay on the effect of stage violence on the audience's "pleasure" provides a suitable coda to the book's argument. Although seven authors contribute, the book often reads as though written by one voice, a remarkable achievement in scholarship.

Another contributing factor to the book's unity is the repeated conclusion that these recent dramas portray "a shift from victimhood to agency by the different characters-victims-perpetrators" (113–14). Such agency by the central female characters includes a wide range of acts of resistance, such as rage, suicide, killing one's offspring, and revenge against a male aggressor. As Pineda-Hernández states, "There is a clear tendency to use violence, to transform the victim role into a victim-perpetrator role with different results for each character." Such acts of agency, Pineda-Hernández notes, are sometimes designed "to create an uncomfortable atmosphere so that their audiences feel the need to react somehow" (115). While not all of these acts of agency are viewed as positive resolutions to women's abuse, they are often seen as resulting from women who find themselves in positions of isolation and powerlessness. Thus, some essays, such as the one by Narbona-Carrión, stress the importance of relationships and female solidarity as a means "to overcome women's victimization" (78).

One more recurring note that runs throughout this text pertains to the most effective and appropriate style with which stage violence should be portrayed. Occasionally, the authors express uneasiness that stage representations of violent acts, especially when presented in the style of realism, may produce unintended consequences in the audience. The book's editors pose the question: "Should it be understood that there is a vicarious pleasure in witnessing violence?" (34). Consequently, the authors often favor theatrical styles that involve either some form of Brechtian distancing or poeticized staging. For example, Saal praises the "self-conscious performance" found in Raffo's *9 Parts of Desire* that merges "the documentary genre with theatrical ritual" (150). Similarly, Ozieblo concludes that the "horrific experiences" found in *Self Defense Or Death of Some Salesmen* are "made tolerable by the epic structure of Kreitzer's fast-paced play" (165).

This volume of essays by European scholars significantly advances the critical dialogue on gender violence in American drama by women. One only hopes this research group at the University of Málaga continues its ambitious scholarly agenda.

—**JERRY DICKEY**
University of Florida

Performing Remains: Art and War in Times of Theatrical Reenactment. By Rebecca Schneider. London: Routledge, 2011. pp. 260. $34.95 paper.

As an epigraph to the first chapter of her dazzling—and sometimes dizzying—book, Rebecca Schneider takes the motto of the Association of Lincoln Presenters: "Now he belongs to the stages" (32). It's the kind of pun that Schneider delights in, not only because it collapses into a clever quip on one of the book's main claims—that the goal of history, like the goal of performance, should not be to recover some pure past but rather to understand an event through reenacting it as part of a continuous present—but also because it plays on the coincidental and yet uncannily appropriate conjunctions between ideas that seem worlds apart in space and time.

This is a book that makes much of seemingly impossible juxtapositions: medieval tableaux vivants with Abu Ghraib, John Wilkes Booth with Gertrude Stein, Civil War reenactment with feminist performance art. As disparate as these subjects seem, Schneider's wide-ranging analyses and perceptive close-readings expose their striking similarities. Yet the real point of Schneider's book is to dismantle the binaries on which performance studies has come to depend: live versus archive, authentic versus mimetic, present versus past. *Performing Remains* promises not only to rewrite where performance studies is going but also to rethink what it's been.

But this book is not for the faint of heart, and readers hoping to peruse a chapter or two will balk at its theoretical density and deliberately circular prose. Illustrating her nonlinear approach to history, Schneider often drops names only to loop back, pages later, making her point less through articulation than through accretion. Characteristic is a foreword "which is not one" (1), in that it does less to explain than to touch upon the pairings that the book will develop and dissolve. Focusing on Marina Abramović's 2010 installation *The Artist Is Present*, queer artist-activist Allison Smith's 2005 performance *The Muster*, and interviews with Civil War reenactors, Schneider argues that "elite" artists and Civil War hobbyists share the assumption that history gains more in the reenacting—that the errors and revisions that reenactment entails have as much to teach us about the past as an exacting examination of its archive.

Chapter 1 develops this assertion by pairing Civil War reenactments with the queer performance art of Miranda July. These performances share the assumption that all present events or performances are citations of the past. Thus the idea of the theater as mimesis—the imitation of an action—is both false (because it depends on an impossible distinction between imitation and action, citation and original) and antitheatrical (because it regards the imitation as an always-imperfect attempt to recover the original). If there is no such thing as an original act—no such thing as an unsullied present—perhaps the best way to practice history is to reenact it.

Reenactment therefore becomes a critical act and its errors productive differences that prevent history from repeating itself uncritically, an assertion Schneider takes up in chapter 2. She focuses on Suzan-Lori Parks's *The America Play*, in which an African American character impersonates Lincoln in a theme park, and Linda Mussman's *Cross Way Cross*, in which a blond woman impersonates Lincoln on a solo road trip. Parks's commentary on race and Mussman's on gender, Schneider observes, depend on their characters' deviation from the exact replication of a past event or person. In this way, it is the error of historical reenactment that "does things" (69). Conversely, it is the reenactment that makes us aware of the error: "If the 'familiar' was not in some way induced, it could not be essentially disturbed" (78).

Chapter 3 is the heart of *Performing Remains*, and the moment (which we've all been waiting for) when Schneider wrestles most articulately with the ghosts of performance theorists past. In addition to continuing the dismantling of "liveness" that she began in chapter 1, she critiques Diana Taylor's influential *The Archive and the Repertoire* as reinforcing the "logic of the archive" by characterizing performance as always already lost. If we define performance as disappearing as soon as its present becomes past, Schneider asks, are we not already assuming a linear model of time? What if we characterize performance as that which remains?

If chapter 3 dissolves the binary of live performance and the archive, chapter 4 dissolves that of work and play through a reading of Jerzy Grotowski's 1965 staging of Stanislaw Wyspiański's 1904 *Akropolis* and the Wooster Group's 2004 restaging of Grotowski's staging. Schneider challenges us to regard reenactment as labor in itself, the way that Grotowski's *Akropolis* emphasizes acting as physical activity—or that Civil War reenactors promote their hobby as historical research.

From *Akropolis*'s depiction of statues brought to life, Schneider moves to a discussion of still images that achieve liveness. Chapter 5 examines medieval paintings reenacted in tableaux vivants, the self-performances of Cindy Sherman frozen into "film stills," and the photographs of Abu Ghraib. Arguing that the Abu Ghraib photographs reperform and make live their dehumanizing purpose each time someone views them, Schneider arrives at a key question of the chapter and the book: if we honor the distinction between a still image and the live arts, are we not just reiterating the old, creaky Enlightenment concept of time as linear and the past as irrecoverable?

Schneider's discussion of Abu Ghraib reintroduces the political stakes of her argument, which her foreword announces she will temporarily "suspend" (2). In the afterword, Schneider returns to Allison Smith's queer reenactments of Civil War "camp" (pun intended), as well as Mark Tribe's Port Huron Project, in order to illustrate the ways that reenactment might be used not only to preserve or to repeat history but also to protest and to change it. It's an ambitious task for a fifteen-page afterword, and, ironically, it's in her attempt to return to the concrete implications of her argument that the book's theoretical density becomes overwhelming.

Schneider thus falls a bit short of articulating the political implications of her argument, though we might infer them from her assertion that "the minor, forgotten, overlooked, disavowed, unsung, second, double, and 'lesser' gain a kind of agency in the re-do" (180). At times the book overreaches its own evidence and methodology, as if Schneider is trying to make a metaphysical argument about how time works rather than a theoretical argument about how performance represents it. Yet readers who allow the book's thrillingly nontraditional approach or theoretical complexity to deter them are missing out. Anyone hoping to use performance theory in the future will have to contend with this book, and those who used it in the past would be well advised to reexamine that earlier work in light of Schneider's new ideas. *Performing Remains* rewrites what performance studies was and is and can be—what history is and was and can be—in brilliant and paradigm-shifting ways.

—JULIA FAWCETT
Ryerson University

Violence in American Drama: Essays on Its Staging, Meanings and Effects. Edited by Alfonso Ceballos Muñoz, Ramón Espejo Romero, and Bernardo Muñoz Martinez. Jefferson, NC: McFarland, 2011. pp. vi + 288. $55.00 cloth.

How American drama represents and addresses the role of violence in U.S. society is the topic of this timely volume, drawn primarily from papers given at the third International Conference on American Theatre and Drama. This lively collection, which includes essays by established names, as well as by names new to English-speaking readers, has strengths in several areas: gendered behaviors, chiefly violence against and by women, structural and cultural violence, and wartime aggressions and attitudes.

Single-author studies form an important part of the collection. The editors observe that Dorothy Chansky's essay, "The Violence at the Top of the Stairs: Domestic Dystopia in Inge's Heartland," may be the first to examine domestic violence in the work of Inge by distinguishing between "situational couple violence" and the more devastating "intimate terrorism" (114). Dana Rufolo, in "Psychodrama Strategies That Protect Tennessee Williams' Late-Play Characters from a Violent World," argues that Williams moved from recreating memory to creating characters who use "coping strategies" (141) to develop a protective circle of relationships.

Perhaps the most cohesive discussion emerges from essays on women committing violence in response to a threatening environment. In "The Thrust for Freedom from Systems of Oppression: A Century of Suicide, Prolicide and Viricide in Plays by American Women," Cheryl Black examines acts by which "women meet violence with violence" (45) in plays from 1916 to the present. Noelia Hernando-Real goes so far as to suggest, in "Sane Enough to Kill: On Women, Madness and the Theatricality of Violence in Susan Glaspell's *The Verge*," that Glaspell's female protagonist breaks free of realist parameters for acceptable women's behavior and, in that new context, *must* take life. In "New Critical Approaches to *Machinal:* Sophie Treadwell's Response to Structural Violence," Miriam López Rodríguez sets aside the usual evaluation of *Machinal* as an innovative expressionist play in order to cast the protagonist as a young woman much like Treadwell herself, who felt victimized by "the American mechanized and sexist society of the 1920s" (81). Jerry Dickey considers in "Working Women and Violence in Jazz Era American Drama" how the public debate over women entering the workplace, particularly the business office, revealed a fracturing of women's sense of self. Besides the familiar *Machinal*, Dickey discusses Maureen Watkins's *Chicago*, Francis Faragoh's *Pinwheel*, and Elmer Rice's *The Subway*, lesser-known plays that muted the distinction between the virtuous angel of the house and the worldly, sensual temptress. Moving from modernist to contemporary drama, María Dolores Narbona Carrión, in "'Arms in Women's Hands': The Subversion of the Victim Role of Women in Heather McDonald's *Dream of a Common Language*," recognizes "brave initiatives" (187) that female characters take.

Structural violence (embedded in unequal power relations) and cultural (ideological) violence, whether gendered, racial, or ethnic, receive careful attention. While not excusing male perpetrators, Michael Solomonson focuses on the cultural objectification of women in "Rebecca Gilman's Exploration of Gender Conditioning as a Factor in Violence Against Women." Diana Rosenhagen grapples with the question of whether violence *against* structural and cultural racial oppression can be justified. In "'Actual Explosions and Actual Brutality': Baraka, Violence and the Black Arts Stage," she finds Baraka's plays of the mid-1960s to be "acts of violence in themselves" (144). Like Rosenhagen, Irma Mayorga, in "Invisibility's Contusions: Violence in Cherríe Moraga's *Heroes and Saints* and *The Hungry Woman* and Luis Valdez's *Zoot Suit*," considers how stage violence can illuminate oppressive circumstances and outline forms of agency for Latinos/as, enabling a progressive "politics of visibility" (158). N. J. Stanley examines the "urge to [commit] violence" as "an inability to function ethically"

(222) in "Neil LaBute, Vigilante of Violence: An Examination of His Trilogy *The Shape of Things*, *Fat Pig*, and *Reasons to Be Pretty*." And in "Challenging the American Dream: U.S. Theater and the Continuum of State Violence," Marta Fernández Morales approaches *The Exonerated* as an exemplary documentary play—that is, political but not propagandistic.

Verbal or representational violence forms a notable subset of structural and cultural violence in the discussion. In "Violence Averted Only to Return: Visiting the Archive of 'Pocahontas Plays,'" Tamara Underiner sketches a genealogy of Pocahontas narratives from 1808 to 2007, focusing on the extent to which Indian characters are granted dramatic agency. Yiyi López Gándara's essay, "Threats, Bad Language and Imperatives: Verbal Violence in Politically (In)Correct Institutional Speech in American Drama at the End of the Millennium," focuses on *Oleanna* and *Angels in America* to illustrate the abusive nature of institutional speech.

Several essays articulate the complexities of staging attitudes toward wartime violence, including the "War on Terror." In "Revolution and After: Heroism and Violence in Early National Plays about the American Revolution," Amelia Howe Kritzer finds that these plays largely removed violent action from the stage, recasting wartime behavior as the upholding of moral principles important to issues of reconciliation in the postwar period. In "The Guns Sing in Harmony: *Johnny Johnson* and the Musical War," Anne Beggs argues for *Johnny Johnson* as a "comprehensively *American* musical" (110) that blends Kurt Weill's score with Paul Green's dialogue and lyrics to create "a powerful political satire that is at once a piece of folk-Americana and a modernist evocation of violence" (109). In "Terrorist Violence and Its (Dis)Figurations in Three American Post-9/11 Plays," Markus Wessendorf captures the "deep-seated skepticism towards the rhetoric of patriotism" (247) evidenced by Neil LaBute, Christopher Shinn, and Craig Wright. Virginia Dakari links the hegemonic figure of General Ulysses S. Grant to a post-9/11 "reconstructing [of] history as a cancerous nightmare" (251) in "The Cancer Body (Politic) of American Violence: John Guare's *A Few Stout Individuals*."

Violence in American Drama offers a coherent, coordinated selection of essays on an important topic. It also points to areas for further research. Barbara Ozieblo, for example, notes that scholars have paid scant attention to audience affect in regard to stage violence. The volume thus ends appropriately with her study, "Affecting the Audience: Gina Gionfriddo's *After Ashley*," which reveals the limitations of familiar notions such as catharsis and defamiliarization. Ozieblo looks to cognitive studies for new tools to address this topic.

—**IRIS FISCHER**
University of Kansas

Changed for Good: A Feminist History of the Broadway Musical. By Stacy Wolf. New York: Oxford University Press, 2011. pp. xiv + 306. $24.95 paper.

Stacy Wolf's *Changed for Good: A Feminist History of the Broadway Musical* is an important addition to the burgeoning field of musical theatre scholarship. In his 2004 *Theatre Survey* article, "Toward a Historiography of the Popular," David Savran maintained that, although the field has become "more fashionable of late," inept scholarship predominates: "What passes for musical-theatre scholarship—with a handful of notable exceptions—oscillates between dreary, encyclopedic catalogs and wildly impressionistic flights of the imagination. Certainly no other theatre form has inspired such a cornucopia of idolatrous and anecdotal narratives that scorn analysis in favor of narcissistic rumination and fantasy" (213). Even more recently, in their introduction to *Women in American Musical Theatre* (2008), Bud Coleman and Judith A. Sebesta observed that "although a number of works have treated the subject of musical theatre from a fairly traditional, almost 'positivist' historical perspective, few have approached it theoretically or using a less 'traditional' historical methodology, such as feminism, Marxism, postmodernism, etc." (3). Such is Wolf's intention in *Changed for Good.* Building upon the work of Raymond Knapp and Scott McMillin, Wolf utilizes an impressive array of theories, from cultural studies, queer studies, ethnoracial studies, and musicology, to analyze and interpret the representation of women in American musicals and to demonstrate women's centrality to the form, both on- and offstage. Importantly, Wolf acknowledges where her work intersects with other musical theatre scholars and announces her intention to "open a politicized, historicized conversation with Knapp's and McMillin's books to interrogate musical theatre's conventions and how they work from a feminist perspective" (247).

Wolf begins her study with an account of "Defying Gravity," the Act 1 finale of the blockbuster musical *Wicked*, in which the green-skinned societal outcast Elphaba soars above the heads of her would-be captors and belts an anthem of self-assertion. Wolf's description of this spectacular moment, and the ensuing discussion of how the song converses with similar numbers in musical theatre history, frames her study. "Defying Gravity," Wolf contends, signifies how *Wicked* is Elphaba and G(a)linda's show and, likewise, how "musical theatre has always been the terrain of women and girls" (5). "Defying Gravity," Wolf continues, also exemplifies how *Wicked* embodies the generic conventions of musical theatre as championed by Rodgers and Hammerstein in the mid-twentieth century. Wolf asserts that from the 1950s to the 2000s, "virtually all Broadway musicals had to contend with the formidable legacy of Rodgers and Hammerstein"; consequently, "their conventions have been internalized by musical theatre audiences" (10). However, here and throughout the book, Wolf is interested not in how *Wicked* and other musicals perpetuate the Rodgers and Hammerstein hegemony, but rather in how they can signify as queer by "turning away from heterosexual couples and presumptive heterosexual romance and toward women" (18).

A particular strength of Wolf's study is her methodology, which can serve as a model for others in the field. In the introduction, she states that one purpose of her book is "to demonstrate a methodology for taking apart the total experience to understand how the pieces of a richly multivalent performance make meaning" (5). Wolf thereby examines a constellation of materials that comprise the performance "text," including the libretto, music, lyrics, casting, staging, spectacle, and performances. That she examines the score as a vital component of each performance text is noteworthy, as most scholarly considerations of musical theatre have approached the genre from either a theatrical or musicological perspective and have rarely synthesized the two. A notable exception is Knapp's two-volume *The American Musical and the Formation/Performance of National/Personal Identity* (2006), which includes abundant musical analysis. Additionally, Wolf emphasizes how musicals are products of a historical moment, thereby answering Bruce Kirle's call, in *Unfinished Show Business: Broadway Musicals as Works-in-Process* (2005), for an analysis of musicals that recognizes their incompleteness by deconstructing the privileging of an autonomous text.

Organized by decade, the five chapters following the introduction examine a representative group of musicals in the context of the changing roles of women in U.S. culture from the 1950s to the 2000s, beginning with *Guys and Dolls* and ending with *In the Heights*. Rather than provide an exhaustive reading of each musical, Wolf focuses on one convention "that bubbled to the surface" in each decade: the female duet in the 1950s, the solo female dancer in the 1960s, the ensemble number in the 1970s, scenography in the 1980s, and the female principal's first song and the eleven o'clock number in the late 1990s–2000s. With the final two chapters Wolf returns to *Wicked*, concluding that the musical adopts Golden Age conventions but replaces the typical heterosexual romance with a homosocial friendship between two women, a relationship that, if read through a queer lens, can empower girls and women while also pointing to the need for a queer, feminist Broadway musical theatre. Of special interest is the final chapter, "'It's All About Popular': *Wicked* Divas and Internet Girl Fans," which analyzes girls' participation on Internet fansites and blogs to demonstrate "the energy and acuity of girl fans of musicals, and how they carry the torch of the form's continuation and its ongoing reinvention as a vehicle for female empowerment" (23). Wolf's use of Internet sources to study musical theatre as both social event and commercial product offers yet another interpretive tool to gauge how this indigenous American art form engages with its cultural context and, as Wolf affirms, enables women "through the doing of performance" (18).

Changed for Good argues persuasively that women have dominated the Broadway musical as performers, creators, and spectators since the mid-twentieth century. Answering Savran, Sebesta, Coleman, and Kirle's call for an analysis of musicals as works-in-process, Wolf explores the relationship between gender and genre in a study that is not only insightful but also beautifully written. Wolf's passion for musical theatre infuses every page, and, importantly, her vibrant descriptions of the musicals in performance allow the reader to envision the "doing" that, Wolf argues, "brings feminist possibilities into being" (63). In the epilogue Wolf contends, "A feminist history of the Broadway musical is an argument and a story but it's also a method and a perspective" (239). One hopes that her study will prompt further investigations of a feminist musical theatre and that the field will be "changed for good."

—BRETT D. JOHNSON
Mercyhurst University

Self and Space in the Theater of Susan Glaspell. By Noelia Hernando-Real. Jefferson, NC: McFarland & Company, Inc., 2011. pp. x + 204. $55 paper.

Following in the footsteps of scholars like Barbara Ozieblo, J. Ellen Gainor, or Kristina Hinz-Bode, all authors of recent monographs on Susan Glaspell's plays, Noelia Hernando-Real, vice president of the International Susan Glaspell Society, has contributed *Self and Space in the Theater of Susan Glaspell*, a groundbreaking book demonstrating once more that the playwright rightly deserves the honorific title of mother of modern American drama. This fascinating book was published by McFarland & Company, which, it is worth noting, has previously issued several works devoted to Glaspell: *The Road to the Temple*, edited by Linda Ben-Zvi, in 2005; Kristina Hinz-Bode's *Susan Glaspell and the Anxiety of Expression*, in 2006; and *Susan Glaspell: The Complete Plays*, an anthology of Glaspell's dramatic works edited by Linda Ben-Zvi and J. Ellen Gainor, in 2010. Hernando-Real's contribution to the understanding of the importance of

Glaspell in the history of American drama is notable for its originality, as the author explores largely uncharted territories. If she pays tribute to her Glaspellian predecessors whose works are thoroughly discussed throughout her book, Hernando-Real goes beyond the existing studies to open up new perspectives on Glaspell's plays by focusing on the dramatization of space. Whereas many scholars have recognized the significance of space in the dramatic corpus of this cofounder of the Provincetown Players, it has never been the subject of a comprehensive analysis. In notably reading Glaspell's plays through the prism of "geopathology," a concept devised by Una Chaudhuri in *Staging Place: The Geography of Modern Drama* (1995), Hernando-Real considers the synergy between the construction of space and the construction of self.

"Geopathology" refers to the problem of space and the tensions between inclusion and exclusion, home and homelessness. Hernando-Real shows in *Self and Space in the Theater of Susan Glaspell* that the struggle with the problem of space reflects the struggle with the problem of self. According to Hernando-Real, this dialogue between belonging and exile, this tension between feeling at home and feeling estranged, mainly concerns female protagonists; consequently, the study concentrates on Glaspellian heroines, with some references to male characters. Adopting a semiotic approach, Hernando-Real examines how the spatialization of the self is *textually* codified: it is indeed Glaspell's dramatic texts rather than performances of the plays that are studied. Hernando-Real's corpus includes here those of Glaspell's plays that are set in a home—that is, most of the playwright's pieces: *Suppressed Desires* (1915), a play cowritten with George Cram Cook, *Trifles* (1916), *The Outside* (1917), *Close the Book* (1917), *Bernice* (1919), *Chains of Dew* (1922), *Inheritors* (1921), *The Verge* (1921), *The Comic Artist* (1928), a play cowritten with Norman Matson, *Alison's House* (1930), and *Spring Eternal* (1943). The originality of Hernando-Real's book lies not only in the centrality of space in her approach, which offers a new vision of Glaspell's plays, but also in the way she structures her analysis, departing from the traditional play-to-play pattern. Rather, she has divided her study into subthemes, discussing the different pieces following these thematic threads in order to bring out their specificities or similarities.

Having devoted her first chapter to the definitions of key notions—such as "space" and "place," "geopathology," "home," "gender," and "realism"—the author discusses the playwright's staging of "American geomythologies" by paying specific attention in chapter 2 to the American myth of mobility: she thus notably considers how Glaspell's female protagonists play an active part in the frontier myth and the pioneer myth, which have traditionally been conceptualized as primarily male myths. Hernando-Real then proceeds to analyze in chapter 3 the tensions between isolation and community by studying the representation of the home as a prison or a shelter in Glaspell's plays. Chapter 4 centers on the link between space and time and on Glaspell's spatial representation of the past. Hernando-Real shows that Glaspell displays two opposing conceptions of the notion of heritage, which appears either as a driving force for the assertion of one's identity or as an obstacle hampering the female protagonists' emancipation from stifling traditions. As demonstrated in chapter 5, death pervades many of Glaspell's plays, in which, Hernando-Real argues, the house is turned into a grave haunted by absent characters or wartime memories that influence the present of the protagonists on stage. Finally, the author concentrates on the means devised by Glaspellian heroines to escape the physical and social places in which they feel trapped. Noelia Hernando-Real's conclusion in her afterword about the significance of space in the formation of identity in Susan Glaspell's plays, as demonstrated throughout her book, is entirely persuasive. Her readers will have been convinced by the author's conclusions, informed by her deep insight into the plays themselves and her mastery of theoretical concepts that broaden our understanding of them.

Self and Space in the Theater of Susan Glaspell is an important addition to the scholarly literature on Susan Glaspell's plays, as it not only contributes to the recognition of the playwright's importance in the history of American drama but also opens up new perspectives on the interpretation of her works.

—EMELINE JOUVE
Toulouse II University, France

The Making of Cabaret. 2nd ed. By Keith Garebian. New York, NY: Oxford University Press, 2011. pp. xiv + 232. $19.95 paper.

"*Cabaret* is not *just* a musical," Keith Garebian asserts in the new preface to his second edition of *The Making of Cabaret.* Rather, he argues, it is "a rare balancing act that is both entertaining and instructive and that manages to make music, dance, dialogue, and décor part of the action rather than restrict them to serving as mere *divertissements*" (xiv, xi). Garebian's work on *Cabaret*, which is part of his larger body of work on groundbreaking musicals such as *West Side Story*, *Gypsy*, and *My Fair Lady*, is also an impressive balancing act of entertainment and instruction as he deftly and deeply explores the historical, artistic, and structural process of creating and producing a groundbreaking musical.

In this new edition, which updates and expands the 1999 original, Garebian has cut "much of the extraneous biographical background on the major collaborators in order to concentrate more sharply on aesthetic and sociocultural issues that did not receive much discussion in the first edition" and has included several images of the most recent revivals (xiv).

Garebian begins with "Bowles and Berlin" and "Prince of Broadway," detailing the origination of the Sally Bowles character and the adaptation process from her inception to her arrival on Broadway. He introduces Christopher Isherwood's biography and his *Berlin Stories*, the tales chronicling his experiences in pre-World War II Germany. Garebian then traces John Van Druten's stage and film adaptations of Isherwood's character in *I Am a Camera*, including biographical information on Julie Harris, who starred as Sally Bowles in both versions. The focus of the chapter then shifts to Harold Prince, the innovative director of the 1966 Broadway original production of *Cabaret*, whose imprimatur, Garebian argues, is indelible.

In "Curtain of Light, Tilted Mirror," and "Cabaret Ambience," Garebian examines *Cabaret*'s original production design, with a particularly useful analysis of the political and social milieu of real German cabaret and the ways in which Prince and his team both utilized and missed opportunities to exploit the Brechtian elements available to them in the richness of their Kit Kat Klub setting. Garebian specifically focuses on Boris Aronson and Patricia Zipprodt's work in sets and costumes and thoroughly examines the production's "single greatest design element," the giant mirror that hung over and reflected the audience, which he uses as a metaphor throughout the text (49).

After providing thorough biographies of composer John Kander and lyricist Fred Ebb, Garebian insightfully analyzes the incorporation and application of a camp aesthetic in their musicals and specifically in the Kit Kat Klub performances of Sally Bowles and the emcee in *Cabaret*. He also examines each song in the original score, detailing the writing process for each collaborator as well as their decision-making, rehearsal, and revision processes as the musical found its final form. Wading into content that could easily become mind-numbing, Garebian's work here is balanced by his inclusion both of descriptive passages of character work and plot concerns and of analytical details concerning orchestration and complex rhyme schemes.

Throughout *The Making of Cabaret*, Garebian provides biographical material for the stars of the musical, as well as anecdotes that enhance both the context and interest of the narrative. In "Casting" and "Rehearsals and Boston," he covers the major players in the original production, Lotte Lenya, Joel Grey, and Jack Gifford, among others. He also provides some of the most comprehensive research collected on Ron Field, *Cabaret*'s choreographer in 1966 and 1987. In the chapter "Broadway Presentational," Garebian provides a balanced assessment of the original production's achievements and faults, covering both financial details and the reviewers' responses to the Broadway opening and the cast, with particular attention to the much maligned Jill Haworth as Sally Bowles. Overall, his work on the original production firmly institutes it as a pivotal musical in its historical moment.

In "Reincarnations and Revisions" Garebian examines the two major *Cabaret* reincarnations, the 1972 Bob Fosse film and the 1998 Sam Mendes production that transferred from London's Donmar Warehouse. Here he focuses on actors who have reinvigorated the roles over time on Broadway (Natasha Richardson and Alan Cumming) and film (Liza Minelli) as well as in London and Stratford. For this new edition, Garebian has added a detailed analysis of the important 2008 production at the Stratford Shakespeare Festival, which is a particularly useful resource since it rarely receives the attention the Mendes production is given. He asserts that the research behind the direction, concept, and design of the Stratford production was groundbreaking and provides striking images to support this claim. Although he ultimately argues that "no matter how significant a new version, it never truly obscures the original signatures of the first Broadway production," throughout the book Garebian consistently works to establish *Cabaret* as a complex and flexible piece of theatre that illuminates the ways in which "a great musical mirrors social and cultural history" (xiv).

The Making of Cabaret honors every artistic collaborator who has shaped *Cabaret*'s production history and makes good on Garebian's promise to "capture the collaborative excitement" involved in producing one of the greatest musicals of the twentieth century. The book is enriched by Garebian's intricate research, which relies on a wide variety of updated sources, including print, radio, and video interviews, letters, biographies, reviews, original drafts and designs, videotaped performances, academic essays, photographs, and program notes. His jargon-free analysis of the musical and its various productions make this "compendious reference" a resource suited to dramaturgs, theatre historians, directors, and musical theatre enthusiasts (xiii).

—VALERIE JOYCE
Villanova University

How It Feels to Be Free: Black Women Entertainers and the Civil Rights Movement. By Ruth Feldstein. New York: Oxford University Press, 2013. pp. 304. $29.95 hardcover.

Engagements with and interrogations of race and gender equality guide Ruth Feldstein's study of five well-known African American entertainers—Nina Simone, Miriam Makeba, Abbey Lincoln, Cicely Tyson, and Diahann Carroll—during the height of the American civil rights movement of the 1960s. At its core, Feldstein's book provides insight into the mobilization efforts of her iconic subjects as each assisted in the struggle for a multilayered equality. Those efforts, manifested in what Feldstein labels "performed civil rights," identify multiple performances beyond a mere referencing of all-important racial aspects of that struggle through the inclusion of an oft forgotten yet ever present struggle for gender equality. *How It Feels to Be Free* presents multiple sites of cohesion between each of Feldstein's subjects and the organizations they supported and maintained through performances in lounges, coffee houses, cocktail venues, and large halls. Each of these women followed in the footsteps of Lena Horne and others who, in their own time, utilized popularity garnered through film and radio performances to bolster support for the African American cause. By way of widely available avenues of access such as recording, print media, and the still emerging technology of television—newly available to most blacks and whites—this next wave of "Black Women Entertainers" (22) cultivated culturally vibrant connections by way of daily incursions into American households. The women in Feldstein's study thrive through a connectedness of lives and actions promoting the African American civil rights struggle as a shared narrative. Each individual Feldstein discusses was keenly focused on engaging and elaborating a newly situated American experience.

Feldstein uses as her starting point two iconic events central to the history of multiple civil rights struggles. The February 1, 1960, sit-ins in Greensboro, North Carolina, and the March 21 white South African murder of peaceful protesters in Sharpeville served as points of departure from which Miriam Makeba, Nina Simone, and Abbey Lincoln first inserted themselves into "politicized musical subcultures." (37)

When thinking back to African American performers who engaged the subject of violence visited upon black bodies seen on nightly news telecasts of the day, one likely calls to mind works like the Sam Cooke hit "A Change Is Gonna Come" or Martha Reeves's ever-popular "Dancin' in the Streets." Feldstein, however, provides a deeper exploration, not only of specific instances of performance but also of the journeys traveled by the performers themselves. In one such case, singer Miriam Makeba struggles to find clarity in her own experiences with South Africa's apartheid government and its harsh treatment of black South Africans through the lens of the similarly violent and harsh treatment of African Americans. Through that personal search, her performance of a particular song, "The Click Song," became recontextualized through those experiences, and, according to Feldstein, a song that "did not at first glance seem to be political in any way" (7) did, through performance, gain political meaning. Thus, a celebratory melody most often sung on the occasion of a young woman's wedding was transformed. A festive musical passage becomes one of defiance so that literal rather than figurative meanings were recontextualized and brought to the fore. According to Feldstein, "performances and reactions to these performances together shaped dialogues about race relations and gender" (8). While for some, as in the case of Makeba, geographical shifts provided new insights and awakenings, for others, as in the case of singer Abbey Lincoln, multiple name changes paralleled equally vibrant shifts in social, cultural, and political contexts. Naming and renaming became an action representative of such epic change. Lincoln's change from Anna Marie Wooldridge to Gaby Wooldridge to the *sexier* Gaby Lee (the "sepia Marilyn Monroe") and finally to the well-known Abbey Lincoln exemplified the shifting currents of individual mediations of identity (31).

While individual personal journeys serve as the focus of the book, it is a lens keenly focused on shared experiences and trajectories that truly directs the narrative Feldstein presents. From the start, Feldstein clarifies aspects of previous scholarship on the struggles for civil rights with interrogations of overused terms like "movement" and "struggle." In one instance, Feldstein correctly reinterrogates references to the term "movement" as potentially misleading, in part because of "how many strands were braided together in struggles for black freedom" (135), developing over time and across national and international boundaries. In part, Feldstein suggests a temporal arc of sorts, mapping struggles that marked those entertainers who performed civil rights and in doing so increased the value of "black power perspectives as currency" (35) toward successful movement outcomes. Feldstein also identifies multiple instances of change through close readings of specific musical performances and their sites. Through multilayered references to locations such as Stanley's Bar, "the meeting place of choice for black activists," (27) or New York's Village Gate, Village Vanguard, and Bitter End, Feldstein shows how each venue provided the performers access to the ears of those supportive of the struggle at hand.

The work unfolds in five concisely structured chapters and concentrates on the previously mentioned connections among the artists. The collective Feldstein presents moves the reader to recognize the continued political action of subjects well known for their efforts in performance, as well as how each subject shifted those performances in the service of deciphering negative connotations of race and gender not only in the struggle for equal recognition but also as a continuing clarification of the American identity.

—KEITH BYRON KIRK
University of Houston

There's a Place for Us: The Musical Theatre Works of Leonard Bernstein. By Helen Smith. Burlington, VT: Ashgate, 2011. pp. xviii + 300. $99.95 cloth.

Helen Smith's study is among the first to consider the musical theatre works of Leonard Bernstein collectively. Her aim is to "survey the musical theatre works of Bernstein as a whole, and, through consideration of the musicals, operas and theatre pieces to observe how both his compositional technique and his approach to composing developed and evolved" (2). The book is organized in a chronological fashion, with each chapter devoted to a musical theatre work (*On the Town, Trouble in Tahiti, Wonderful Town, Candide, West Side Story, Mass, 1600 Pennsylvania Avenue, A Quiet Place*) composed between 1944 and 1983.

In each chapter, Smith begins by briefly situating the musical in its general historical context, considering influences emanating from the years in which the musical work was written, such as the wartime climate of *On the Town* (1944) or the McCarthy investigations that are paralleled in *Candide* (1956). The contextual information is followed by a short plot summary, which is useful as not all readers will be familiar with every work. An almost exclusive focus on music is perhaps a departure from other studies of musical theatre works, which frequently devote equal space to detailing the complex (and at times torturous) process of creating a musical, from its inception to its Broadway premiere. While Smith certainly does not discount the fact that Bernstein wrote his musical theatre works as a member of a production team—noting that the "study . . . is complicated by the fact that the composer is only one part of a team"—Smith's understanding that "Bernstein [is] totally and individually responsible for the music for each show" (2), coupled with her study's musical emphasis, ultimately means that she pays significantly less attention to the librettos, books, lyrics, rehearsal processes, or pre-Broadway tryouts than might be expected. (An exception to this is the chapter on *Candide*, which details changes in Lillian Hellman's book and subsequent versions of the entire work spanning thirty years.) Once again, Smith does not ignore these factors, but they are mentioned only if directly affecting Bernstein's compositions. For instance, director George Abbott's decision to cut "Gabey's Comin'" from *On the Town* had ramifications on the audience's initial introduction to important musical motifs for the entire musical score. Similarly, the amount of time taken to create a show, which spanned anything from four-and-a-half weeks to years, is noted only in terms of how it affected Bernstein's compositional output; in the short time allotted to compose the score for *Wonderful Town*, Smith reflects on Bernstein's employing the "practice of using 'trunk' music—that is, music that remained initially unused or in the composer's 'trunk' following its composition, or reuse of melodies and music in different shows" (90). The importance of choreography and dance, however, is privileged, particularly as Jerome Robbins's visions for *On the Town* and *West Side Story* were so integral to their creation.

The bulk of each chapter is given to extensive analysis of the music; Smith interacts with earlier scholarship, including work by Paul Laird, Jack Gottlieb, and Ethan Mordden, both acknowledging foundational research done by others and signaling where her work departs from or revises current exchanges. Significant attention is paid to the composers who influenced Bernstein, from contemporaries and mentors such as Igor Stravinsky, Aaron Copeland, and Marc Blitzstein, to earlier influences such as Beethoven, Mozart, Britten, Bellini, and Bartók. One of the strengths of Smith's writing is that she gives her reader clear and concise definitions of important terminology the book employs; for instance, she delineates pastiche as a "method of defining a period through musical means" (79) versus parody, which is "inclusion of music for an ironic or comic effect, by implication or ridicule" (122). This distinction is particularly useful, as Bernstein employs both methods of musical composition in setting the scene and developing characterization in his works.

The majority of Smith's analysis focuses on Bernstein's compositional techniques and their development, such as his use of motifs and musical intervals, patterns and structures, canon and fugue, chromaticism, serialism, and rhythm. In particular, Smith argues that Bernstein employs all of these methods to further the integrated musical theater form, resulting in an inherent "organicism and . . . unity of sound" (272). Although some examples Smith gives are readily accessible, more complex analysis—consider, "the first chord could be D major or B minor, creating either a I-IV^7 or a I-VI^7 pattern; the overall tonality of the song appears to be B minor, with a Phrygian tinge" (218)—may not be as readily comprehensible to all. Hence, it is unfortunate that a CD or website with audio clips could not also have been included; despite almost 150 examples from the musical score and detailed tables, Smith's in-depth musical analysis simply may not be accessible to readers without some background in music theory and knowledge of Western music, particularly jazz and classical.

Despite these minor concerns, Smith's book is an excellent addition to existing scholarship on musical theatre in general and to studies devoted to the output of Leonard Bernstein in particular. Especially important is her comprehensive consideration of all Bernstein's musical theatre works; frequently musicals and operas are studied in isolation from one another. Smith sets a standard for other musicologists who are turning their attention to the Broadway musical and paves the way for further integration in the study of opera, musical works written for the theatre, and the Broadway-style musical.

—JENNA L. KUBLY
Independent Scholar
St. Paul, Minnesota

Simming: Participatory Performance and the Making of Meaning. By Scott Magelssen. Ann Arbor: University of Michigan Press, 2014. pp. xii + 249. $35.00 paper, $75.00 hardcover.

Few scholarly books open with as enticing a hook as Scott Magelssen's excellent study of participatory performance, *Simming*. Magelssen seemed destined to write this book since his career as a simulator began in infancy when he subbed for an ersatz baby Jesus, stolen from a life-size Christmas crèche in Wisconsin, to create, to the delight of onlookers, a living nativity. He reprised his role as Christ, now as an adult, at Bible camps and then went on to tackle multifarious role simulations as field research for this book, including as a runaway African American slave, illegal Mexican migrant, and the corpse of a Civil War soldier for a demonstration of embalming practices. That Magelssen not only immersed himself as a role-player in these simulated performances but also wrote about them with both scholarly and artistic aplomb makes this book both good research and very good reading. It's a rare work of scholarship that is also a page turner. I couldn't wait to see what outlandish situation he would get himself into next and, equally importantly, how he would contextualize these bizarre experiences within the frames of performance studies and U.S. cultural phenomena of the early twenty-first century.

Magelssen borrows the term "simming" from the online gaming universe, defined here as "deliberate, embodied practice" within "live, three-dimensional, immersive environments" where "spectator-participants engage in the intentionally simulated production of some aspect of real or imagined society, recognized as such by all parties" (5). He is particularly interested in simulations that incorporate some component of pedagogy or social justice through which participants can transform their perspectives and way of being in the world, although he is cautious in pronouncing outcomes and rigorous in examining how to assess efficacy. His work is inspired by Augusto Boal, whose own theatre, like that of these simulations, empowered spectators to become actors in what Boal termed a "rehearsal for life."

Magelssen organizes the book into three broad sections that demonstrate how simming can be employed to explore past, present, and future situations, both real and imagined. All three of the engagements with past history in part 1 fall into the larger category of tourist simmings, although one of these was virtual—an online chat program conducted with Magelssen and his students by historic interpreter/educators from Old Sturbridge Village. It is in the two live experiences, at Conner Prairie interactive history park in Indiana and the Museum of Funeral Customs in Illinois, that Magelssen gets to play two of his more adventuresome roles, as a fugitive slave and a Civil War corpse, respectively. As a corpse, Magelssen found himself naked on an embalming table, with only a modesty sheet to cover his lower extremities and silver half-dollar coins to inhibit eyelid twitching. At Conner Prairie, which he visited twice as a role-playing participant in its simulation of the Underground Railroad, he was surprised to learn how eagerly staffers embraced the theatricality of the work. "This is a drama and you are characters," the tourists were told as they were assigned roles and briefed on the scenario (40). Magelssen found this kind of experiential learning physiologically impressive—literally—as role-players "knelt in abject submission before our racial betters, dashed from our pursuers, or huddled on the floor of a Quaker family's candlelit kitchen with a meager repast of cornbread and water" (33–34).

He encountered still more rigorous—even dangerous—role-playing in Mexico in *Caminata Nocturna*, a six-hour Spanish-language simming of an illegal crossing of the U.S.-Mexico border, which he describes as "an extreme sports event with a bit of proscenium theater thrown in" (107). This "action-adventure story" features prominently in part 2, which focuses on learner-driven simming that helps participants bear witness to the present. Visitors are given information, invited to role-play, presented with dilemmas, and encouraged to make their own choices based on their recently acquired knowledge. This focus on deep learning and the agency afforded the actor-simulators is further expanded in part 3, where engagement involves rehearsing for the future. In this section, Magelssen investigates real-life entities—schools, churches, the military—that employ simulations to prepare participants for life-and-death situations including biochemical attacks, mock drunk-driving car crashes, and war in Iraq and Afghanistan. In each scenario throughout the book, Magelssen tells a compelling story spun from personal involvement and observations, investigates the issues from a multitude of perspectives, and cites prominent theoretical scholarship that supports, critiques, or interrogates the work and its potential efficacy as a tool for learning and/or effecting change.

What is most remarkable about this book is not so much its contribution to the growing field of performance studies—and certainly it has a proud place in that literature—but its penetrating study of early twenty-first-century American culture and politics. Magelssen carefully demonstrates how all of the simulations described have blatant or covert political agendas, reified through a remarkable employment of sophisticated theatre techniques. How many of these simmings are truly open-ended immersions in "deep learning" and personal agency for the actor-participants rather than arguments for a particular world view advanced by the creator-producers? The sheer theatricality Magelssen describes is mind-boggling. The minute detail that goes into creating the mock car crash "to hell and back" simulations; the "Dispensing Drill for Anthrax from the Strategic National Stockpile," where citizens are goaded into participating by signs declaring "Patriotism is not enough"; and the simulated Iraqi villages peopled with Arabic-speaking émigrés used to rehearse soldiers deployed to war zones theoretically should keep all of our collegiate theatre majors employed for years. Magelssen ultimately chooses an optimistic perspective—"simming practices are being employed more and more to understand the world—and even to save it," he contends—but he ends with a cautionary note, exhorting simming producers "to invite us to co-produce a world worthy of keeping, without scaring us into maintaining the one they want us to have" (190).

—**MARTHA S. LOMONACO**
Fairfield University

Theatre and Museums. By Susan Bennett. New York: Palgrave, 2013. pp. viii + 88. $11 paper.

Susan Bennett calls out the age-old divide separating museum and theatre in the first pages of this little volume (the books in Palgrave's Theatre & series, which aim to "explore connections between theatre and some aspect of the wider world," are designed to be "readable in one sitting by anyone with a curiosity about the subject" [viii]). Bennett begins by pointing out the seeming irreconcilability between the two: the museum, traditionally conceived, collects and preserves the past; theatre, on the other hand, elapses in the present, leaving barely a trace behind to be archived, right?

In the pages that follow, Bennett not only points out the flaws in this binary but also surveys and unpacks a number of ways in which the museum has been resisting and even collapsing this binary by becoming more performative or, drawing on Diana Taylor's work, "repertoiric" (that is, creating and transmitting meaning through the non-text-based repertoire versus solely through the text-based archive). In so doing, Bennett articulates compelling relationships between the seeming "antonyms" of theatre and museums. Indeed, one gets the impression the exercise is aimed at those stubborn readers for whom the binary is still a convenient discursive structure, since "cultural policymakers, urban and regional planners, arts and other marketing agencies, and, of course, visitors" have long stopped parsing them out thusly, if they ever did in the first place (77).

Unlike books offering a history of or best practices for traditional museum theatre or live interpretation (Catherine Hughes's *Museum Theatre* [1998], Tessa Bridal's *Exploring Museum Theatre* [2004], and *Effective Exhibit Interpretation and Design* [2013]), *Theatre and Museums* is a rich and fresh meditation by way of several case studies in which the goals and practices of these two traditions dovetail in what she calls one "matrix of investigation" at a timely moment for crossover cultural analyses (73).

The first section offers a brief review of recent scholarship on museums and performance, as well as a thumbnail history of museums, which have of late exhibited what we in performance studies recognize as a turn to "theatricality." This turn accompanies a shift in institutional focus from the visitor as a passive spectator to one who is a "participant in a multivalent dynamic designed to animate the museum space, outside and within" (20–21). The series of examples that comprise the rest of the book closely hew to this trajectory. Those at the outset tend more toward traditional forms of display. Bennett begins with a couple of more obvious examples of a museum-theatre relationship. These include performance events within the traditional exhibit space, like Marina Abramović's high-profile performance art retrospective at MoMA. They also include the museum exhibition of theatre ephemera, for example, the Victoria and Albert's display of its theatre-related collection, first in the short-lived London Theatre Museum and more recently in the Theatre and Performance Galleries, which opened in 2009.

But as the case studies unfold, they move to more innovative and surprising programming where "repertoire intrudes upon the narrative of museum-as-archive" (29). These are the sites in which the visitor becomes more and more actively engaged. Bennett examines whole museums designed to be interactive, such as the Experience Music Project in Seattle, where "visitor-performers" not only view musical artifacts but engage with the exhibits to make music of their own. "[W]hile visitors may well have an identical response at admiring a guitar once played by Hendrix, the iconic silver glove worn by Michael Jackson, or the turntables used by Grandmaster Flash," she writes, "they also get to lay down a track that puts them into the story through embodied experience" (46–47). Though the subject matter and quality of experience are of a more serious nature at museums dedicated to remembering the Holocaust (the Jewish Museum in Berlin, the United States Holocaust Memorial Museum in Washington, D.C., the Simon Wiesenthal Center's Museum of Tolerance in Los Angeles), Bennett demonstrates how each of these spaces similarly offers "choreographed" surrogation experiences to their visitors. Such practices, she says, quoting Vivian Patraka, enable visitors the change "from spectators/bystanders" of trauma and injustice "to witnesses" (55).

In this manner, Bennett maps "a trajectory of general movements in museum practice from collection and display to pedagogy and participation" (8). And she demonstrates that this trajectory is not simply a trend to appeal to more crowds but one that demonstrates a deeper political shift in the position of museums in the cultural landscape. For along with greater visitor participation comes a general movement away from the museum as an institution of governance and power. Once designed to produce well-behaving citizens and affirm and advance the superiority of Western cultures by displaying the collected "primitivism of everywhere else" (13), newer museum models empower the visitor to collaborate in the generating of meaning in museum spaces (60), decentering traditional structures of authority.

The book's final three examples (the National Museum of the American Indian in Washington, D.C., the Heard Museum in Phoenix, and Blackfoot Historical Crossing Park in the Siksika Nation reserve in Alberta) are devoted to indigenous culture and experience and stand "outside curatorial logic as it has developed in the west" (63). The last case study, for instance, Blackfoot Historical Crossing Park, is the institution closest to Bennett's home but the least obviously either theatre or museum. Blackfoot Historical Crossing Park does not use the word "museum" to describe itself, and "the visitor must move outside [the building] and literally walk the site to begin experiencing the long history of place" (71). Yet, Bennett writes convincingly of the ways in which the visitors' interaction with the site through walking is a "deliberately meditative experience of place history" (71). This is a museum that moves fully into the repertoiric and dismantles the model of museum as an archive of the past. Blackfoot Historical Crossing Park, like all three of her final examples, is "construed as a living place" and is therefore as much about the present as it is about the Siksika people's ten-thousand-year relationship with that place.

While it might be ambitious for most of us to read *Theatre and Museums* "in one sitting," it is indeed a compact and elegant volume that opens up a complex and rich discussion of the connections between theatre and museums. On a more profound level, however, Bennett shows how theatricality and performance can be democratizing tools toward more progressive models for museums' function in the world.

—SCOTT MAGELSSEN
University of Washington

Ecocriticism and Shakespeare: Reading Ecophobia. By Simon C. Estok. New York: Palgrave Macmillan, 2011. pp. 173. $80.00 cloth.

Ecocriticism and Shakespeare: Reading Ecophobia contributes to the growing "green" conversation about the bard and his times and clearly demonstrates ecocriticism's theoretical edge. Through a subframe of "ecophobia," Estok illuminates the subtle ideologies that shaped the early modern environmental thought and behavior. The book is part of the Palgrave Macmillan Literatures, Cultures, and the Environment series, edited by Ursula K. Heise (Stanford University), which "explores how ideas of nature and environmental concerns are expressed in different cultural contexts and different historical moments" (editor's statement, front matter).

Firmly grounded in literary ecocriticism, Estok builds on and complicates a tradition of "green" studies of Shakespeare, such as Bruce Boehrer's Shakespeare *Among the Animals* (2002), Gabriel Egan's *Green Shakespeare* (2006), and Robert Watson's *Back to Nature: The Green and the Real in the Late Renaissance* (2006). Thankfully, however, Estok eschews the knee-jerk interpretation that all fairies, forests, and heaths are representations of "nature." Instead

Estok conducts a smart interrogation of the spirit of control and domination with which early moderns met the ecological challenges of their epoch. In particular, Estok takes issue with so-called green Shakespeare studies that avoid ecocriticism's political edge, arguing for the viability of an ecocritical approach that "encompasses feminism, queer theory, critical racial theory, food studies, cultural anthropology, ecopsychology, post-structuralism, and deconstruction" (12). Following this approach, Estok's close reading of Shakespeare's texts reinforces recent trends in ecocriticism to overtly expose the connections between and among race, class and gender oppression, ecological thought, and environmental degradation. A lively exploration of the concept and reaches of "ecophobia" is at the center of the book. Estok lays out this central theory in the first two chapters and then unfolds its elements through six subsequent chapters. Two chapters focus on single plays (*King Lear* and *Coriolanus*); two chapters conduct comparative analyses of several texts in light of significant theoretical frames (*Henry VI* and *Henry IV*, both parts, *Othello*, and *Pericles*); and the final two chapters move in and out of several texts in their eco-theoretical exploration of gender and metaphor (85), exotica and ecophobia (99), and the "ecocritical unconscious" (111).

According to Estok, ecophobia is that general repulsion from the so-called natural world and its varied expressions that characterizes the modern and now contemporary world. In Shakespeare's texts and times, Estok argues, we can see "an irrational and groundless fear or hatred of the natural world, as present in our daily lives and literature as homophobia and racism and sexism. . . . It is about power and control; it is what makes looting and plundering of animal and nonanimal resources possible" (4). In what is both a study of Shakespeare and a treatise on ecophobia, Estok offers "vocabulary for conceptualizing something we do (and have been doing for a long time) and for which we haven't had appropriate descriptive or theoretical words" (5).

Estok calls out our society's fears and forebodings about a nature (read climate change) that is a "hostile opponent who is responding angrily to our incursions and actions, an opponent to be feared and, with any luck, controlled," revealing "ecophobic stances that posit nature as the scapegoat for social problems" (6–7). In his second chapter, Estok reframes *King Lear* as a play about a "king who is victimized by the weather" (6). He argues, as Una Chauhuri did in her 1994 *Theater* article "Toward an Ecological Theatre," that metaphors are also material indicators. The weather in *King Lear* is not a mere analog for Lear's inner turmoil but must be seen as a very real clue to the atmospheric and geological conditions of the times. Noting that "colder temperatures, crop failures, and poor fishing . . . were so very much a part of the early modern daily realities,"

Estok looks "at the actual weather of Shakespeare's England and its relationship with things such as economic growth, with early modern notions about witchcraft, and with the obviously changing views toward nature (from organicism to mechanism)" (13, 19). The Little Ice Age (from 1560 to 1600 in Estok's reference, but defined by NASA as a period between 1550 and 1850 CE) throws new light onto the storms of the stage as potential signifiers, as Robert Markley has asserted, of "complex connections between climactic instability and its potential consequences: the loss of agricultural harvests and the fracturing of ideologies of national unity, patriarchal authority, and socioeconomic stability" (quoted by Estok, 21).

In chapters 5 and 6 Estok presses deeper into the ecological and social impact of ecophobia. "The air was especially bad in the cities. London air was filthy, largely the result of coal burning and deforestation" (9). Citing Henry VIII's 1543 *Act for the Preservation of the Woods*, Estok argues that "concerns about the state of England's forests" were popularly (as well as royally) felt in Shakespeare's time (9). Finally, exploring England's ecophobic treatment of so-called New World people and environments, Estok argues that, as "the opening of vast new worlds of resources . . . had to be controlled before they could be hocked as commodities, ecophobia plays a central role in the environmentally hostile imagination that sought control and domination" (16).

The book's strength lies in the close readings of texts through which Estok unpacks and deconstructs early modern ecophobic responses to gender (*A Winter's Tale*), racial difference (*Othello*), and the new, sometimes monstrous, biotic and behavioral diversity flooding into England as a result of colonization. Estok argues that the "semiotics of cannibalism" marks an important overlapping of postcolonial theory and ecocriticism, as is oft exemplified in *The Tempest*. Estok unpacks *Pericles* with an eye to exposing the ecophobia implicit in the Elizabethan construction of a "monstrous other" (76–83).

The book's weakness lies in its loyalty to a singular academic discipline. Estok engages only those well-known voices of literary ecocriticism (such as Garrard, Glotfelty, Slovic, Rosendale), positioning his book squarely within the discipline of literature and literary theory to the exclusion of the very discipline in which Shakespeare himself lived and worked—the theatre. Surprisingly, as if Shakespeare had roots in the production of literature rather than the production of stage plays, the words "drama," "theatre," "performance," and their derivatives do not appear in the book's index. In a book so much about the role and rhythms of place, sites such as The Rose, The Globe, The Swan, The Curtain, and all the others are invisible. The book fails to mention, much less treat through analysis, the fact that these renowned texts were once "sides" held in the sweating hands of a company of actors who *together with Shakespeare* (some would argue collaboratively) heaved these stories into embodied life on a physical stage before a flesh-and-blood audience that they (the players) knew and strove to please. When scholars forget that Shakespeare's plays were shaped by the confrontation and community of unstable artistic enterprise, they not only reinscribe the faulty notion that Shakespeare's works are the mere literary record of individual genius but also miss much of what made and makes these texts living ecological forces. Shakespeare's company left a body of work, traces of live performance in a living society whose ecological values and sensibilities carried us smack into the Industrial Age. Shakespeare's plays are documents of living artistic practice, and without at least acknowledgment that meaning-making is contingent on that very lively (read ecological) context, textual analyses are suspect. What are we about in ecocriticism if not the return and remembrance of the body—the earth's, the animals', and our own?

If theatre and performance studies scholars and artists are to make use of Estok's book, they will need to make the connections on their own. Within theatre studies, Estok's book will make a useful pairing with recent publications such as *Ecology and Environment in European Drama* (2010) by Downing Cless, and *Readings in Performance and Ecology* (2012) edited by Wendy Arons and Theresa May. Likewise, Estok's exploration of ecophobia resonates with Cless's chapter on Marlow's *Dr. Faustus*, providing directors with a theoretical foundation for imagining productions that foreground ecological perspectives. Estok echoes earlier works such as Garrett Sullivan's geographical analysis of early modern English drama in *The Drama of Landscape: Land, Property, and Social Relations on the Early Modern Stage* (1999). Sullivan's chapter on *King Lear*, and Estok's chapter 1 set up a curious dialogue about how both ecological events and sociogeographic events (e.g., the Enclosure Acts) showed up in English drama. Estok's articulation of ecophobia loops back in interesting ways to Una Chaudhuri's theories of how "homelessness" and "exile" thread through contemporary drama in *Staging Place: The Geography of Modern Drama* (1994). In making connections between theatrical performances and environments, Estok's *Ecocritism and Shakespeare: Reading Ecophobia* makes a valuable contribution to theatre and performance studies, as well as literary ecocriticism.

—THERESA J. MAY
University of Oregon

Alfred Jarry: A Pataphysical Life. By Alastair Brotchie. Cambridge, MA: MIT Press, 2011. pp. xii + 405 + 156 illustrations. $34.95 cloth.

One of the most pleasurable and exciting aspects about studying biographies of Alfred Jarry is tracking the development and resolution of so many legendary anecdotes and seemingly irreconcilable elements of his life. As is typical in biographical research, Jarry scholars regularly make new discoveries or revelations, and along with the contingency of historical contexts, the value of what is included in the scholarship shifts as well. The latest biography on the enigmatic avant-gardist who altered theatre history with his *Ubu Roi*, Alastair Brotchie's *Alfred Jarry: A Pataphysical Life*, is the most comprehensive yet in English. At the forefront of current Jarry scholarship as a regent of the Collège de 'Pataphysique, Brotchie delivers to English-language Jarry scholars and enthusiasts a convincing narrative of Jarry's life in which he attempts to nail down certain dubious moments in the received biography of Père Ubu (as Jarry's closest friends called him). Brotchie's will remain a key contribution to the field for many years and will add to the pleasure of tracking those Jarry legends moving forward.

The book is written in chronological narrative format and contains fourteen chapters. Appropriating some of Jarry's own strategies of doubling and opposition, Brotchie alternates each biographical chapter (even numbered) with a short "intercalary" chapter (odd numbered), which is intended "to offer a glimpse of undercurrents which connect the most apparently disparate aspects of Jarry's thought and personality" (x), to explain, for example, his philosophy of pataphysics or to position him within the late-nineteenth-century modernization of Europe. Some biographical chapters seem long and bog down amid lengthy descriptions of mostly vital, but sometimes inconsequential, players and events in the narrative, which makes Brotchie's decision to avoid "discursive footnoting" (x) a bit frustrating. The breakdown of Jarry's timeline, however, is clear and effective.

Brotchie states that he considers Jarry the man and Jarry the writer as one, but he does not necessarily offer a critical biography in the strictest sense, such as Keith Beaumont's *Alfred Jarry* (1985) or Linda Kleiger Stillman's 1983 critical biography of the same title. His evaluations of Jarry's oeuvre are secondary to the conditions surrounding those works. What Brotchie conveys is a deep evaluation of Jarry's actions and behaviors within the context of his milieu, which sheds light on how his writing and life were equally affected by Jarry's contingent geographical, financial, and personal relations.

Brotchie's narrative fills many gaps in previous English-language biographies (e.g., Roger Shattuck's *The Banquet Years* [1968]; Claude Schumacher's *Alfred Jarry and Guillaume Apollinaire* [1984]), including the details of Jarry's military service and other life events between 1894 and 1896, and from 1901 to his death in 1907. Another distinction that separates Brotchie's work from that of recent biographer Jill Fell is his ability to argue convincingly the validity of many disputed details of Jarry's life. Fell, on the other hand, who published her biography *Alfred Jarry* in 2010, leaves many of those details in question. Brotchie reveals that during Jarry's time in the military he was given frequent leave to Paris, thanks to his father's connections at the Rennes base, and that the supposedly self-manufactured reason for Jarry's discharge—that he poisoned himself—may not have been fabricated at all. Brotchie also shows that Jarry had, appropriately, installed a state-of-the-art toilet in his Rue de Cassette apartment. Toward the end of his life, Jarry was dogged by his creditors between Paris, Laval, and his "Tripod" home in Le Coudray, as he moved in and out of the care of his sister while his undiagnosed meningeal tuberculosis progressed.

Among the book's 156 illustrations are what seem to be nearly all the available photos, portraits, and sketches of Jarry. Also included are images of the places he resided and those with whom he surrounded himself, as well as images of his works, literary and artistic, all of which aid tremendously in bringing the narrative to life. This collection of images is unsurpassed in any other Jarry biography, English or French. Many of Brotchie's translations make their first appearance in English in the book. Featured among these is the last letter Jarry ever wrote, to Madame Rachilde, on his deathbed, asking when her Tuesday evening salon soirees would recommence. The letter exposes one last time how optimistically Brotchie casts Jarry throughout his life, a distinct departure from most previous English-language biographies.

Another important new contribution Brotchie makes to our field includes his take on the 1896 *Ubu Roi*. Contrary to many biographers, Brotchie concludes that Gémier danced his jig to regain the audience's attention at the invited dress rehearsal on December 9, not the premiere on the tenth, and not until after an actor's hand was used for the lockbox on the cell door holding Bordure prisoner. According to Brotchie, the audience at the premiere performance on the tenth—including all of the Parisian literary critics—started the violence with Gémier's initial "*merdre*" and continued throughout the performance. Brotchie also details Jarry's collaborative relationship with Claude Terrasse (and its gradual deterioration) on the librettos for *Pantagruel* and other ill-fated operas beginning in 1901. These interactions were heretofore unclear, but Brotchie reveals how jaded Jarry became, as an impoverished absinthe and ether addict desperate for money, having constantly to change his work to please potential producers/actors.

In his otherwise meticulous account, Brotchie glosses over a point that some theatre scholars are currently working to revise. Brotchie seems to take for granted that with the premiere of *Ubu Roi*, Jarry initiates a brand-new set of performance practices. But in works such as *Symbolist Theater* (1993) and *The Cambridge Introduction to Theatre Historiography* (2009), Frantisek Deak and Thomas Postlewait respectively have argued that *Ubu Roi* merely continues a set of symbolist performance practices established long before 1896. This miss tarnishes only slightly the strong work Brotchie does overall.

Despite its excellence, *Alfred Jarry: A Pataphysical Life* will probably not remain the definitive biography of the legendary man of letters forever; I will revel in seeing newly revealed documents alter yet again our understanding of Alfred Jarry. For now, though, Brotchie has provided a thoroughly researched and carefully articulated story of a man whose life was one of the most fascinating in theatre history.

—LANCE MEKEEL
Bowling Green State University

La Voz Latina: Contemporary Plays and Performance Pieces by Latinas. By Elizabeth C. Ramírez and Catherine Casiano, eds. Urbana: University of Illinois Press, 2011. pp. ix + 365. $60.00 cloth.

In the past thirty years, Latina playwrights have proliferated in the United States. A handful, like Josefina López and Quiara A. Hudes, have gained mainstream recognition. Others remain on the fringe, like theatre collectives Butchlalies de Panochtitlan and solo performers Karina Casiano and Susana Cook. Regardless of fame, Latina performance has gained critical attention in scholarly works like Alicia Arrizón's *Latina Performance: Traversing the Stage* (1999). However, the playtexts themselves have largely remained unpublished.

Elizabeth C. Ramírez's and Catherine Casiano's anthology *La Voz Latina: Contemporary Plays and Performance Pieces by Latinas* attempts "to bring the growing body of performance work by Latinas to theatre practitioners, researchers, and the widest audience possible" (2). In the first volume of what promises to be a larger collection, the editors present the work of twelve authors, who are also practitioners. Most of the playtexts have never been published, yet all have been produced. This is remarkable since, as many of the artists expressed in interviews included in the book, producing their work has been challenging. Furthermore, as critic Kathy Perkins argues in one of the anthology's concluding essays, "Contributions by Women of Color," while there are a significant number of plays written by women of color, these works "receive countless workshops, but very few full productions" (360). This criterion reflects the editors' own experience as practitioners and the value they place on a play's labor, process, and life.

The introduction summarizes the editors' goals and their ten-year journey with the book project. It also provides an overview for new readers on Latina/o culture (i.e., a definition of Latina/o; demographic, cultural, and economic impacts on Latina/os in U.S society, etc.). Those interested in scholarship will also find a brief literature review of published anthologies and of critical analyses of Latina plays. In this review they chose to start with a book by Luis Valdez and Teatro Campesino following Yolanda Boyles-Gónzalez's argument that the plays in the anthology were a collective creation and thus were cowritten by the women members. However, as they continue the conversation and discuss other critical works, they overemphasize Valdez's figure, reifying the genealogy that puts Luis Valdez as the prodigious father of Latino theatre. This genealogy is problematic, since it ignores other artists and groups, predecessors to and contemporaries of Valdez, who were significant, especially in cities on the East Coast. The introduction concludes with an explanation of the book's structure, general comments about the plays included, and a warning that "while we have strived for uniformity throughout, as we have already pointed out, each playtext entry will not be quite like another almost in every case" (18).

This anthology is divided into six thematic sections, each with an introductory essay. For instance, part 2, "Chicanas and Chicano Teatro: Staging Identity," gives a short history of the Chicana movement and theatre, and part 5 "Where Is Home and How Do We Get There?," focuses on "home" as a recurring theme in Latina plays. Each section devotes a chapter to the artist it presents. The chapters include the artist's biography, the play's history and reception, an interview with the artist about her artistic development, goals and challenges, the production history, the artist's contact information, and the playtext. As a result, readers learn about the significance of the plays both through the editors' interpretation and through the artists' own voices. It also gives to those interested in producing or writing about the plays access to the artist.

La Voz Latina showcases diversity not only in style, length, genre, and theme but also in the ethnic, racial, cultural, and class background of the artists.

Included are works by renowned artists, like Chicana Cherríe Moraga's short play *Waiting for da God*, a bittersweet play about the painful processes of aging and Alzheimer's. It also showcases the work of veterans whose names are recognized mostly in alternative, academic, and international circles, for example, works by Chichimeca-Otomi, Elvira and Hortencia Colorado, and Dominican Josefina Báez. In the Colorado Sisters' play *Chicomoztoc Mimixcoa*, the artists travel through time, space, and dreams in search of their father's birthplace and their indigenous ancestry. In *Dominicanish*, Báez's playful nonlinear performative text, the artist reflects and shares stories and sounds about being a black Dominican woman living between cultures. All the playtexts in this collection challenge the stereotypes of the sacrificing mother or the sex bomb that according to cultural scholar Arlene Dávila circulate in Hispanic and mainstream media (*Latinos, Inc.*, 125). The Colorado Sisters and Báez also challenge the idea of whitened Latina/os. Furthermore, by proudly claiming their racial background, they confront the centuries-old legacy of racism and shame instituted by European colonialism in the Americas.

This collection also stands out because it includes a significant number of solo performance texts. As Alberto Sandoval-Sánchez and Nancy Saporta Sternbach argue in their book *Stages of Life: Transcultural Performance and Identity in U.S. Latina Theater* (2001), Latina solo performance is "the most highly original, irreverent, and innovative theatrical art form Latinas are producing" (95). This format requires fewer resources than do traditional plays and allows the artist to tell her story without mediation and to be on center stage, a political response to the lack of representation and characters available for Latina performers. An example of a solo performance piece is Carmen Paláez's *My Cuba*. In it, Paláez recounts her first encounter with Cuba and with her great-aunt, who received her lovingly, despite suspicions of her intentions. This play illustrates unspoken tensions between those who left Cuba and those who stayed behind.

The anthology concludes in part 6, "Commentary on Latina Theatre in the United States," with two essays. The first is the aforementioned critical essay by Kathy Perkins in which she reviews the efforts, dialogues, and actions that women artists of color are taking to give visibility to their work and their stories. In the second, award-winning playwright Caridad Svich offers a reflection on the writer's duty to tell stories regardless of their own specific identities and experiences and on her hopes for a more inclusive American scene where the voices of Latinas, and all those currently marginalized, are heard.

Overall, *La Voz Latina* accomplishes its main goal to make the playtexts of contemporary Latina artists available and visible. Furthermore, it brings attention to contemporary artists who, because of their vast experience in theatre making and the quality of their work, deserve wide recognition. Undoubtedly, this book is an important contribution to Latina and U.S. theatre, as it offers a diverse, rich, and exciting example of contemporary Latina plays. Hopefully, there will be more volumes to come!

—**BELIZA TORRES NARVÁEZ**
University of Texas at Austin

Racial Innocence: Performing American Childhood from Slavery to Civil Rights. By Robin Bernstein. New York: New York University Press, 2011. pp. 318. $24.00 paper.

The enduring popularity of the trope of "internalized racism" in the pedagogy of minority empowerment has always been somewhat paradoxical. The explanatory power of this catchphrase would appear weak. Since racism is targeted at people, how could it be other than internalized, given that it hits its mark? Furthermore, the strategic value of this trope is hard to see, insofar as it redirects attention from the perpetrators of hatred and racism and toward their victims, among whom an invidious distinction is drawn between those who manage to ward off the racist interpellation and those who reenact it upon themselves and all who share their identity. Such a pernicious dualism between good and bad victims of racism would appear counterproductive to any robust psychology of empowerment and liberation. But this has not prevented the dualism from being drawn, as taxonomies of racial self-hatred continue to proliferate in the vernacular.

Robin Bernstein's impressively researched, cogently written, and deeply theorized new book, *Racial Innocence*, offers one ingenious answer, at least in the case of the U.S. black/white dichotomy, to the popularity of internalized self-hatred as an explanatory model. Turning to the rich archive of childhood as lived, imagined, and performed, she argues that we must turn to a critical genealogy of the concept of childhood innocence to understand the paradoxical appeal of "damage." Children, she reminds us, were not always considered innocent, vulnerable subjects, but (at least within Calvinist orthodoxy) as guilty of original sin. When children began to be reimagined as innocent in romantic and sentimental American culture, their innocence found a privileged figure in the little white girl. It wasn't American childhood as such that became innocent but a specifically raced and gendered childhood. This had important consequences for abolitionist and, later, civil rights activists. Embracing the culture (or was it the cult?) of the child, antiracists sought to extend this privilege of innocence to black boys and girls, in part by demonstrating their equal capacity to suffer.

But, as Bernstein shows with depressingly exhaustive evidence, the culture of white supremacy inculcated an ideology of black insensateness, contrasting with white sensibility. White supremacy excused performed and real violence against black bodies because of their allegedly greater capacity to endure pain and be obliviously happy. Pedagogies of childhood play—evidence of which Bernstein finds in novels, memoirs, illustrations, playbills, figurines, songsheets, photographs, and dolls, to sample just some of the range of her evidence—reinforced this white supremacist dichotomy between white fragility and black obdurateness. Harriet Beecher Stowe, who sought to demonstrate the damage slavery did to black children through her character Topsy, found that her own creation became one of the most enduring sites for the reproduction in performance of the mythically insensate black child. Harmless, innocent fun (as evidenced in an astonishing chapter on the minstrel roots of Raggedy Ann and Andy) became a disavowed site for the reproduction of white supremacy.

Elements of this argument have been outlined in the literature, for instance in Saidiya Hartman's influential *Scenes of Subjection* (1997). What Bernstein contributes is a novel methodology for interpreting the archival record for its performances, or "scripts" as she calls them. Her chosen term is deliberately situated between the historical/textual and the embodied/live. It draws upon performance studies, thing theory, material culture, visual culture, and literary analysis to propose that objects in the archive leave evidence as to how they "want" to be used. That is, much as a playscript inclines the performance derived from it toward particular ends, even if a particular staging is revisionist or resistant toward those ends, things possess "scripts" that direct their users toward forms of model behavior. These directions can be derived both from their contexts (descriptions and prescriptions of their uses) and a close analysis of the things themselves. Much of the book is engaged in tracking these everyday scripts of childhood: crying, cuddling, laughing; touching, breaking, beating; playing, learning, resisting. These quotidian activities are not often seen as related to the larger political story of slavery and freedom, segregation and its overthrow. *Racial Innocence* reveals to us what an oversight we have made. In the process, it makes an understated but highly persuasive case for the contribution of a historically oriented performance studies to the interdisciplinary conversations surrounding the politics of the everyday.

Racial Innocence thus convincingly intervenes in debates over narratives of psychological harm. Its arc is long, with the greater weight in the nineteenth century. But, at least for this reader, its political dividends pay off in the final chapter devoted to the use of dolls in the child studies of the black psychologists Mamie and Kenneth Clark, begun in the 1930s. These doll studies are very widely known for their contributing role in the 1954 *Brown v. Board of Education* U.S. Supreme Court decision overturning segregation in public schools. The Clarks' demonstration, through the doll play of black children, that a color hierarchy of white over black had already been "internalized" by their youthful subjects, became an enduring script in American pop psychology. As Bernstein notes, "The Clarks implanted in American common sense the belief, which remains prominent today, that any black child who prefers white dolls is necessarily showing symptoms of individual and societal pathology: internalized racism" (197).

Racial Innocence makes two important contributions to the ongoing assessment of the Clarks' legacy for black liberation and empowerment. First, through her genealogy of racial innocence, Bernstein untangles the paradox as to *why* the emphasis upon black susceptibility to damage was so strong at the time, and why it overruled any concern that such models might reinscribe belief in black inferiority or sustain a reductionist ego psychology. And second, she demonstrates a historical method that, while valuing the Clarks' strategy, preserves historical evidence of the agency and resistance of black children's doll play, within and against the Clarks' intentions and interpretations. By centering the *scriptive thing*, Bernstein enhances our ability to read both with and against its grain. This is, perhaps, another paradox that the book leaves us with, one more performative than psychological. But it is a more theoretically productive one than the now exhausted model of "internalized racism," and for that reason alone we ought to make room on our shelves and syllabi for this important new study.

—TAVIA NYONG'O
New York University

Keith Johnstone: A Critical Biography. By Theresa Robbins Dudeck. London: Bloomsbury Methuen Drama, 2013. pp. 232. $25.95 cloth.

In *Keith Johnstone: A Critical Biography*, Theresa Robbins Dudeck provides a rich and much-needed exploration into one of improvisational theatre's most influential figures. While readers interested primarily in Johnstone's philosophy of improvisation will find a wealth of information pertinent to nonscripted performance, Dudeck investigates her subject across various dimensions, including playwright, director, and above all, teacher. The resulting chronological history of Johnstone's life culminates in a critical analysis of his pedagogy, casting Johnstone as an ever-evolving educator whose spontaneity, imagination, and commitment to risk continue to shape contemporary theatre practice.

As an experienced teacher of improvisation herself, Dudeck deftly weaves Johnstone's pedagogic theories together with examples from his workshops, effectively balancing the more cut-and-dried elements of a strictly biographical approach. Furthermore, as a personal friend of Johnstone who he has named the literary executor of his estate, there is perhaps no one else so well qualified as Dudeck to conduct such an in-depth study. Dudeck is quick to acknowledge her distinctive position in relation to her subject, as well as the potential complications this closeness may pose. However, readers will be happy to find a well-rounded critique that benefits from her unique perspective while maintaining critical acumen. Of particular interest is the host of primary source documents from Johnstone's personal papers included throughout the book that will certainly prove generative of further scholarship.

To draw attention to the development of Johnstone's pedagogy, Dudeck employs the classroom as a metaphor to structure her analysis. While her study is largely rooted in the physical spaces in which Johnstone trained, created, and taught, she also extends this metaphor to include "conceptual spaces which informed his pedagogy" (1). To this end, each chapter focuses on a designated "classroom" space, moving the reader from Johnstone's early childhood, to his teaching career, and, finally, into the present. Dudeck's classroom frame is helpful in positioning Johnstone as both teacher and student simultaneously, connecting his artistic theories to the circumstances that informed their growth. While those already acquainted with Johnstone's theories may find that the metaphor pulls focus from her rich analysis of Johnstone in order to devote attention to the frame, newcomers to his philosophy will certainly benefit from Dudeck's careful hand-holding.

After setting up this classroom metaphor, chapter 1, "Introducing Keith Johnstone and His Impro System," does just what the title promises. By adding the word "system" to "impro," Dudeck provides a term that connects the various spheres of Johnstone's practical and theoretical work, including but not limited to the improvisatory work for which he is best known. Dudeck defines the Impro System as "an approach to actor training and theatre practice that encourages spontaneous, collaborative creation using the intuitive, uncensored imaginative responses of the participants" (2). This definition not only highlights the various applications of Johnstone's theory but also grounds his work squarely in the realm of theatrical practice. Drawing on Johnstone's claim that the theatre itself is an informal classroom, Dudeck moves to his work as the author of *Impro: Improvisation and the Theatre* (1979), giving a brief overview of each chapter that effectively acquaints unfamiliar readers with the core tenets of his System.

Building on this foundation, chapter 2, "The Formative Years," details Johnstone's early childhood, homing in on what he describes as "damage inflicted mostly by secondary school education" (20). Framing Johnstone's later insistence on spontaneity as redressive action, Dudeck works meticulously to chart the development of his philosophy. She then devotes the balance of the chapter to Johnstone's work at the Royal Court Theatre. Here, Dudeck contextualizes Johnstone's role in British theatre of the 1950s and 1960s, exploring in particular his relationships with influential theatremakers including George Devine, William Gaskill, Ann Jellicoe, Arnold Wesker, Wole Soyinka, Edward Bond, and Samuel Beckett.

"All the World's a Classroom," chapter 3, tracks the end of Johnstone's activity at the Royal Court Theatre and the transition to his teaching career at the Royal Academy of Dramatic Art and subsequent international workshops given alongside Eugenio Barba, Jerzy Grotowski, and Dario Fo. Of particular note is Dudeck's commitment to understanding Johnstone's development through the international context of his professional history. Books such as Jeffery Sweet's *Something Wonderful Right Away* (1987), Janet Coleman's *The Compass* (1991), and Mike Thomas's *The Second City Unscripted* (2012) are but a few of the works focused on the formation of Chicago improv specifically. By contrast, in this first biography of Johnstone, Dudeck calls attention to his innovative approach through the Impro System while connecting this System to the global circumstances in which it developed.

Chapters 4 and 5, "The Master Teacher in the University Classroom" and "From Company to World Stage: The Loose Moose Theatre Company," overlap chronologically, with the former focusing on Johnstone's twenty-three-year tenure as a professor of acting at the University of Calgary and the latter detailing the formation of Johnstone's most prominent artistic team, the Loose Moose Theatre Company. Dudeck charts the relative success Johnstone enjoyed in these "classrooms" while also noting the challenges he faced within academia and his own company. Although her respect for Johnstone remains evident in her analysis, Dudeck does not shy away from her critical task, attributing Johnstone's later professional difficulties in part to his own antisocial behavior and lack of business skills.

Despite the detrimental effects of his personal shortcomings, Dudeck relies on Johnstone's insistence on positing moments of struggle as opportunities for growth. Reflecting on the preceding chapters, she writes: "Students will remember Keith Johnstone as the teacher . . . who told them to take risks and gave them the right to fail because, having tried and failed so many times himself, Keith understood that failure is a component of a problem-posing pedagogy" (194). She then follows this assertion by expanding the classroom frame to the global sphere, asking, as the final chapter title indicates, "What now? What comes next?" Dudeck offers several possibilities, exploring Johnstone's current work teaching workshops as well as assessing the international reputation he has garnered. Through its forward-looking formulation, chapter 5 serves as the book's crescendo, taking as its form the process-driven pedagogy Dudeck so effectively explores.

In *Keith Johnstone: A Critical Biography*, Dudeck presents an engaging and much-needed scholarly analysis of Johnstone and his work, masterfully weaving theory and practice together in a text that is certain to find diverse and appreciative audiences. Appropriate for scholars, theatremakers, and theatergoers alike, Dudeck's study serves as a welcome invitation for future explorations, many of which will certainly build on this rich and informative text.

—ALEXIS RILEY
Bowling Green State University

An Actress Prepares: Women and "the Method." By Rosemary Malague. New York, NY: Routledge, 2012. pp. x + 254. $125.00 cloth, $31.95 paper.

An Actress Prepares: Women and "the Method" bears the somewhat surprising distinction of being the first thorough, in-depth analysis of Stanislavski-based actor training from a decidedly feminist point of view. Focusing on Stanislavski's System as it was (mis)understood in the United States, Rosemary Malague examines the theories and techniques of four main teachers who turned "the Method" into *the* standard in American acting: Lee Strasberg, Stella Adler, Sanford Meisner, and Uta Hagen. Malague dedicates a chapter to each individual, relying primarily on publications written by the practitioners themselves, transcriptions and video recordings of their training sessions, and previously conducted and published interviews, as well as the criticism and analyses of prior scholars. She argues that such close examination reveals an inherent gender bias, particularly within the patriarchal model established in the creation of "the Method" as we understand it today.

The first chapter, aptly titled "The 'Given Circumstances,'" provides valuable background information that helps place the rest of the book in proper context. Malague offers personal anecdotes from her experiences as an acting student, which serve as an entry point into a preliminary examination of the nature of Method training. Acknowledging previous criticisms of "the Method," as well as prior feminist critiques regarding theatre practices, she then establishes the niche into which her study fits, ultimately defending the urgent need for a feminist examination of acting pedagogies.

With chapter 2, Malague embarks on the first of her detailed analyses of the four main progenitors of Method training in the United States. Beginning with Strasberg's early work with the Group Theatre, Malague examines the unhealthy power dynamic this guru-in-the-making set up with students (including his most famous student, Marilyn Monroe) as he helped them work on themselves, finding and "fixing" their problems in order to improve their acting. Stories of students' emotional and psychological breakdowns are infamous, of course, but Malague points out that Strasberg himself repeatedly cites many more "problems"—and more difficult problems—in his female students than in his male.

In chapter 3, Malague suggests that when Stella Adler traveled to Russia to study with Stanislavski, returning to the Group Theatre with a new and different understanding of his System, she was deliberately undermining Strasberg's power. Malague further proposes that, though Adler's teaching technique had its own flaws, her emphasis on imagination and "the given circumstances," which encourages actors to work on *characters* rather than on themselves and allows actors to develop an intellectual engagement and eventual independence from their teachers, represents what might been seen as a "(proto-) feminist" agenda (27).

Chapter 4, which focuses on Sanford Meisner, is perhaps the most immediately captivating chapter in the book, in part because, as Malague points out, interest in and specific study of "Meisner technique" has continued to grow and expand, finding a cult like popularity in the years after his death. Focusing on his repetition exercise, which is intended to reveal "natural impulses" and "instincts," Malague reveals that, in practice, Meisner ended up engaging in patriarchal control similar to that of Strasberg (whom he ostensibly opposed). When students displayed the "wrong" instinct in an exercise, Meisner was quick to correct them, explaining what the "correct" (often gendered) impulse *should* have been.

In chapter 5, Malague reveals a clear admiration for the work of Uta Hagen, largely because Hagen, much like Adler (and unlike their male counterparts), encouraged her students to think *and* act. Though concerned about the potential damage actresses may face when they are asked to "substitute" their personal experiences for those of their (all too often) weak, damaged, subservient characters, Malague nevertheless has great respect for Hagen's supportive and encouraging teaching style. As the sole teacher (among these four) who simultaneously maintained a professional acting career, Hagen strongly encouraged her students to work on exercises independently and, more importantly, warned her students about the dangers of working with a teacher who took too much control.

Finally, in the chapter titled "The 'Magic If': Forward-Looking Conclusions," Malague reaffirms her belief that "the Method," despite its flaws, has been and could continue to be highly effective training for aspiring actors. She posits that, through careful examination of the theories, histories, and practices of Method training, as well as consideration of some alternative actor-training techniques, we may be able to reassess the value of "the Method" for the contemporary actor (or actress), emphasizing its strengths, avoiding its biased traps, and modifying it to include, rather than exclude, the variety of truths that students bring with them to the classroom.

What makes Malague's critical investigation of "the Method" so exceptional is her ability to simultaneously utilize two distinct perspectives. Her analysis offers both the theory-based, rational eye of a skilled feminist scholar, as well as the personal, "behind-the-scenes" experience—as a student and as a teacher—of Method-based actor training. Interestingly, though, while she purposefully points out that some version of Method training has made its way into virtually every conservatory and university acting program in the United States, she does not take a hard look at any of them—even those that claim direct lineage, like the Actors Studio Drama School. Admittedly, a large part of Malague's agenda includes challenging those who currently teach some version(s) of Method acting to analyze their *own* pedagogical practices. However, I am suggesting that it might be equally eye-opening, perhaps within the confines of another venture, to conduct a thorough investigation of some of these specific institutions, questioning what happens to *inherited* versions of "the Method" as they are transferred from professional studio settings to degree-granting programs.

Ultimately, *An Actress Prepares* is an invaluable contribution to the ongoing discourse regarding theatre practice and pedagogy. Malague's specific and mindful criticism of "the Method" from a feminist perspective is beyond timely; it is long overdue.

—KRISTEN ROGERS
Texas Tech University

Mabou Mines: Making Avant-Garde Theater in the 1970s. By Iris Smith Fischer. Ann Arbor: University of Michigan Press, 2011. pp. 266. $60.00 cloth, $29.95 paper.

Iris Smith Fischer's monograph fills a significant gap in experimental performance history, as it is the first text dedicated exclusively to examining the work of Mabou Mines, one of the most important avant-garde theatre groups in the United States. Although the New York–based company received its first Obie (Off and Off-Off Broadway Theater) Award in recognition of its work in 1974, Mabou Mines came to prominence in the 1980s with groundbreaking productions such as *A Prelude to Death in Venice* (1980), script and direction by Lee Breuer, and *Dead End Kids* (1980), conceived and directed by JoAnne Akalaitis.

Beginning with a clearly written and insightful introduction, the book is organized chronologically in five chapters, ending with a brief epilogue. *Mabou Mines: Making Avant-Garde Theater in the 1970s* also includes a section of excellent production photographs and a useful appendix with a timeline of members' activities and company achievements, from 1957 to 1980.

Writing about a group that "set out to create indescribable performance" (v), Smith Fischer carefully documents the first and lesser-known decade of Mabou Mines's production history, beginning in 1970, when the company was supported in its first three years by Ellen Stewart, director of La MaMa Experimental Theatre, and then, over a ten-year period, by Joe Papp of the Public Theater. Smith Fischer weaves together accounts of core members' artistic backgrounds as she tells the story of how Mabou Mines's multidisciplinary performances came about. In her introduction Smith Fischer states that detailing company members' biographies is not her intent here. Her focus is on the "coming together" of the multitalented founders, JoAnne Akalaitis, Lee Breuer, Philip Glass, Ruth Maleczech, and David Warrilow, and the group's rehearsal processes and productions. Actors Frederick Neumann and Bill Raymond joined the group in 1971; Terry O'Reilly joined in 1973. Smith Fischer also suggests why some members had moved apart or left the group by the end of the 1970s.

Smith Fischer argues that Mabou Mines rejected the notion of the actor as an interpretative artist, and instead, performers were seen as "creative agents" (1). This company of individual artists—"Co-Artistic Directors"—sometimes with disparate visions, often struggled with collaboration as they consistently "made new" and often provocative work together. The group ultimately evolved into what Smith Fischer describes as a "company of directors," with Breuer acknowledged as the "first" director and Akalaitis as "the second director" with a "sensibility and vocabulary of her own" (120).

In the introduction, Smith Fischer situates Mabou Mines's work in the 1970s within the context of longer, ongoing conversations in theater and performance studies about the avant-garde—or avant-gardes. In Smith Fischer's analysis, the idea of and adherence to the "Avant Garde as Community" is crucial to an understanding of how Mabou Mines functions: members support each other through their efforts to create and foster a common language and techniques and through sharing responsibility (organizing childcare within the group is but one example).

In the first chapter, "Coming Together," Smith Fischer charts the complex movements of the couples, Breuer and Malaczeck and Glass and Akalaitis, from coast to coast in the United States and throughout Europe, where they encountered English actor David Warrilow. The five determined to make New York City's downtown arts scene their base. In this section and throughout the volume Smith Fischer clarifies the connections and the distinctions between Mabou Mines and experimental theatre troupes associated with 1960s radicalism—the Living Theatre, the Open Theatre, the Performance Group, and the San Francisco Mime Troupe. Mabou Mines in the 1970s "was not political" (in Akalaitis's words): "There was no ideal about politics, or what theatre should be, could be, or how we wanted to change it. . . . [The ideal was] excellence, and finding a performing technique that was American—one that was personal, yet very stylized and technical" (35). Working in art galleries and with visual artists, which Mabou Mines did in the early 1970s, was unique among theatre collectives at the time. Teachers and directors Herbert Blau, R. G. Davis, and Jerzy Grotowski were powerful influences on the development of Mabou Mines's working processes.

Chapters 2, 3, 4, and 5 are devoted to the group's production history. Chapter 2 centers on two of the company's early original works and on Lee Breuer's development as an artist. *The Red Horse Animation* and *The B. Beaver Animation*, which Smith Fischer describes as a meld of high and low culture, draw attention to the artist/self in U.S. society (as represented in the first piece by a moving Red Horse and in the next by a "dammed up" Beaver). This, according to Breuer, was really about him, "a dammed up writer" (77). Chapter 3 moves on to an exploration of company members' intensely fruitful and sometimes fraught connections with Samuel Beckett; Mabou Mines gained critical attention by producing his plays and adapting some of his nondramatic pieces, usually with great success. Smith Fischer points out that in the 1970s (notwithstanding some critics' accounts to the contrary) Mabou Mines maintained "warm" relations with Beckett, despite the fact that some of their productions (*The Lost Ones* in particular) went well beyond a "straight reading" of the author's words (116, 117). In chapter 4, "See Yourself as a Heavyweight," Smith Fischer juxtaposes the rehearsal processes of two important productions of the mid/late 1970s—Breuer's *Shaggy Dog Animation* and Akalaitis's *Dressed Like an Egg*, which was based on the writings of Colette. Smith Fischer frames this comparison with an analysis of gender stereotypes in Breuer's work versus the multiplicity of gender identities in Akalaitis's. Although I find Smith Fischer's analysis of Breuer's "master narrative which carries the weight of memory" compelling, I am less sure what Smith Fischer means by her description of Akalaitis's "deliberate forgetfulness" in her work (121, 154). Based on the description of Akalaitis's directorial process in this chapter, which was propelled by her direct response to the women's movement and her gender-conscious perspective, I found this description of her practice confusing. Chapter 5 expands on Smith Fischer's sense of Mabou Mines as a "company of directors" or "being bosses together" (165) as it examines Frederick Neumann's directorial experiences with Mabou Mines in the late 1970s and Ruth Malaczech's direction of *Vanishing Pictures* and her founding with Breuer and Raymond of the actors'/ designers'/directors' studio, Re.Cher. Chez.

Smith Fischer launches her narrative in the first few pages of the book with a description of two evocative images from lauded Mabou Mines's productions of later periods: *Lear* with Malaczeck in the title role (1987) and *Dollhouse* (2003), where all the male roles were "played by actors no more than four and a half feet tall" (1). There is an energy and liveliness in these descriptions that characterize Smith Fischer's production histories in the first two thirds of the book; the lengthier final chapters, however, lack the pace and the spark of the earlier sections. That being said, the vibrant personalities and extraordinary, diverse gifts of "the company of directors" compel the reader's interest throughout this volume, which sheds light on a formative period of a group whose work happily continues to astound spectators and fascinate scholars today.

—**CINDY ROSENTHAL**
Hofstra University

Transposing Broadway: Jews, Assimilation, and the American Musical. By Stuart J. Hecht. New York: Palgrave Macmillan, 2011. pp. 240. $85 cloth.

One might think that the subject of Jews and the American musical has been all but exhausted; after all, during the past decade, Andrea Most in *Making Americans: Jews and the Broadway Musical* (2004) and Henry Bial in *Acting Jewish: Negotiating Ethnicity on the American Stage and Screen* (2005) have provided insightful explorations of the topic, as has John Bush Jones in *Our Musicals, Ourselves* (2004), among others. But Stuart Hecht, in his entertaining and downright brilliant *Transposing Broadway*, proves that scholars have only just scratched the surface of this significant subject, opening a deep vein of gold that reveals just how important the contributions of Jewish artists have been in developing the American musical.

His thesis is that "Jews shaped the musical, aside from its entertainment value, to represent their grappling with the promise of the American Dream and the methods of assimilation that might help one achieve it" (4); Broadway musicals are, he asserts, our "cultural Ellis Island" as they provide access to U.S. culture just as Ellis Island welcomed immigrants to America (5). The book focuses on transposition as change—changing styles of music, form and structure, the characters, and subjects in musicals—to reflect an ever-changing audience and nation (13). I knew I was going to love this volume when, right off the bat in the introduction, Hecht gives consideration to the noteworthy but oft-dismissed work of Jerry Herman, pointing out that although the form and structure of his shows, like *Hello, Dolly!*, *Mame*, and *La Cage Aux Folles*, are conventional, their subjects are not. They are models of characters attempting to integrate into mainstream American culture and life.

The author's method is primarily dramaturgical, with the volume organized topically by chapter; within each topic, Hecht engages in a close study of representative shows, analyzing how each works onstage "for both the immediate audience and for the larger community which that audience represents" (13). For example, chapter 2 focuses on how the use of the double couple expressed larger societal issues, with *Guys and Dolls* the quintessential double couple format and its assimilative associations. Like the introduction, chapter 3, "The Melting Pot Paradigm of Irving Berlin," focuses on a Jewish writer of some of the most popular songs in musical theatre history, usually given short shrift in that history (including by Most), when his "legacy has not been as recognized or acknowledged as his degree of popularity and artistry might dictate" (43). As Hecht suggests, Berlin embodied the American Dream.

Chapter 4 explores musicals that offer instruction on how to achieve that dream, with an interesting examination of depictions of gambling as a short cut to it, as well as portrayals of labor unions and outsiders. He finishes this section with an assessment of Sondheim shows that both celebrate and question the American Dream. One of Hecht's most brilliant moments occurs in this chapter when he briefly analyzes "You Gotta Get a Gimmick" from *Gypsy* as an assimilation advice (87), taking a seemingly fluff, vaudevillian number and turning it into socio political statement. His good work on "Cinderella Musicals" in the next chapter leads to the climax of the book, and it is in the penultimate chapters 6 and 7 that I sensed that the author feels the closest personal connection to the shows examined, namely, *Ragtime*, *Parade*, and *Fiddler on the Roof*. Hecht opens up the latter to new readings by suggesting a through line from it to later musicals like *Hair*, *Rent*, *In the Heights*, and *The Color Purple*, arguing that, based in part on this legacy, *Fiddler* was "one of the most important American musicals ever produced" (185). (In fact, he so convinces me that I likely will be adding it to my syllabus next time I teach musical theatre history, when before I have glossed over it in that course.)

And if these two chapters were not enough to convince me that I have encountered a model of fresh, productive scholarship in Hecht's book, I reached the epilogue, a brief but brilliant consideration of the recent trend of "Lovable Monsters" as characters in musicals such as *Bat Boy*, *Shrek*, and *Avenue Q*. This final gift of an epilogue focuses briefly on *The Producers* and argues that the recent spate of "quirky heroes and heroines" suggests that America is now more accepting of people for who they are. "Assimilation has become reversed: 'the other' has become a new dominant cultural force" (202), making, as he concludes, "assimilation . . . no longer necessary" (204).

The only minor complaints I have (and they are indeed minor) is that Hecht adopts the not uncommon but in my opinion short-sighted position that book musicals ended with the rise of rock and roll (32), whereas book musicals are still somewhat prevalent, and that there are quite a few typos, misspellings, and some improper grammar, which detract from the content at times—but I would blame more the editors than the author for this shortcoming (they are rife enough, however, that I would hesitate to approach Palgrave with a book proposal). But these are nothing in the face of what I love about the book, which in addition to the above includes Hecht's analysis of music, not just libretto and lyrics, to undergird his arguments; his belief in the importance of commercial, popular appeal when studying the shows; and the delightful, occasional infusion of personal anecdotes into his narrative. His description of his shtetl-raised grandmother's outrage upon attending *Fiddler* ("It was never like that! It was never pretty, never so nice!" [180]) confirmed for me the personal connection that Hecht feels to his material, and that connection could be what makes, for me, *Transposing Broadway* the current apotheosis of musical theatre studies.

—JUDITH SEBESTA
Lamar University

Native Acts: Indian Performance, 1603–1832. Edited by Joshua David Bellin and Laura L. Mielke. Lincoln, Nebraska: University of Nebraska Press, 2011. pp. 333. $35.00 paper.

Ceremony, Spirituality, and Ritual in Native American Performance: A Creative Notebook. By Hanay Geiogamah. Los Angeles: UCLA American Indian Studies Center, 2011. pp. 144. $16.00 paper.

Given the disappointing lack of books published each year on Native American drama, these two new works are prime considerations not only for literary review but also for use in cultural and performance studies. Both of these works speak to the "Indianness" of Native American performance and, perhaps more importantly, are written from a distinctly Native American perspective. Editor Laura L. Mielke's explication of the terms "Indianness" and "performance" in her introduction to *Native Acts*, is relevant to both works: "When we refer to Indianness in this volume, we mean the acknowledged attribute of direct association with American Indian peoples and cultures; who identifies American Indian attributes determines the substance of Indianness at specific moments" (5). Mielke defines performance in three ways: to present to an audience, to carry out a command or particular action, and to participate in a formal public function or ritual (2).

Native Acts: Indian Performance, 1603–1832 includes ten insightful essays on the performance of being "Indian" that explore said performance from the perspective of the indigenous peoples. Mielke's introduction is a superlative beginning that not only defines terms and explains the selection of essays but also raises some pertinent questions about the performance of Indianness for the indigenous peoples of North America. She begins with an example of her own, the legend of Pocahontas, dissecting the various interpretations of the story and calling for an examination of the intent behind those who reported what has now become an American legend that perpetuates a romantic myth of indigenous peoples in North America. The chronologically organized essays first explore the essentialist attitudes of the Europeans who colonized America and the impact of those attitudes on the native people, concluding with the performance of Indianness in the early formation of the United States. As Mielke asserts, "In early North America, Europeans' conceptions of Indianness were inextricable from the moral, religious, teleological, political, and economic justifications for their [European] presence" (5). The significance of this collection of essays lies in the deliberate intent to recognize the proprietorship of Native Americans, characterized by Mielke as "a critical intervention in the scholarship treating the performance of Indianness" that restores "Indian peoples to the intercultural matrix from which such performances arose" (10).

The first four essays, by scholars Matt Cohen, Nan Goodman, John H. Pollack, and Olivia Bloechl, expose essentialist interpretations that pervade historical representations of Indians. All four scholars argue that specific essentialist assumptions led to misrepresentations of the Native American peoples and the subsequent public attitudes that defined native and Euroamerican relationships during the colonial era. Each author also provides a brief historical background of the text or events that are being examined. In "Lying Inventions: Native Dissimulation in Early Colonial New England," Cohen analyzes Native American acts of strategic simulation and dissimulation as challenges to perceptions of stable national identities. Goodman's essay, "The Deer Island Indians and Common Law Performance," examines the European attitudes that deprived Indians of legal status in common law. Bloechl's essay, "Wendat Song and Carnival Noise in the Jesuit *Relations*," reveals the Jesuits' assessment of Wendat healing ceremonies as superstitious, a grave charge at the time. Pollack's essay, "Native Performances of Diplomacy and Religion in Early New France," focuses on the misinterpretation of native ritual of the Innu, Algonquin, and Maliseet as a negotiated treaty, documented by François Gravé Du Pont and Samuel de Champlain in *Des Sauvages, ou, Voyage de Samuel Champlain* in 1603. The French understood the oration of Anadabijou as a chief or king commanding his people to accept French settlement and military aid. Pollack explains, however, that allied tribes were not interested in military aid nor did they concede any territory to the French; they were interested solely in economic advantages to be gained by trade.

Stephanie Fitzgerald's essay, "I Wunnatuckquannum, This Is My Hand," is the first of three essays in the collection to discuss the performance of writing. She argues that the writing in the Massachusetts Indian Deeds constituted a ritual that was concerned not only with negotiations between the English and the Wampanoag but also future generations of indigenous peoples. The essays "Performing Indian Publics," by Philip H. Round, and "Editing as Indian Performance," by Theresa Strouth Gaul, continue with analysis of the performance of writing. Gaul's examination of the performance of editing by Elias Boudinot, a Cherokee editor of the *Cherokee Phoenix* in the early 1800s, is particularly insightful. For example, in her analysis of Boudinot's inclusion of the poem "Nature's Farewell" in the September 17, 1828, edition, Gaul reveals how "context transforms the romantic quest motif of the poem into a presentiment of what the Cherokees would experience should they bow to the government's demands" (293), suggesting that the theme of death in the poem may be a subtle protest against forced removal (293). This is a new perspective on the political finesse Boudinot exhibits, a previously neglected aspect of Boudinot's editorial career.

Fitzgerald's essay is also the first of three essays that analyze the contribution of particular individuals to native performance. As Fitzgerald scrutinizes a Wampanoag sachem named Wunnatuckquannum, Caroline Wigginton similarly recovers the importance of Coosaponakeesa, a Creek woman, as one of the first native authors in her essay, "In A Red Petticoat." Jenny Hale Pulsipher's "Playing John White" is the third essay to examine the performance of an individual as representative of culture. Pulsipher focuses on a man named John White, born a Nipmuc Indian named Wompas. All three essays investigate the contributions of specific individuals to the discourse of native performance by comparing the accepted Western view of them with their probable intent from a native peoples' perspective. Pulsipher stresses the importance of realizing that individuals do not necessarily represent their cultures, but that sometimes their performance, such as Wompas' portrayal of himself as English, simply reflects their motives as individuals.

Timothy J. Shannon's "This Wretched Scene of British Curiosity and Savage Debauchery" describes what happened when Indian "kings" were brought to England under varying pretexts. He notes that at first visiting Indians were designated "kings" and extended every courtesy given a visiting dignitary. As relations changed after the Seven Years' War (1756–1763), however, government officials were reluctant to arrange for them to visit King George III or to pay for their accommodations (221). Shannon indicates that at that time imposters, "other Indians and Britons," dressed in Indian style, displaying false representations of

"Indians" for public consumption (236). For example, a Scot named Peter Williamson, who called himself "King of the Indians," performed narratives that included scalping and torture while dressed as an Indian, wearing war paint and brandishing a scalping knife. This is a prime example of how Europeans subjected indigenous peoples to appropriation and ridicule, ultimately placing natives in a subordinate role.

In his afterward, Philip J. Deloria states, "Historiography, like history itself, avoids origins and proliferates beginnings" (310). He suggests that these essays ignore their origins in history and other areas such as performance studies and anthropology to proliferate new areas of interdisciplinarity. I agree with his assessment of these essays in that the academic community can use them across many different disciplines, contributing to the scholarship of history, performance studies, literary studies, cultural studies, and more. These essays add to the general history of the peoples, bringing forth arguments for renewed interpretations of historical events, individuals, and texts and providing a solid foundation for continued research, especially for those who are initiates in the field of Native American studies.

In *Ceremony, Spirituality, and Ritual in Native American Performance: A Creative Notebook* Hanay Geiogamah, professor of theater at UCLA and founding artistic director of the American Indian Dance Theatre, deconstructs his work in ceremonial theatre in scholarly terms, as well as providing a practical guide on how to reproduce it. He uses the term "deconstruct" to describe his reflections on the process of development used in his original work *49*. While he speaks to the specificity of Native American ceremonial theatre, I was struck by the universality of the elements he describes. This universality is supported by the comparisons he makes to many different works in the Western theatre canon. The book is comprised of a brief section on each of the elements of ceremonial theatre followed by the script for *49* with detailed notes by the author on every aspect of reproducing this work.

Geiogamah begins with a brief overview of his career, beginning with his work with the experimental theatre La MaMa in New York City during the 1970s, and the development of *49*, collaboratively devised with the Native American Theatre Ensemble (NATE), in 1974. The title *49* is derived from a "popular post-powwow knock-down, drag-out funfest then in full practice all over Indian Country" (1). In appendix 1, he explains the origins of the powwow *49* and offers several stories regarding the origin of the name (none of them conclusive). Geiogamah then describes his journey, from the creation of the piece through his scholarly analysis of it, his understanding of the process, and the impact *49* had on Native American theatre.

For those unfamiliar with *49* or La MaMa, Geiogamah gives a vivid description of the type of work being done in the 1970s from the perspective of an active participant. His introspection is an inspiration for today's artists, Native American and nonnative alike. His account of how *49* developed in opposition to conventional Western practice and the questions the artists had while making the piece illuminate the creative risk an artist must make when charting new territory. "At the time, we didn't have a developed sense of the western dramatic process of act one build, act two climax, act three descending action. So, in our search for a workable performance context, we started by trusting our sense of rhythmic structure, rhythmic beat, and our feeling of the energy that drives all Indian dance and performance" (1). One of the risks an artist encounters when diverging from the norm is that of being misunderstood by the audience. I think Geiogamah encounters this risk a second time in writing this book. It seems to me that if the reader has not attended a powwow *49* or a performance of Geiogamah's *49* it will be difficult to envision the piece even though Geiogamah includes the script with detailed staging notes.

49 opens with the shaman Night Walker "enacting the traditional custom of calling people together for a purpose related to the well-being of the tribal community" (72). The shaman appears throughout the play as the connecting element in this journey from a community's awakening to their culture's value and the experience of its loss to a rebirth filled with hope and solidarity. Following the shaman's call to the people in scene 1, the mood of expectancy is shattered with police sirens and police officers, who, spewing racial slurs, assume the gathering of young Indians will be destructive. The shock is meant to be an Artaudian device inducing the audience to feel the same apprehension the actors re-create. The police are used as a "ritual structuring device," and their presence is repeated throughout the work (73). The play is meant to build awareness in young Native Americans of their past and their present, engaging them in a cathartic process that leads them to envision and create a positive and meaningful new future. Traditions of Native American culture, including vision quests, the teaching of weaving, and cleansing through ritual, are re-created throughout the work.

Geiogamah discusses ceremony, spirituality, and ritual in separate chapters, in which he describes possible source material, the role of the ceremonial director, and several questions that should be addressed when planning a ceremonial work like *49*. Some of the questions he lists are "Who is the ceremony for? What will the text be? Will a myth, a legend, a story of the tribe be helpful? What music will be performed? Do any of these dances, music, stories, elements of décor belong to a member of the tribe or family?" (12).

In the chapter on ceremony Geiogamah discusses his dramaturgical intervention, in 2005, with the long-standing Eastern Cherokee drama *Unto These Hills*, providing a brief history of the piece, how he became involved with it, and the outcome of his experience. This section of the book is important not only for practitioners of Native American ceremonial theatre but also for dramaturgs in assessing the impact of change to any well-established work. *Unto These Hills* was originally written by Kermit Hunter, a non-Indian, and it centered almost entirely on the history of Cherokee encounters with white men. The principal roles were played by white actors, whereas the Cherokee actors functioned in the background. Geiogamah, who believed that the play should reflect a Cherokee perspective, wanted to "incorporate elements from every aspect of the Cherokee tribal cultural heritage: music, dance, myth, legends, stories, historical memory, art, design, and language" (16). For example, for the required representation of the removal of the Cherokee from their lands in the East he filled the stage with eight hoop dancers and forty-eight hoops and used black lighting to illuminate the glow paint on the hoops for great effect when darkness fell on the evening production. Although attendance picked up with these new changes, there were those in the tribe who were not happy with the new production and wanted a return to the old play. Subsequently the tribe has continued to make changes to the play over the years as it continues its annual production.

In a separate chapter, Geiogamah delineates what he labels "Six Propellers of Ritual": repetition, counterpoint, indirection, irony, audience as tribe, and spectacle (30). In this chapter he also compares Western definitions and thought with Native American use of ritual. He describes how elements in Kushner's *Angels in America* are manifested in *49*, and how *49*, like the works of German dramatist Georg Büchner, replaces traditional dramatic development with a vital emotional center (35). As he continues to analyze the components of ceremonial theatre, he intricately weaves together musical, literary, and theatrical terms. For instance, he includes the terms "coda" and "counterpoint" in his explanations of archetypes, catharsis, and foreshadowing. In his consideration of the elements in ceremonial theatre he draws on Artaud and Aristotle to support his arguments.

The meticulous director's notes that Geiogamah includes with the script of *49* are among the most valuable components of this book, providing readers with a detailed description of the piece, how it should be staged, and what should be achieved through its performance. The notes also give nonnatives a better understanding of Native Ceremonial Performance. The elements that he describes are not restricted to dramatizing only Native American experience but could be used to create a devised theatre piece from any cultural or sociopolitical experience. Although the workshop descriptions in appendix 2 may have been intended to aid practitioners in creating a Native Ceremonial Performance, they are also excellent resources for exercises to include in any performance studies or devised theatre class. This "Creative Notebook" will be of considerable interest to artists and scholars, and it constitutes a valuable contribution to the fields of theatre, dramaturgy, performance studies, cultural studies, and Native American studies.

—**TERESA STANKIEWICZ**
University of Missouri

Suzan-Lori Parks: Essays on the Plays and Other Works. Edited by Philip C. Kolin. Jefferson, NC: McFarland & Company, Inc., 2010. pp. vi + 213. $39.95 paper.

Suzan-Lori Parks's work has dominated American theatre for the last decade. From being the first African-American woman to win the Pulitzer Prize for drama to her massive, multiple, simultaneous premiere of *365 Days/365 Plays*, which resulted in a year long production all over the world, Parks has changed the world of theatre, and the recent spate of scholarship about her now expands with this excellent body of scholarship.

Kolin's dynamic anthology offers twelve essays, two interviews, and a production chronology that scholars will find invaluable. On the whole, the essays are eclectic and insightful and many point the way toward new and further directions in the study and understanding of Parks's work. Readers will find a great breadth of analysis here, but the brief length of each piece allows for only some depth, making it this reviewer's hope that many of the authors here will expand and develop their ideas.

The book opens, after a brief preface summarizing each piece, with an essay by editor Kolin, who writes on biography and performativity. The essay is a synthesis of interviews and statements by Parks that, once one moves past the occasional hyperbole about her genius, sets the tone and resonates with the rest of the volume. Kolin sees Parks as publicly performing "Parks," a conclusion that Parks refutes in the interview near the end of the book, in which she argues she does not act when she is onstage in a play: "I don't think I was acting. I was just being. I was just up there being me" (187). The tension between these two observations perfectly captures the challenge of analyzing Parks, as both statements are true, yet they display the paradoxes of Parks that are beautifully illuminated throughout this volume.

Rena Fraden analyzes the political and religious nature of Parks's "radical inclusion," locating her spirituality in a vague new age mysticism rather than in the Catholicism of her youth. Fraden also presents Parks's approach to American history as "radically inclusive," cannily observing that the playwright rejects all essentialisms and deconstructs both history and ethnicity. Jacqueline Wood employs Jazz as a metaphor to understand the female self in three early works: *Betting on the Dust Commander*, *Pickling*, and *Devotees in the Garden of Love*. Referring to what Parks does as "Beckettian Jazz" (a poetic and apt description), Wood sees these three plays as "examples of such interrogations of African-American female selfhood in relation to time and memory, blackness and social tradition" (34, 35).

Philip C. Kolin's second offering is an essay on memory in Parks's *Imperceptible Mutabilities in the Third Kingdom*, finding "the production of memory is at the heart" of the play (46). He also considers the linguistic play between mind, mine, and mines in the play's dialogue and the specific role black bodies play on stage. In one of the more cutting-edge essays in the book, Nicole Hodges Persley employs hip hop theory to probe *Death of the Last Black Man in the Whole Entire World* and *The America Play*. Viewing Parks's work as employing the techniques of sampling and remixing, as well as tropes of emulation and reference, Persley makes a compelling argument for understanding Parks through hip hop culture. This essay is a perfect example of a study that could easily have been a book-length investigation on its own.

Shawn Marie Garrett, one of the most prolific Parks scholars working today, contributes an investigation into the premiere production of *Venus* and, later in the volume, an interview with Parks herself. The essay argues for a reevaluation of the understanding of the premiere of *Venus* at the Yale Repertory Theatre and subsequently at the Public Theatre in New York, directed by Richard Foreman, "a story more of fruitful collusion than collaboration" (77). What makes the essay interesting is that Garrett argues that one should understand *Venus* through the critical lens of love. The interview, one of many that Parks has given, provides many similar statements to those given in previous interviews (indeed, Fraden observes earlier that Parks is "remarkably consistent in interviews" [20]) but also has many new ideas and thoroughly demonstrates that Parks is a protean, Eshu-like figure herself, for whom language is fluid and deeply interconnected.

Money in the *Red Letter* plays is the overarching theme of Jon Dietrick's essay, which also deals with the relationship between the symbolic and the real and between profit and reproduction. Jochen Achilles studies the ludic elements of *Top Dog/Underdog*, finding a variety of games that range from fun to deadly. Parks's inter-intertextualities and the evolution of the idea of the "(w)hole of history," especially in the *365* plays, is the topic of Jennifer Larson's fascinating investigation. Christine Woodworth studies the traumas of childhood in Parks's plays, both in the form of traumatized children in *In the Blood* and adult characters haunted by a childhood that ultimately kills them, as in *Fucking A* and *Topdog*. All four essays provide genuine insights into their respective plays and like Persley provide a launching point for new ways to consider Parks.

Leaving drama behind (albeit never entirely), Glenda Dicker/sun considers the mythic foundations of Parks's sole published novel *Getting Mother's Body*, finding echoes of the Demeter/Persephone story and also links to the dramatic canon. Charlene Regester likewise scrutinizes Parks's screenplays for their dramatization of the unconscious. Rounding out the volume are two of the more valuable contributions: Richard E. Kramer's production history of the plays and, perhaps even more significant, an interview with longtime Parks collaborator Liz Diamond by Faedra Chatard Carpenter. Students and scholars alike will find both pieces invaluable for understanding and contextualizing Parks's work.

I have noted elsewhere that every new Parks play both expands her canon and shifts it, making it impossible to describe the typical "Suzan-Lori Parks play." As Kolin himself observes, her canon is "compellingly experimental, unsettling. It is at once comic and cosmic, absurd and tragic, erotic and fervent, historical and iconoclastic" (10). A protean dramatist, her work continues to challenge audiences and academics, who, in the case of this volume, rise to the challenge admirably and reward the reader with interesting insights and new ways to view Parks, both the character and the canon.

—**KEVIN J. WETMORE, JR.**
Loyola Marymount University

The Problem of the Color[blind]: Racial Transgression and the Politics of Black Performance. By Brandi Wilkins Catanese. Ann Arbor: University of Michigan Press, 2011. pp. ix + 214. $75.00 cloth, $28.95 paper.

In *The Problem of the Color[blind]*, Brandi Wilkins Catanese turns back the clock to the 1990s and spotlights that decade's debates, tensions, and anxieties related to the adoption of colorblind practices within theatre and, to a lesser extent, film. The author's deep research into the period results in the creation of a book that is so richly detailed that it almost seems as though it were recovered from a time capsule. Of course, no such book was published in the 1990s, and that is why this book is so valuable. It frames a historical moment in which open conversations occurred about the meanings of race, gender, and disability and their continuing impact on the American theatre.

As one century ends and another dawns, it is typical to look back on past achievements and to predict what the future may hold. Evidence of this appears in the extensive literature relating to the late nineteenth century. With her book, Catanese joins the growing ranks of authors, particularly those within the area of critical race studies, who have revisited the period of the late twentieth century in an effort to better understand the evolution of race relations across the century and/or to predict the future of race relations in the twenty-first century. If, as sociologist W. E. B. Du Bois famously noted, the twentieth century is the century of the "color line," then what role (if any) will race play in the twenty-first century? Will we move beyond the "line" into a colorblind society? Catanese engages these questions from the temporal perspective of the 1990s and gives the reader the feeling of having a front-row seat in the replaying of the debates and tensions of that historical moment.

Catanese outlines her project in her first chapter, "Bad Manners: Talking about Race." In an early subheading, the author attempts to head off readers' assumptions about the content of the book: "THIS IS NOT A BOOK ABOUT NONTRADITIONAL CASTING" (9). Although Catanese concedes that the book "emerged from an effort to understand my own experiences relative to nontraditional casting in the theater and to imagine alternatives," the author asserts that it "evolved into a broader meditation on the integration of black performance into our conversations about the future of race in national culture" (10). The traces of her original motivation can be felt, particularly in her incorporation of a detailed overview of nontraditional casting and re-presentation of definitions of different types of casting (societal, cross-cultural, conceptual, and blind), thus making the book somewhat about nontraditional casting. By design, it does not have the same exacting engagement with the topic as Angela Pao's *No Safe Spaces* (2010), but it still contributes meaningfully to the discussion and exists as a worthy companion text for readers interested in nontraditional casting.

The majesty of Catanese's book anchors itself in her shift away from the history and mechanics of nontraditional casting and in her critical engagement with the concept of colorblindness. Rather than framing colorblind theatre as the venue (and process) through which a person can "transcend" color or race, the author contends that such an analytical lens overlooks the materiality of bodies. She argues persuasively for the adoption of a new frame, one that privileges the optic of "transgression" in considerations of the limits and possibilities of colorblindness. Catanese writes, "Transgression exposes the moral limitations of transcendence as a viable strategy for social change by acknowledging the histories of social location that people wear on their bodies and that inform all of our interpretive frameworks" (22).

In the second chapter, Catanese recounts the colorblind theatre debates that were ignited by August Wilson's 1996 address to the Theatre Communications Group in which the esteemed playwright made "a plea for institutionalized support for black theater and an antidote to the color-blind casting practices used as recompense for racialized inequities in American theater" (37). This chapter, which is probably the most useful published scholarly study of Wilson's debates with theatre critic Robert Brustein, engages the complexities of the various arguments and, through an embrace of critical nuance, stakes out a middle position that praises Wilson for his desire to support the creation of black theater while challenging him on the narrowness of his definition of blackness.

In the third chapter, Catanese shifts medium and discusses the operation of colorblindness in the cinema. She closely reads two mid-1990s films starring actor Denzel Washington: *The Pelican Brief* and *Devil in a Blue Dress*. The selection of these films, which arguably are not the most noteworthy titles in the actor's extensive filmography, allows the author to maintain her focus squarely on the last decade of the twentieth century and the topic of colorblindness. Washington assists Catanese's study by being a person who can be cast in roles that were not originally imagined for a black actor. Challenging the notion of blindness and racial transcendence, the casting of Washington frequently entails changes to the script or story, typically consisting of the editing out of interracial heterosexual relationships and expressions of desire. The alterations, which are supported by both actor and producers, reveal the legibility and effect of color even within a blind framework.

In the fourth chapter, the author discusses Suzan-Lori Parks's play *Venus*. Although other scholars similarly have written about how the playwright simultaneously engages and troubles history, Catanese contributes to the study of Parks's oeuvre by incorporating such analyses within the larger frame of racial transgression. She gives her reader a way of understanding Parks's work not solely as the product of an auteur but also as influenced by the culture and concerns of the 1990s.

The final chapter, which functions more as an epilogue, moves the clock forward a decade, from the mid-1990s to the mid-2000s and points to the continuing conversation related to colorblindness. Catanese introduces the concepts of "postblack" and "postrace" and expresses a preference for the former because "the moniker of postblackness does what postrace does not: it names and thereby keeps blackness alive even while demanding that its significance to the public sphere be renegotiated" (145). The remainder of the chapter explores the materiality of race through close readings of film and televisual representations, including an analysis of a short-lived reality television show premised upon *Black Like Me*, in which "black and white families would 'trade' races, passing for the other." These more recent examples demonstrate the usefulness of reentering the 1990s debate and evaluating conceptions of appropriation, authenticity, transcendence, and transgression in relation to colorblindness within the performing arts and, more generally, society at large.

—HARVEY YOUNG
Northwestern University

BOOKS RECEIVED

Berger, Thomas L., and Sonia Massai, eds. *Paratexts in English Printed Drama to 1642*. New York: Cambridge University Press, 2014.

Bryer, Jackson R., and Robert M. Dowling, eds. Eugene O'Neill: *The Contemporary Reviews*. New York: Cambridge University Press, 2014.

Bryer, Jackson R., and Mary C. Hartig, eds. *William Inge: Essays and Reminiscences on the Plays and the Man*. Jefferson, NC: McFarland, 2014.

Crombez, Thomas, and Luk Van den Dries, eds. *Mass Theatre in Interwar Europe: Flanders and the Netherlands in an International Perspective*. Leuven, Belgium: Leuven University Press, 2014.

Dillon, Elizabeth Maddock. *New World Drama: The Performative Commons in the Atlantic World, 1649–1849*. Durham, NC: Duke University Press, 2014.

Dowling, Robert M. *Eugene O'Neill: A Life in Four Acts*. New Haven, CT: Yale University Press, 2014.

Faroqhi, Suraiya, and Arzu Öztürkmen, eds. *Celebration, Entertainment and Theatre in the Ottoman World*. New York: Seagull Books, 2014.

Hagher, Iyorwuese. *The Kwagh-hir Theater: A Weapon for Social Action*. Lanham, MD: University Press of America, 2014.

Lee, Rachel C. *The Exquisite Corpse of Asian America: Biopolitics, Biosociality, and Posthuman Ecologies*. New York: New York University Press, 2014.

Leiter, Samuel L. *Historical Dictionary of Japanese Traditional Theatre*. 2nd ed. New York: Rowman & Littlefield, 2014.

Lim, Eng-Beng. *Brown Boys and Rice Queens: Spellbinding Performance in the Asias*. New York: New York University Press, 2014.

Magelssen, Scott. *Simming: Participatory Performance and the Making of Meaning*. Ann Arbor: University of Michigan Press, 2014.

Malia, Scott. *Giorgio Strehler Directs Carlo Goldini*. Lanham, MD: Lexington, 2014.

Peschel, Lisa, ed. *Performing Captivity, Performing Escape: Cabarets and Plays from the Terezin/Theresienstadt Ghetto*. London: Seagull, 2014.

Prentiss, Craig R. *Staging Faith: Religion and African American Theatre from the Harlem Renaissance to World War II*. New York: New York University Press, 2014.

Prizant, Yael. *Cuba Inside Out: Revolutionary and Contemporary Theatre*. Carbondale: Southern Illinois University Press, 2014.

Robalino, Gladys, ed. *Female Amerindians in Early Modern Spanish Theatre*. Lanham, MD: Rowman & Littlefield, 2014.

Schreyer, Kurt A. *Shakespeare's Medieval Craft: Remnants of the Mysteries on the London Stage*. Ithaca, NY: Cornell University Press, 2014.

Senelick, Laurence, and Sergei Ostrovsky, eds. *The Soviet Theatre: A Documentary History*. New Haven, CT: Yale University Press, 2014.

Westgate, J. Chris. *Staging the Slums, Slumming the Stage: Class Poverty, Ethnicity, and Sexuality in American Theatre, 1890–1916*. New York: Palgrave Macmillan, 2014.

Wills, Garry. *Making Make-Believe Real: Politics as Theatre in Shakespeare's Time*. New Haven, CT: Yale University Press, 2014.

CONTRIBUTORS

ALAN SIKES is an assistant professor in the Department of Theatre at Louisiana State University, where he teaches courses in theatre history and dramatic theory. He received his M.F.A. in theatre directing at the University of Wisconsin-Madison and his Ph.D. at the University of Minnesota-Twin Cities. Alan researches the role of theatre in the formation and contestation of class and gender identities; his monograph on this topic, *Representation and Identity from Versailles to the Present: The Performing Subject*, is published by Palgrave Macmillan. Alan also has essays in the anthologies *Querying Difference in Theatre History*, *Theatre Historiography: Critical Questions*, and *Public Theatres and Theatre Publics*, as well as several theatre and performance journals.

HEIDI L. NEES is an assistant professor in the Theatre and Dance Department at California Polytechnic State University, San Luis Obispo. She received her Ph.D. from Bowling Green State University in 2012 and has shared her research at the American Society for Theatre Research, the Association for Theatre in Higher Education, and the Mid-America Theatre Conference.

NICOLE BERKIN recently completed her Ph.D. in Theatre Studies at the CUNY Graduate Center. Her dissertation examines the social and material conditions of touring in nineteenth-century American performance culture. She has published essays in *New England Theatre Journal* and in the edited collection, *Performing Objects and Theatrical Things* (Palgrave, 2014).

ANDREW GIBB is an assistant professor of theatre history, theory, and criticism in the Department of Theatre and Dance at Texas Tech University. He is currently working on a book about theatre and performance in nineteenth-century California, a project that combines his research interests in U.S. theatre history and Chicana/o theatre.

MEGAN GEIGNER is a candidate in the Interdisciplinary Ph.D. in Theatre and Drama program at Northwestern University. She has an M.A. in liberal studies from Reed College and an M.A. in theatre studies from Illinois State University. Her dissertation examines the creation of American hyphenate identity through ethnic public performance in early-twentieth-century Chicago. Her work has been published in *New England Theatre Journal* and *Modern Drama*. She is the Graduate Rep for the Theatre History Focus Group at Association for Theatre in Higher Education and an officer for the Ethnic Studies Graduate Student Colloquium at Northwestern. She also works as a professional dramaturg in Chicago.